EAST HARTFORD
CONNECTICUT

Its History
and Traditions

Joseph O. Goodwin

HERITAGE BOOKS
2014

HERITAGE BOOKS
AN IMPRINT OF HERITAGE BOOKS, INC.

Books, CDs, and more—Worldwide

For our listing of thousands of titles see our website
at
www.HeritageBooks.com

A Facsimile Reprint
Published 2014 by
HERITAGE BOOKS, INC.
Publishing Division
5810 Ruatan Street
Berwyn Heights, Md. 20740

Copyright © 1879 Joseph O. Goodwin

— Publisher's Notice —
In reprints such as this, it is often not possible to remove blemishes from the original. We feel the contents of this book warrant its reissue despite these blemishes and hope you will agree and read it with pleasure.

International Standard Book Numbers
Paperbound: 978-0-7884-3320-7
Clothbound: 978-0-7884-9072-9

CONTENTS

PREFACE, ... ix

DESCRIPTION.—1879, ... xii

CHAPTER I.—THE INDIANS.

The River Tribes.—The Podunks.—Places of living.— Fort Hill.—Burial Places.— Offer inducements to settlers.—Lieut. Holmes.—Assist starving settlers.—Their villages.—Restricted by the Whites; laws regarding them.— Quarrel with Sequassen.— John Eliot.— To return to Podunk.— Podunk lands in controversy.— Deeds to Thomas Burnham.— Podunks unsettled.— Trouble with Uncas.— Adjustment of bounds with Mohegans.— Sowgonosk marries Joshua.— Joshua's gifts of land.—The Five Miles.— Podunks join Philip.— Apprehensions and alarms.— Fortification, 1675.— William Hill shot.—Garrisons ordered.— Menowniet.— Cohause, a "child of death."— Trill and Wood.— Remnant of Podunks.— Four houses fortified, 1704.— Decay of Podunk tribe.—Bull's servant.—Stealing cider.—Stories of Indians.— Last of the tribe, ... 17

CHAPTER II.—EARLY OCCUPANCY.—1635-1666.

Settlements on the river.— Association.— Indian deeds.— Charter.— Proprietors &c.— Lands.— Bounds.— Division and grants of lands.— Fence.— Division of upland, ... 38

CHAPTER III.—SETTLERS AND INHABITANTS.—1648-1800.

Growth.— Settlers, names of.— Inventory, Richard Risley, . . 48

CHAPTER IV.—EARLY HISTORY.— Continued.— 1670-1774.

Main Street.— Bounds extended five miles.— Garrisons.— Bounds with Windsor.— Pounds.— East-side officers.— First meeting house.— Hockanum Bridge.— Progress of the settlement, 1700 — Forts, 1704. — Names of residents.— The Five Miles.— Burial place.— Public houses.— Line between the Three and the Five Miles.— Bolton line.— Draining "Eason's Hollow."— Divident lines of lots.— Lister this side.— Sign-posts or "whipping-posts."— French war, names of our company to Crown Point.— Neutral French.— Glastonbury line. — Preaching in Five Miles.— Line of Orford Parish, . . 68

CHAPTER V.— DURING THE REVOLUTION.— 1770-1783.

Our town no suburb.— Hartford votes.— Company for Boston, 1775.— Exploit of Gideon Olmsted.— Names of soldiers.— Battalion in Hartford.— Soldiers provided for.— Prisoners of war.— Confederation.— Embargoed provisions.— Bounties.— Men in service, and drafts.— The debt.— Distrust, ... 81

CHAPTER VI.— THE FRENCH ENCAMPMENT.

Rochambeau and Washington meet here.— Barbecues.— A gay time, etc. — Silver Lane.— Boats impressed.— Lafayette's tour, 1824, . 88

CHAPTER VII.— TOWN HISTORY.

Town privileges asked.— Petitions.— Town incorporated.— Bounds.— First meeting.— Officers.— Accounts with Hartford.— Guns sold.— Meetings in Orford Parish and in meeting houses. Manner of voting.— Town officers, 1784-1878, ... 92

CHAPTER VIII.— THE TOWN'S POOR.

Division with Hartford.— House for.— House sold, and poor let out.— A new house.— Burned.— "Out-door poor," 102

CHAPTER IX.— PEST HOUSE AND INOCULATION.

House built 1761.— Inoculation set up 1791.— Private house.— Privilege taken away.— Hospital described, and methods, . . . 104

CHAPTER X.— PUBLIC HOUSES AND SALE OF LIQUORS.

Ordinaries.— Abuse in resorting to.— Sadler's ordinary.— Philip Smith's public house.— Thomas Olcott's.— Wells's tavern.— President Monroe.— Phelps's tavern.— Lafayette.— Daniel Pitkin's.— John P. Jones's.— Joseph P. Jones's.— Cotton's.— Other taverns.— A mysterious disappearance.— Sale of liquors regulated.— "Old red store." Pitkin's store.— John Cotton's store, ... 107

CHAPTER XI.—BURYING GROUNDS.

First yard.—Additions, and votes.—Description.—Spencer street yard.—South Burying Ground.—South Middle.—In Burnside, not laid out.—Isolated graves.—Funeral customs and appointments.—Sextons; some odd characters.—The Phelps family, ... 114

CHAPTER XII.—ECCLESIASTICAL HISTORY.

The Puritans.—Early confederation.—William Pitkin's complaint.—First society, 1694.—Reluctants.—Meeting house, 1699.—Rev. Mr. Rood.—Rev. Samuel Woodbridge.—Minister's house.—Salary, etc.—A colleague.—First meeting house described.—Second meeting house described.—"Dignifying" it.—To be colored.—Steeple, not built.—A stove.—Further description.—The psalmody.—"Dignifying."—"Advice to the next seaters."—Rev. Dr. Williams.—Anecdotes of, and characteristics.—His house.—His sermons.—Rev. Andrew Yates.—Among the children.—A temperance advocate.—Rev. Joy H. Fairchild.—Rev. Asa Mead, died here.—Rev. Dr. Samuel Spring.—Rev. Theodore J. Holmes.—Mr. F. H. Buffum.—Mr. Richard Meredith.—Salaries.—Preaching in Five Miles.—First Society, first so-called, 1784.—Sunday ferry.—Third meeting house.—New bell and tower clock.—Material of old house.—A center at old meeting house.—Noonings.—Coming to meeting.—The old site, ... 123

Other Societies.—The Baptists and Methodists.—Spencer street Methodists.—Thomas Spencer.—Hockanum Methodists.—Burnside Methodists.—St. John's Parish, once Grace church.—St. Mary's church.—Hockanum Ecclesiastical Society, ... 145

CHAPTER XIII.—PARISH OF ORFORD.

Its territory purchased, etc.—200 acres for the minister.—To be divided.—Taken possession of.—To be laid out.—Grant to Burnham and Williams.—First division, 1731.—Line between the three mile lots and the Five Miles.—Encroachments.—A further division.—Settlers.—School.—A Parish in 1773.—Line with old society.—Wants to be a town, 1812.—Town meeting in, 1813.—Made town of Manchester, 1823, ... 149

CHAPTER XIV.—INDUSTRIES.

Saw Mill River, or Hockanum.—Early Mills at Burnside and eastward.—On Hop Brook.—At Burnside.—Story of Bidwell's sleep.—Fulling mills.—Copper Mines.—Iron slitting.—Powder making.—Snuff.—Guns cast.—Paper mills in Orford.—A lottery.—Glass working.—Another lottery.—Silk culture.—Paper mills in Scotland.—Cotton mill in Buckland.—Other mills.—Oil mills.—Nail Cutting.—Hat making.—Other mills.—Willow Brook. Other mills and industries.—A "shoddy" mill, ... 154

CHAPTER XV.—SCHOOLS.

Early provisions.—First school this side, 1708.—Two schools here.—Story of the "Goose pond."—One teacher only.—How supported.—School in Scotland.—In Hockanum.—School Society Fund.—School in the Five Miles.—Near the meeting house.—North of Gilman's Brook.—Four schools on Main street.—One in Scotland.—Near the Olcott's.—On "Jamstone Plain."—At "Hillstown"? etc.—Money divided.—Old houses on Main street divided.—South and Second South districts formed.—School districts formed by law.—New district, South-east.—Scotland district extended east.—Three districts north of Hockanum river.—The Center, and its school house.—The Second North and its houses.—The North and its house.—The Meadow district.—The School Society.—School Fund.—Long Hill District.—North district changed.—Scotland school house, and division of the district.—Named Burnside.—Hockanum district.—South Middle district.—Bounds of districts.—Present support of schools.—Town Deposit Fund.—"The Academy."—Other private schools, ... 164

CHAPTER XVI.—ROADS, BRIDGES, AND FERRIES.

Early roads.—To Windsor.—To Thomas Burnham's.—To Burnside.—Road on Meadow Hill.—Bridges, 1663.—Main street.—Highway near Willow brook.—North Meadow road.—Gilbert's Island, and landing place.—Hockanum Bridge.—North Prospect street.—Burnside avenue.—"Bear Swamp."—From mills toward Bolton.—Silver Lane.—North of Gilman's brook.—Along Windsor line.—Brewer lane.—"New road" in Podunk.—To Pratt's Ferry.—South Meadow road.—New London turnpike.—Other roads.—Burnham road made public.—Tolland turnpike.—Middle turnpike.—Ellington road.—Other roads.—Ferries.—Repair of roads.—Sewers.—By-laws de highways and sidewalks, and bathing.—Plank walks, 175

CHAPTER XVII.—THE STREET ELMS.

Traditions concerning, ... 192

CHAPTER XVIII.—HARTFORD FERRY AND BRIDGE.

First ferry.—Fares.—Money from for schools, etc.—One-half the ferry given to East Hartford, 1783.—Two ferries.—Bridge Company.—Differences, and ferry suppressed.—Free bridge wanted, . 194

CHAPTER XIX.—MILITARY AFFAIRS.

To train east side.— Training days, and grounds.—Companies and commanders.— Higher officers of our town.— Vote *de* standard, etc.— The artillery company.— Its guns.— Commanders.— Higher officers. — Grand reviews, etc.— *The war of* 1812:— A draft.—The artillery in it.— List of members, and pay-roll.— Reminiscences.— Privateering. — Effect of draft on home troops, ... 198
THE WAR OF THE REBELLION.— Equipment of troops, bounties, etc.— Town bonds.— Drafts and quotas.— Statistics.— Monument.— Memorial Day.—List of Volunteers, 1861 to 1865, ... 205

CHAPTER XX.— OLD HOUSES.

First houses.— Old fashioned houses described.— Earliest in town, names of owners, etc.— Other old houses, some standing, and occupants, ... 212

CHAPTER XXI.—THE PITKIN FAMILY.

A noted race.— Names of prominent members, and sketches of them.— Governor William, ... 225

CHAPTER XXII.— CUSTOMS AND LAWS.

Early government.— Punishments.— Church membership. — Bachelors not tolerated.— Strangers not entertained.— Labor, price regulated. — Excess in apparel forbidden.— Lecture day.— Sunday travel.— Guards at meetings.— Arms.— Early rising.— Town crier.— Black birds and wolves.—Inhabitants to be admitted.— Freemen, obliged to attend meetings.— Townsmen.— Slaves, curious records.— "Old Flo'."— Old Sylvia.— Matilda Scott.— Vehicles.— Chaises, etc.— Tobacco.— Household arts.— Bad boys.— A case of witchcraft.— Causeway haunted, ... 231

ADDENDA.—The Review of 1843.—The "Gulf," a correction, . 241

INDEX, ... 243

PREFACE.

When the writer began, some ten years ago, to interest himself in the history of his native town, he had no idea that his researches would ever attain to the dignity of a printed volume. But, led beyond his original intent by the opportunities which the custody of the town records gave him, he has extended his inquiry to the records of the "ancient town of Hartford," and to the records and files of the State, and found so much that was new and interesting to him, that he would fain communicate something of his own gratification to his fellow-townsmen. And, indeed, nothing has more incited him to pursue his work,—often almost a burden when added to other pressing cares,—than the constant expressions of interest and approval that have met him on every side since the reading of his paper on our town history in Elm Hall last winter. He is confident that something of interest will be found in the following pages for all to whom the past takes on a mellower tinge with its added years, and feels that he need make no apology for its publication.

Not the least pleasant of the experiences of the compiler of local history is the hunt for local traditions and reminiscences, those bits of sentient history that are the property of the fireside rather than the public, and which lead us, so to speak, behind the dignified front which each generation presents to its successors in its business records. The true flavor of these fireside talks cannot be given upon a printed page, and the author suspects that the public will not know all the pleasures which his inquiries have afforded him. Among those whom he has "interviewed" with much profit to himself and much gain to his history are, Mr. Timothy Deming,—whose well-stored memory was clear and active until his death in his ninety-third year, Aug. 14, 1879,—Mr. Chauncey Lester, Mr.

Allen Wadsworth, Mr. Thomas Burnham, Miss Martha Roberts, Mr. Thomas Dowd, Mr. Aaron G. Olmsted, Dr. Henry K. Olmsted, genealogist of the Olmsted family, Mr. Agis Easton, Mr. William M. Stanley, Mr. Walter A. Riley, and many others. The genealogical papers of the late Capt. Charles H. Olmsted have been serviceable in many ways.

The documents and authorities upon which the main body of this history rests are, DeForest's History of the Indians of Connecticut, the printed volumes of the Colonial Records of this State, together with the many manuscript volumes and files of the State library, and of the Town Clerk's office in the towns of Hartford and East Hartford. To Mr. Charles J. Hoadly, the State librarian, the author is indebted for valuable assistance, and to Mr. Walter A. Riley, whose familiarity with the records of our town, and whose independent researches have made him an authority in local antiquarian matters. Most of the references to houses and house sites may be verified upon the maps of the " Atlas of Hartford City and County ; Baker & Tilden, 1869."

Some roads as frequently spoken of are as follows : South Meadow road is the first road running to the Connecticut River from Main street, north of the Hockanum ; Mill street runs west from the Post Office ; below the meadow hill it is known as the North Meadow road. Prospect street runs along the meadow hill north from the last named road, and east until it ends on Main street. Orchard street runs between Prospect and Main streets ; its eastern end is nearly opposite Burnside avenue. The latter is the main traveled way to the eastward from Main street. Silver lane is the first road running east, south of the Hockanum. " Tobacco avenue " runs south from Silver lane and ends on Main street.

The author has been obliged to repel all temptations to genealogical study in his volume, and to relegate that sort of work to the members of the different families. That his work might be helpful to such inquiries, he has been careful to give most of the names associated with our earlier history.

In regard to any errors that may be found in this volume, the author wishes to say that he will be glad to be notified of

PREFACE.

them, that a corrected copy may be preserved, to be re-published, perhaps, at some future day. For anything that will add to a fuller knowledge of our town history, or of the people who helped to make it, he will also be grateful, meaning not to let his interest abate, although his work has, as it were, passed out of his hands.

For warm sympathy in his work and for cordial material aid, without which his history could not be published at this time, the author is indebted to the following persons:

Albert C. Raymond,
Ralph G. Spencer,
Aaron G. Olmsted,
Henry L. Goodwin,
William M. Stanley,
Ira T. Roberts,
Edward O. Goodwin.

Mrs. Edward S. Goodwin,
Henry R. Hayden,
Henry K. Olmsted, M.D.,
George W. Pratt,
Francis Hanmer,
Alfred Kilbourne,

EAST HARTFORD, CONN., Sept. 1879.

JOSEPH OLCOTT GOODWIN.

DESCRIPTION—1879.

The town of East Hartford is bounded north by the town of South Windsor, east by Manchester, south by Glastonbury, and west by Connecticut River. It has a population of about 3,000 souls. A good map of the town may be found in Baker & Tilden's Atlas of Hartford County, published in 1869, and to it references may be made in reading the descriptive parts of this volume.

The town covers a territory of about five miles in extent, north and south, and about three and a half miles, east and west, including the meadows. It geographical center is a point a little east of the house of George W. Pratt, Esq., on Silver lane. It is divided into ten school districts, two of which are joint districts—one including a section of South Windsor, and one a section of Manchester.

Main street runs through the town from north to south, with substantial dwellings, and good farms along its entire length. For miles it is grandly shaded by immense elms, and other trees. Two highways and the Bridge road connect Main street with Hartford, by means of the Hartford Bridge Company's bridge; and two important highways connect it with Burnside and Manchester. Other highways give communication to other parts of this and contiguous towns. The New York & New England Railroad crosses the town east and west, with a station on Main street and one at Burnside. The Connecticut Central Railroad enters the town near the center of its northern boundary and makes a junction with the New York & New England road at its station on Main street. This road has a station, "Burnham's," close to the South Windsor town line.

In 1866 a horse railroad company was chartered to connect Burnside and Glastonbury with Hartford, but the project is, at least temporarily, abandoned. Omnibuses make two trips daily from Burnside to Hartford, and four trips from the Center to Hartford. The mail wagon from Glastonbury passes through Hockanum and the Center to Hartford, and returns, daily.

East Hartford is remarkably level in its topography. The meadows lie along the Great River, like a vast park. They are about a half mile in width, and, interrupted only by a stretch of higher ground below the mouth of the Hockanum, extend the whole length of the town. They are annually flooded by the spring freshets, and yield abundant crops of hay without fertilizing. On the east these meadows are bounded by the Meadow Hill, a rise of fifteen or twenty feet to the upland. Excepting a few slight elevations, as at the Center Burying Ground and elsewhere, there are no noticeable hills in the town, save near its eastern and northern borders. Spencer Hill, southeast of Burnside, is a beautiful rounded knoll, from which a fine view may be had. North of it lie Great Hills, covered with forest; while still farther north, and across the Hockanum, Long Hill stretches its gentle cultivated slopes into South Windsor. In Podunk (North District) rises "Pirate Hill," probably named after some fable of Kidd and his treasures, and north of it several other moderate eminences. The arable lands are light and dry, and remarkably free from stone. A hidden ledge of rocks forms the falls at Burnside and extends beneath the surface southerly through the town. Some rough quarrying has been done on this ledge.

The Hockanum (by some called Solomon's) River enters the town from the east, furnishing power for the powder mills, and for the paper mills at Burnside. Between Burnside and the Connecticut the river has worn a valley a quarter of a mile or so wide, with irregularly projecting hillsides. This valley is flooded every spring by high water from the Connecticut, and makes a good pasturage in summer. A number of brooks cross the town from east to west, running at the bottom of their little valleys, and pleasantly interrupting the level of the landscape. Talcott Mountain on the west, and the Bolton range on the east, are prominently in sight from almost any point in town, while from some places may be seen Mount Tom and Holyoke in the north, and the Strait Hills below Middletown, and the Meriden mountains in the south.

EAST HARTFORD CENTER has three churches, Congregational, Episcopal, and Roman Catholic. In the basement of the Congregational church the town meetings are held. Here, also, are two general stores and the East Hartford post-office; two meat markets, two harness shops, a blacksmith's shop, a tin shop, a livery stable, four tobacco warehouses, a lumber yard, two florists' gardens, manufactories of patent seed-sowers and weeders, of knife straps, of silver spoons, etc.

BURNSIDE (formerly Scotland*) village lies about two miles east of Main street. It has one church, Methodist Episcopal. Here are three large paper mills on the Hockanum, the upper one owned by F. R. Walker & Co., the "middle mill" by the East Hartford Manufacturing Company, the lower mill, on the old grist mill site, by The Hanmer & Forbes Company. These mills are kept constantly busy with their orders, and have each won a reputation for fine goods, the first for newspapers, the second for fine writing papers, the last for manilla and envelope papers. Near the east town line are the powder mills, now owned by the Hazard Powder Company, of Enfield. These have been idle since the last war. In Burnside are also two general stores and the Burnside post-office, a blacksmith's shop, a wagon shop, etc.

In WILLOW BROOK (Second South District,) there are three general stores, a coal yard, a blacksmith's shop, a wagon shop, two tobacco warehouses, etc.

---

* The name of Scotland was changed to Burnside in 1862, when it was made a post station, as there was already one Scotland in the State. The name was chosen because of its Scotch derivation, signifying a *burn's side*, and was the suggestion of Miss Susan Goodwin. Its former name of Scotland was given it by the Forbes settlers, who were of Scotch antecedents.

In HOCKANUM (South District) there are two churches, Congregational and Methodist Episcopal. There are two general stores, a post-office (Hockanum), a tobacco warehouse, a grist mill on Pewter Pot Brook, etc. Many alewives and shad are caught here in nets during the spring freshets.

The MEADOW DISTRICT lies along the Connecticut river, and has quite a populous village. Here is Morse's Hotel, two general stores, a provender store, lumber yard, marble cutting works, a carriage shop, blacksmith's shop, tin shop, ice houses, etc.

The Southeast district is sometimes called Hillstown. Farming is its chief industry.

The various industries we have named are, with a few exceptions, merely accessory to the principal occupation of the people, which is farming, the raising of fruits and produce for the Hartford markets, and the culture of tobacco. This town is one of the largest tobacco growing towns in New England.

The town has no parks or public grounds, unless the unkempt plot north of the Hockanum causeway, on which the old meeting house stood, may be called so. But Mr. Albert C. Raymond has lately given to the Village Improvement Society (chartered in January, 1879, though organized two or three years earlier), in trust, a plot of ground on the corner of Main street and Central avenue, for a site for a public library and park. This it is hoped will be laid out and kept in a manner worthy of the generous spirit in which it was given. Mr. Raymond has also provided a munificent fund with which the library building is to be built, furnished with books and permanently maintained.

INDIANS.

CHAPTER I.

1631-1793.

When first the Connecticut Valley became known to the white men, it was inhabited by what were known as the River Tribes,—a number of small clans of Indians living along the Great River and its tributaries. Of these tribes the Podunks occupied territory now lying in the towns of East Hartford and South Windsor, and numbered, by differing estimates, from sixty to two hundred bowmen. They were governed by two sachems, Waginacut and Arramamet, and were connected in some way with the Indians who lived across the Great River, in Windsor. This is evident from the fact that when the land between the Scantic and the Podunk rivers was sold to the English, Arramamet signed the deed with ten others, among whom were Sheat and Cogrenossett of Poquonnoc in Windsor; and in 1637, Arramamet and other Indians complained to the General Court, alleging that Lieut. Holmes had denied them the planting of the old ground about Plymouth House, in Windsor.

One of the principal places of habitation of the Podunks was near the mouth of the little river, by them called Podunk. Land in this neighborhood was occupied by the Indians after the English settled here, and was reserved to them by the General Court for many years. There are also abundant traces of their former presence all along the meadow bank; while the highlands bordering the valley of the Hockanum have been found especially rich in their implements of flint and stone.

The Indians built their slight summer lodges near the Great river, living sumptuously upon the swarming shad and salmon, and lampreys in their season, and finding an easy prey in the deer that sought the luxuriant feeding ground of the meadows; while the rich alluvium gave them maize and beans in response to their rude tillage. For clothing they hunted the otter, the mink, and beaver, covering their wigwams, perchance, with coarser peltries of deer, wolf, and bear, before the white traders came to beguile them of these luxuries.

The winter habitations of the Podunks were farther inland, along the warm valley brooks, in the deep recesses of the woods. To these they retired when autumn let loose his blasts adown the broad river valley, threatening to lock their fisheries beneath the ice. Here they repatched their sheltered lodges with skins and bark and reeds, and in the bland "Indian summer" conducted their big hunts, over ground familiar to every boy within our borders who owns a gun, afterwards drying their venison and bear meat for their winter's sustenance.

In troublesome times they built their forts of stout posts, or palisades, and gathered into closer habitations, leaving a central space in the village for a camp fire, about which to celebrate their wild and varied ceremonies. Traces of such an enclosure still remain in Goodwin's pasture, one-fourth of a mile east of the post-office—the steep hillside having been its defence and outlook on three sides, and an embankment and palisades upon the north. This neighborhood has been found rich in stone and flint relics, and a tradition of a large stone buried in the center of the hill remains, although no one has as yet been able to find it. The place to-day bears the name of "Fort Hill," and is probably the fort to which "one-eyed" Tantinomo withdrew at the time of his quarrel with Uncas and Sequassen in 1665, when the English so unsuccessfully attempted arbitration between them.

Of an Indian burial place discovered on the highland south of Podunk brook and just west of Main street, Barber (Conn. Hist. Coll.) gives us some particulars.

It was situated, the account says, about half way between their summer quarters by the Great River and their inland village. Skeletons were exhumed here a few years ago by digging from one to four feet below the surface. These indicated that the bodies had been laid on their sides, with their heads toward the south, the knees drawn up to the breast, the arms folded. Remains of blankets and bark coverings were found, and, in one instance, a small brass kettle and hatchet, well preserved. A gun barrel and lock, a number of glass bottles, one half-full of liquid of some sort, a pair of shears, a pistol, leaden pipes for tobacco, strings of wampum, small brass rings, and glass beads were also found. The skeleton of a woman was dug up, and with it a brass comb, with the hair still preserved about it. Most of the articles found had probably been obtained from the Dutch (whose trading house was set up on Dutch Point in Hartford, before the coming of the Englishmen), and are preserved in the rooms of the Hartford Historical Society.

It seems strange that so few articles of Indian manufacture are named among the articles found on this site, for remains of stone and flint are not lacking. I have several arrow-heads, etc., picked up here by Mr. Alfred E. Kilbourne and myself, during a visit to the place.

Another burial place of the Indians lies on the bank of the Connecticut in South Windsor. This I visited with Messrs. Kilbourne and William Andrus in 1877, and we found fragments of coarse pottery, flints, and bones beneath the caving bank. The bones were arm or leg-bones, very friable, and perished with the handling.

Other burial places no doubt exist. Human bones have been dug up in the brick-yard near Colt's Ferry, and parts of a skeleton were unearthed while digging the sewer on Main street, at the head of Orchard street, although neither of the latter were safely referable to the Indians.

From the beginning of their contact with the whites, the history of the Podunks is one in common with that of all the North American tribes,—a gradual deterioration in all the simple and robust characteristics that mark an aboriginal people, ending at last in their total decay and final disappearance. And so slight a hold had they upon the soil, that the farmer's boy might well regard the story of their occupancy as but a tale of the old witch-haunted times, did not his polished hoe click occasionally against the clumsy implements of an earlier husbandry, on rare days when he is afield, giving him a subtle sense of the wonderful interval that separates his own life from that to which such rude appliances administered years ago.

But whatever may be said of the violent change wrought by the white man's coming, it hardly becomes us who owe so much to it to shed any but sentimental tears. Indeed, we may console ourselves with the thought that the white man was no unwelcome intruder here. The tribes of this neighborhood had in themselves but little integral strength, and no certain ties of alliance with each other. In a quarrel with the Pequots they had been driven from their lands. Homeless and in extremity, they sought the protection of the English, who would make powerful allies if they could be induced to settle on the river and espouse their cause. In 1631 Waghinacut, probably a Podunk, went to Boston, and afterwards to Plymouth, with this end in view, offering to provide the settlers with corn, and to give them eighty skins of beaver, if they would accept their offer. The English, however, found that he was a treacherous man, and at war with a greater sachem than himself—Pekoath—and did not accept his proposal. Governor Winslow, of Plymouth, however, made a journey to the river, but nothing came of it until 1633, when rumors of the rich fur trade carried on here by the Dutch began to stir the English to action. In that year Lieut. Holmes with some Plymouth men sailed valorously past the two big guns of the Dutch, at Dutch Point in Hartford, with his house aboard, and set up "Plymouth House" just below the mouth of the Farmington river, in Windsor. He is said to have brought back the sachems who had been driven out of their country by the Pequots; and he bought much land of them, ignoring the recent conquest of the Pequots altogether. This he was the more ready to do because to refuse to recognize the claims of the Pequots was also to ignore those of the Dutch, who had purchased their lands of them. As a consequence the Pequots behaved very badly, murdering Captain Stone and his crew in the Connecticut river, and Captain Oldham at Block Island, and committing other outrages which ended in their destruction in 1637.

The relation of the River Indians to the early settlers prior to the Narragansett war appears to have been for the most part of a friendly nature, although the aborigines were then and always rather unmanageable neighbors. Puritan ideas of law and order could hardly avoid something of friction in contact with a race that knew no restraints save the disorderly troop of its own wild traditions. But we are glad to be able to put at the head of their record here (as a whole by no means a flattering one), the fact that in the dreadful winter of 1635, when the ill-prepared settlers at Hartford were reduced to the farthest verge of extremity, there is no evidence of violence or savagery, but rather the record of kindness and sympathy. They kept the settlers alive with gifts of " malt, and acorns, and grains."

Until about the year 1675, the Indians lived near the settlement; one writer says, having a village at the north end of East Hartford meadows, and one at the south end of the "Island," near the Hockanum river, with others, probably, along the Hockanum, as at Fort Hill and elsewhere. For long intervals the only record in regard to them is in the nature of orders passed by the court. The magistrates evidently found them rather uncouth wards, for so they seemed to treat them. They restricted them in various ways, forbidding trade with them in arms, in horses, dogs, or boats, or in dangerous supplies, as cider, " hot water," etc. Smiths were not to work for them, and none but licensed traders were to buy their corn, beaver, venison, or timber. They were forbidden to enter the houses or handle the arms of the settlers, nor were they to bring their own arms into the towns; and if found in the plantations at night they were to be arrested by the guard, or, resisting arrest, to be shot. They were not allowed to harbor stragglers, or strange Indians in their villages; and in 1653 were required to give up their arms in token of their fidelity. Land was not to be leased to them, nor could they buy or sell land themselves. Culprits were treated according to the English laws, and the long arm of justice gave the fugitive little comfort or safety wherever he fled. They were also the subjects of special enactments of the court, a special chapter in the code of 1650 being devoted to them. In 1667 it was ordered that "whatever Indian or Indians shal labor or play on ye Sabbath within ye English limits on ye English lands, he shal pay five shillings as a fine . . . . or sit in ye stocks one hour." And in 1675, for drunkenness he was to work twelve days with the person that complained of him and proved his fault, one-half the benefit of his labor to go to the complainer, and the other half to the county treasury. In 1675, sundry curious laws were made to govern the conquered Pequots, of which we give two specimens, to further show how uncomfortable the righteous Puritans made it for the once wild and uncurbed "sons of the forest:" one making their very religious rites a crime, in declaring "That whosoever shall powaw [pow-wow], or use wichcraft or any fals god shall be convented and punished;" the other forbidding them to chop or fetch home wood, or to hunt fowl or fish on the "Saboth day." Contumacious criminals were shipped to the West Indies as slaves, in exchange for negroes. Sachems were obliged to answer for the good conduct of their subjects, and compelled to give up offenders to the magistrates.

The wild untrammeled life of the Indians early attracted to it some from among the whites who were restless of the restraints put upon them by the rigid government of the Colony. In 1642, it is recorded that "Whereas diverse persons departe from amongst us, and take up theire aboade with the Indians, in a prophane course of life; for the preventing thereof, it is ordered" that any who should so do should be punished by three years imprisonment and such "further censure, by fyne or corporall punishment," as the court thinks meet. And yet in all this sternness there was a tempering of justice. The rights of the Indians were measurably well protected against the crafty whites; they were admitted to live with or near the English and under their protection when "submissive;" committees were appointed to counsel them, and religious instructors were provided for them, that there might be made known to these " poore, lost, naked sonnes of Adam, twice at least in every yeare, ... the councells of the Lord, and thereby to draw and stirr them vp to direct and order all theire ways and conversations according to the rule of his Worde." How amenable the Indians were to the pious tutelage of the whites is best shown by their history.

For many years the Podunks continued to live, as has been said, upon their lands in the Podunk meadows, and along the valley of the Hockanum river, a stream abundant in fish and lampreys, while the swamps along its course were rich in musquashes and larger game. The fort on Fort Hill in Goodwin's pasture, near this stream, was a stronghold of the Indians, and, during the year 1656 occurred the famous quarrel between the Podunks and Sequassen, which, more than any other known incident in their history, connects them tangibly with Fort Hill and the valley of the Hockanum.

It appears that a young Podunk named Weaseapono murdered a sagamore living near Mattabassett (Middletown). The sagamore was a relative of Sequassen (chief of the Hartford and Wethersfield Indians), and Sequassen demanded the criminal. The Podunks resolved to defend him; whereupon Sequassen sought the aid of Uncas, his old Mohegan enemy, who had also cause against Tantinomo, "the one eyed," for harboring a murderer who had fled from his vengeance, as well as for enticing away his men. Uncas, a crafty friend of the whites, brought the matter before the English magistrates at Hartford, and they attempted an amicable settlement. A quaint account of this affair is entered in the Colonial Records of this State in the following words (page 304, vol. 1):

" A relation of the carriage of the difference that fell out betwixt Vncas & Seoquassen of the one side & Totanimo & the Potunck Indians, At the Generall Court held at Hartford, in May, in the year of o^r Lord, 1656.

" That vpon the murther of a Sachem of Connecticott dwelling neare Mattapeaset, by a young man called Weaseapano, Seoquassen complained to the Magistrates of Hartford of the wrong that the Potunck Indians did to him in entertaining & maintaining of him against all justice, wch said Seoquassen tooke

Vncas in to him for helpe, to bee reuenged for the said Sachems death who was inraged wth the like accident of entertaining a murtherer that runne from Vnquas to the said Potunk, who complained likewise of wrongs done him, to the Magistrates. Vnquas also had complained to the Magistrates of Connecticott for seuerall wrongs done to him by Tantonomo, espetially his intising of many of his men & their protecting a Murtherer ; and therevppon the Magistrates ordered that the Sachems of both sides should appeare at Hartford at the Generall Court ; who all appearing, Seoquassen first declared of the fact done by a meane fellow vppon one that was allyed to him, a great Sachem ; and so Vnquas & Foxen iustified, in many words.

"The Gouerno^r pressed to know what sattisfaction they required, who answered & pressed hard to haue 10 men put to death of his friends that was the murtherer ; the other Sachems pleaded vnjust, because the Sachem that was slayne had murdered the young mans Vncle wilfully. The Court many of them spake their mindes to & fro. The Gouerno^r shewed the Indians what o^r law is in such cases, that onely the murtherer or any that were accessary to it should be punished, & so hee & many Deputies pressed both sides for peace, & not to fight vpon such a quarrell.

"The Potunck Sachems p^{r}ffered to giue wampam in way of sattisfaction, wch wholly was rejected, whereupon the Court spent some time to perswade to peace. Then they fell to be sattisfied wth the death of 6 men. The Court wearied with their speeches pressed the Potunk Indians to deliver vp the murtherer, the wch Totannimo p^{r}mised, but priuately stole out of the Court & went wth the rest of the Sachems to Potunk forte : wherevpon both the English & Indians were offended & agreed to send a messeng^r to deliver vp the murtherer, as Totañimo had p^{r}mised in Court. In the meane time the Court appointed 4 Deputyes to be a Comittee to treat wth the Sachems of both sides, to see what could be done for peace. This Committee priuately brought Vnquas to accept of the murtherer only, for full sattisfaction. But those Potunk Indians said they could not deliver vp the said murther^r, his friends were so many & potent wthin the Forte.

"In the afternoon the Comittee & the Sachems made knowne to the Court, who then agreed that by no meanes the English would bee ingaged in either of their quarrels, but would leave them to themselves, wherevpon the Gou^{r}nor made a long speech desiring to bee at peace one wth another, & take wampam. If they would not, then hee declared that the Court would not hinder them, but left them to themselues, & whatsoeuer fell out afterwards vpon either of them, they brought vpon themselues. But so were engaged, that they should not fight vpon this side of the river of Hartford, nor hurt any of the English houses or any of theirs of the other side of the river; wth many expressions more to the same effect, was spoken by the Gouerno^r & also by some of the Deputies.

"Some expressions many times in agitation thereof was spoken that might carry that sence of advising & counselling of Vnquas not to fight, as some app^{r}hended then, but in conclusion the Gou^{r}no^r, as the mouth of the Court, declared his minde fully to the Indians of both sides, as aforesaid.

"Witnesse our hand, this 20th of August, 1657.

"JONATHAN BREWSTER.
"Aug: 19th, (57).

"The Court voted that this relation should bee transcribed & asserted vnd^r the Sec^{r}s hand, that to their sattisfaction it was euidenced in Court to be a true relation."

Uncas gathered his warriors and marched against the Podunks, but was met near the Hockanum river, probably not far from Fort Hill, by Tantinomo with a nearly equal force of warriors, and was unwilling to hazard a battle. He told Tantinomo he would bring the Mohawks in destruction upon his people if he continued to protect the murderers. He then left. Shortly afterwards by a clever exercise of strategy he obtained Weascapono. A dextrous warrior went to Podunk, fired a wigwam, and left Mohawk weapons upon his trail. These the pursuing Podunks found, and, full of fear of the dreadful Mohawks, they sent to Mohegan for terms of peace, and surrendered the murderer. (DeForest.)

It is not apparent, so far as the Podunks are concerned, that any result followed the appointment of the early religious instructors for the Indians, or that they wrought among them at all. DeForest says the Podunks received their first and perhaps their last call to religious truth from John Eliot, the famous Indian apostle, who, being in Hartford in 1657, began his attempts to christianize the natives by addressing them. The principal men of the tribe assembled in the meeting-house in Hartford, and he spoke to them in their own language. He concluded by asking them whether they would accept Christ or not. They replied, " No ; you have taken away our lands, and now want to make us your servants." And they scornfully departed. Possibly they thought the white man's religion was not adequate to console them for the wrongs which they conceived that he, in its name, had wrought against them. They refused to bow to the maker of the hand that was, apparently, every day against them. And yet their wrongs were imaginary rather than real. They had welcomed the English here, and gladly sold them their lands for a price. And if the contrast between their squalor and unthrift, and the comforts of their hard-working and provident neighbors was a glaring one, yet the cause was not far to seek had they been of a philosophic temper. But of such a temper they obviously were not, for it is recorded by the Rev. Samuel Woodbridge, our first pastor on this side of the river, that it was noted that of these " scoffers " all died soon after, and that in his day not one of the tribe remained.

In this same year (1657) appears an order in the records of the colony, which indicates that the Podunks had left their homes because of their apprehension of Uncas, and Mr. Allen and Jonathan Gilbert were appointed to go and make known the minds of the commissioners in regard to the matter. The commissioners had " ordered that Vnckas bee required to p^rmit the Podunk Indians to return to their dwellings & there abide in peace and safety wthout molestation from him or his, & that the said Indians bee incouraged & invited so to do, by the Governor of Connecticott, ... and to signify to Pocomtick and Norwootick sachems our charge uppon Vnckas in refference to Podunk Indians, and our desire of their return and continuance in peace : therefore we desire & expect they will forbeare all hostility against Vnckas till the next meeting of the commissioners."

A committee of eight were appointed in 1659, to lay out and divide the Podunk lands formerly possessed by those Indians, and likewise to treat with them for what land was not fit for their planting, that they might be willing to part with to those English who had contracted with Tantinomo. And what appears to the committee to be granted and allowed by the Indians as Tantinomo's "perticuler propriety, the court is willing to allow of and confirm to the English, according to their bargain, vidz: to Thomas Burnham and his partners." And what winter grain was sowed on the land was to belong to the Indians who sowed it. And if the Indians were willing to part with some planting land, then the committee were to lay it out to the English as a part of Tantinomo's bargain.

The Thomas Burnham above mentioned, and Jacob Mygatt, had, about the year 1658, procured of Tantinomo a deed of certain lands in Podunk. The extent of these lands and the nature of the conveyance cannot now be known, the instrument having been lost. Probably the Burnham lands in Podunk are the only ones in our town purchased by individuals in their private capacity from the Indians. The court recognized this conveyance to Burnham and Mygatt as a mere lease of the land, the title of which they or their assigns were obliged to purchase of the grantees in the distribution of the three mile purchase in 1666. The troubles which grew out of this loose bargain, or lease, were so speedy and importunate * that the General court found it politic to cut off the

---

* Wm. Pitkin and Barth: Barnard bought the right of Jacob Mygatt in these lands, and a dispute arose with Burnham about the division of them. The matter went to the General Court, which, in 1666, confirmed a decision of the county court in the case against Burnham. But his people did not give up so easily. His wife and children sturdily drove off Pitkin's and Barnard's men when they came to plant, and scattered their seed to the winds. The above decision, however, was confirmed again in 1668, giving Burnham what wheat and pease he had planted, but providing that he should pay land rent for the pease at the rate of 8 shillings for an acre. This was in May, 1668, and an appeal of Burnham's was denied the following October. Burnham afterwards purchased, from the grantees of 1666, much or all of the land which he held by his unrecognized purchase from the Indians.

possibility of other complications of this sort by an order, in 1660, forbidding any person directly or indirectly to buy or rent lands of the Indians at Podunk. But Thomas Burnham was to be allowed, if the Indians departed, to improve their lands (with their consent before a magistrate) in their absence; but to freely surrender the same on their return. This to continue until "his lease" expired.

A month later the court having heard the return of the committee, "respecting Thomas Burnham his contract with Tantimono: It appears that part of the lands laid out to the said Burnham and his copartners doth belong to Foxens' successors by a gift of Foxen to his allies;" and it was ordered that the Podunks should occupy according to the former order, and that the English who had contracted with Tantinomo should possess according to their bargain only "that wch is ye particular proprietie of Tantinomo that the Indians do yield, or that Tanto: can prove to be his propriety." Mr. Allyn and Jonathan Gilbert were to "bound ye said Tanton: part" to Thomas Burnham, and the order was to stand until further proof of Tantinomo's right appeared.

Burnham afterwards secured from Arramamet, Taquis, and four others, Foxen's successors, or a part of them, "for divers good considerations and five coats," a deed of all their land at Podunk; the deed saying that they do, for themselves and successors, make over all their right and title in those lands aforesaid unto Thomas Burnham and his heirs. It is signed "Arramamet, his mark"—a device of a bow and arrow, "Taquis, his mark," and others.

Later deeds in the possession of the Burnham family convey to the descendants of Thomas Burnham the rights of individual Indians in lands in the Podunk meadows. One Popo, a Podunk, deeded to John Burnham land bounded by the Connecticut and Podunk rivers and by land of certain squaws, for six pounds and "other consideration." And in 1711, three squaws quit-claimed to Thomas Burnham 2d, land bounded east by the upland, north by Solomon Gilman, and south by a road, "in consideration of one coat and two shillings and sixpence in cash."

Probably these errant Indians turned up like lost heirs at certain impecunious times to assert some obscure claim to the Podunk lands, and no doubt gave the occupants no little trouble to get rid of them. The last that appears upon the record is the "wife of Squinimo, an Indian man," complaining that she is unjustly kept out of possession of certain lands at Podunk, contrary to the act of March, 1660. Col. Allyn was to enquire and report in May, 1723, but nothing further appears. Probably a coat or two, or a few shillings, sent the wife of Squinimo on her happy way into the oblivion that has fallen upon all of her tribe.

Going back from this digression to the year 1661, and taking up the sequence of events again, we find the restless Podunks again unsettled, and a source of uneasiness to the whites, who appointed a committee, consisting of Major Mason and four others, " to settle the Podunk Indians in that place vppon righteous and honorable terms;" and also the Farmington Indians, and to purge out strangers from among them; and to "enjoyne both to cease their warr and not to entertein strangers; and also to require ye captives."

The Podunks appear to have required a deal of "settling." In 1666, when Arramamet was their sole sachem, the Mohegans under Uncas encroached on their territory by hunting there,—probably while conducting one of their big "drives," which depleted the country driven in a day of its larger game. This was fresh reason for a quarrel, but it resulted bloodlessly. Both parties appealed to the whites, and the General Assembly appointed John Allyn, William Wadsworth, and Thomas Stanton (an interpreter), to hear and adjust the difficulty. The result was an amicable agreement, as follows:

"This writeing witnesseth that Vncass, sachem of Moheag, in behalfe of himselfe and people of Moheage and Nahantick, doe hereby engage him and them to Aramamatt, Seacut & Nessaheagen, Gent^n of Conecticut, in behalfe of the Indian people at Windsor, Podunk, Hartford, that they wil carry it peaceably & neighbourly towards them and the aforesaid Indians, and that they will not either secretly or publiquely contriue or practice any evil or mischiefe against y^m. And the aforesaid Aramamat etc. engage that they & the aforesaid Indians on the Riuer wil carry it peaceably towards ye aforesaid Sachem and his people and that they wil neither plot nor practice any evil against the said Vncass or his people. And whereas there is a difference about the bounds of Lands and Royalties belonging to ye said Sachem and Aramamat, It is agreed between them that the deviding bounds shalbe at Ashowat to Wonggunshoake and soe to Washiack and from thenc northerly, from wch bounds the Land and Royalties on the east shalbe and remaine to Vncass and his heires, and from ye said bounds on ye west to Conecticut Riuer shalbe to Aramamat and his heires ; and this our agreem^t, and that we oblige ourselues & o^r heires to stand to ye same, wee testify by subscribing o^r marks.

"It is agreed that Aramamat shal not imp^rpriate vnto himself any of ye land y^t is on the south of ye path that goes from Thomas Edwards to Monheage.

"Vncass, × his mark.
Aramamat, × his mark.
Seacut, × his mark.
Nesahegen, × his mark.
Quanampewet, × his m^rk."

(See Colonial Records, Vol. II, Page 41.)

It was after the above treaty that Arramamet gave his daughter, the dusky and high-born Sowgonosk, to Attawanhood (called by the English, Joshua), the third son of Uncas, and sachem of the Western Niantics. In confirmation of their marriage Arramamet gave to them all his lands in Podunk and elsewhere, with the condition that it was afterward to go to the children of Sowgonosk, if any survived her, or to her nearest heirs by English law. This land and much other, to which he had but a questionable title, Joshua, at his death in 1675, willed to his two sons, with remainder to his two squaws. Among the larger tracts of from 500 to 5,000 acres which this munificent chieftain gave away, was one to William Pitkin, Thomas Burnham, and twelve others, comprising all the land, excepting 300 acres, lying from the mountains in sight of Hartford, northward to a pond called Shenaps ;

east to Willimantic river; south by said river, and west by Hartford bounds (the present line between Manchester and Bolton). He had agreed prior to 1672 with the town of Hartford for land to extend its bounds five miles eastward— land included in the present town of Manchester, but long known as the Five Miles, or Joshua lands. A deed of this land was procured in 1682, from his administrators, Jas. Fitch, Jr., and Thos. Buckingham. The price is not given.

The breaking out of the Narragansett war in June, 1675, tested the loyalty and good faith of the Indian tribes in a way that no prior event had done. It was the first grand effort of the Indians to exterminate the white men, who were so rapidly encroaching upon their hunting grounds. In this crisis, when the plan of extirpation spared neither women or children, the Mohegans and Pequots were faithful to the English; some other tribes remained neutral; a few Nipmucks of Windham county, and the Podunks, joined Philip. Tradition says the Podunks then numbered two hundred warriors, but DeForest thinks there could have been but about sixty. Few survived this disastrous war to return to their native haunts along the Podunk and the Hockanum, and it was virtually their end as a nation.

In the sunny serenity of our own time, when one may fall asleep in any drowsy nook that invites him in the woods, it is difficult to call up a picture of the real dangers that surrounded our ancestors at this time. It was an age of superstition, when people were credulous of witchcraft, and of black satanic influences; when the dark forests were astir with demoniac savages, and the nights were hag-ridden and full of direful portents and palpitations. In imagination a foe lurked behind every copse, and the evil one had sworn and sealed emissaries among men. But the Indians were for the time the supreme foe, and the records are full of indications of activity against them. Several persons had been shot at by them in this neighborhood, and in Sept., 1675, Major Robert Treat was "commissionated to appoynt about 30 of your Troop of Dragoones to march on the east side of the river and to make what discoueries of the enemy you can in those parts, and seiz all such sculking armed Indians as you shall meet with in your way; and to make search from Hockanum Riuer to Scantic, where they are to quarter this night and to-morrow make further discouerie." Thirty dragoons were also to march on the west side of the river to Wethersfield, and thirty others to Windsor.

Manifold precautions were taken by those living on the outskirts of the settlements. In October, Mr. John Hollister at Nayage (South Glastonbury,) was permitted to hire three or four men to fortify his house and secure his corn. Flankers were to be placed in or near the outside houses, so as to command from flanker to flanker round the town; and in December those who continued on the east side the river were ordered to "repayre into good and sufficient garrisons" to defend themselves; all grain was to be brought into the town, or secured in some garrison on that side; all swine were to be secured or killed; and no arms or ammunition were to be kept save in garrison-houses, except what men carried with them. Good watches were to be kept by night, and ward by day; or else scouts were to be sent "to range the woods by day to discover the approach of an enemie." These orders were declared by the constables in the plantations.

That these precautions were not idle ones, so far as our territory was concerned, is apparent from this entry in the journal of the Council, Feb. 18, 1675-6:

"The enemie having come to Hoccanum and shott at William Hill and sorely wounded him, the Councill sent forth a party of souldiers to make search for the enemie."

February 21, 1675-6, the following order was passed:

"The enemie some of them drawing down into these parts to doe mischiefe (as is evident,) the Councill have thought meet to order that what corn and provisions are on the east side of the river, in the several farms there and not in garrisons, be forthwith transported to the plantations to be secured from the enemie; and the constables in the several plantations are hereby ordered to assist the good people there, by impressing men, boates and teames for the transportation of their corn and provisions afoarsayd. And the people are allso ordered to draw themselves into garrisons for their safety; and to bring their cattell and hay to be under the command of their garrisons, that they may be preserved,—except they bring them over to the towns; and not to goe forth upon their occasions without their armes and in companyes so as they may defend themselves: and that there be garrisons kept at Nath: Bissell's, Tho: Burnham's, Mr. John Crowe's, and at Nabuck, and Mr. Willys his farme; provided in every garrison there be six men at least, and that the garrisons be well fortified, and that noe place but such doe remayn inhabited on the east side the sayd River. And the constables are forthwith to give notice hereof to the people in their respective limitts, and to require their attendance hereunto."

Nath. Bissell ran a ferry in Windsor (now South Windsor); Thos. Burnham lived nearly opposite the house of Mr. Julius Burnham in Podunk; John Crow lived near the late Ozias Roberts place in East Hartford; Nabuck is now Naubuc; and Mr. Willys's farm was still further south.

A vivid picture of the barbarities of this time is given in the examination of one Menowniett, who was "halfe a Moheag and halfe a Naragoncett," who confessed he was in many fights against the English,—at Northampton and above, at Pacomtock (Deerfield), at Hadley, and in many smaller assaults. He was asked, "Who killed G: Elmore at Podunck?" He [said he] was one of them himselfe; there was 9 in company; 3 did the businesse, which were Weauwoss, Johnnot and Mashinott."

"He also sayth Cohas and another Naragancet shot William Hill."

"Cohas burnt G: Coals house."

"He sayth ye Indians hid a great many guns about Pacomptuck" (Deerfield), etc.

To obtain these guns, Lieut. Thos. Hollister was ordered to take ten men, and with the prisoner, march "forthwith to the sayd place where the arms are s^d to be hid; and if yet they remayn, he is hereby ordered to seiz the s^d arms and convey them in safe custody to Hartford." And in case Menowniett did not carry it well, or failed to make the discovery, Lieut. Hollister had liberty to kill him or to return him to prison again.

Cohas, or Cohause, was taken near New Haven by the friendly Indians, who were very serviceable at this time. He was brought before the council and acknowledged his hostility to the English, and was accused by Menowniett of being party to the shooting of William Hill, and of burning Goodman Coals's house, etc. The council found him an open and desperate enemy of the English, and declared him a "child of death." He was accordingly sentenced "to suffer the paynes and terrors of death; and that if the Indians see cause to put him to death, they shall doe it forthwith; if not, he shall be shot to death by som English. The Marshall is appoynted to see execution done. Which was performed by an Indian."

The larger events of the Narragansett war need not be recounted here. Two soldiers, Thomas Trill and Obadiah Wood, who were engaged in it, lived on this side the Great River, and were the first two persons buried in our Center Burying-Ground.

A ragged remnant only of the Podunks remained on their lands to quarrel about them in 1677. That year the court appointed a committee to set out "what of those planting lands at Podunck shall belong to Aramamet, his heires, and what shall belong to the other Indians." These slowly disposed of their rights here as has already been shown, until in 1722 the wife of "Squinimo, an Indian man," makes a last feeble complaint, and disappears from sight.

But the danger to the colonies from the Indians was not ended with the close of Philip's war. In 1689 a committee was appointed for fortifying four houses on this side the river; and when, in 1704, the Eastern Indians fell upon Deerfield, either killing or capturing all of its sleeping inhabitants, precautionary measures were again undertaken. The "great guns" (formerly taken from the Dutch) were ordered mounted, and the four houses on this side were ordered fortified "at their own cost and charge." William Pitkin,

Lieut. Jonathan Hills, Dea. Joseph Olmsted, Daniel Bidwell, Sergt. William Williams were to be a committee to appoint the houses to be fortified, and to "proportion each man's share that he is to doe of said fortification." One of the houses then fortified was that of William Pitkin, who lived on the meadow hill not far from the track of the New York & New England railroad. There is a difference of opinion in regard to the exact site of this house, which is discussed elsewhere.

Into William Pitkin's fort, says a writer in the *Elm Leaf*, the inhabitants were summoned at evening by the ringing of a bell. No serious trouble was had with the Indians in this neighborhood at this time.

The most that remains to record concerning those of the Indians who lingered here, are certain traditions which show them in their pitiable decay, without character or any noble traits, lingering in thievish, dissolute vagabondage, a disgrace even to their savage and turbulent ancestry, often appearing a forlorn and curious spectacle in their tawdry plumage on "election days" and other high days in Hartford.

Some, as we have said, were enslaved for offences against the English. Joseph Bull, who owned part of a saw-mill at Burnside, had an Indian servant, named Jamus, who had voluntarily bound himself to him. Jamus, however, became tired of service, and was flying with others out of the country. He was caught at Bull's "great charge," and was by the council sentenced to continue in his master's service for life, unless his master chose to abate his punishment for good behavior. If he again ran away or misbehaved he was to be sold out of the country.

The love of the Indians for cider and "hot waters" led them to take many risks. The Williams family early settled near the Willow Brook on land just east of Dowd's grove, and the family have a tradition that here an Indian was shot while stealing cider. The shooting was done with an old "queen's arms" musket, which is still preserved. Afterwards another Indian thrust his gun through the window of a neighboring house, just south of the brook, with murderous intent. Mrs. Williams saw the gun and struck up its muzzle just in time to have the charge enter a beam overhead. Other Indians caught stealing cider were thrown into a patch of briers on "Pigeon Hill," near here; and when they struggled out on the other side were caught and tossed back again, until they were thought sufficiently punished. The *Elm Leaf*, a little local newspaper, which lived a few years with us on rather meagre fare, published a few "traditionary papers," from the pen of Mr. George J. Olmsted, in 1863. In them is told the story of an Indian who entered a house, one Sunday, where a woman was alone, and demanded cider. It was refused him, whereupon he drew a knife from his belt and sharpened it upon the table, threatening at the same time to kill her. Suddenly a large dog, before unseen, sprang out upon him, and he escaped only with a torn and bleeding arm.

The following story of the ingenious plan of two Indians to get rum (allowed only at funerals), is from the same source. John persuaded Sam to play he was dead, and then he went to 'Squire [Jonathan] Hills [of Hockanum], and procured the rum. The 'Squire afterwards met Sam alive, and probably the worse for the rum. He met John also, and said, "Look here, you rascal! Why did you lie to me? Sam is not dead." "Me not lie," said John; "me thought him dead; he say so himself."

This also from the same source: A squaw came to the house of a Mr. Forbes (probably in Burnside) for protection. She was allowed to hide under a bed. An Indian soon came and demanded her; and the people, being somewhat afraid, gave her up. The Indian dragged her away to the woods, and scalped and killed her.

The following is from another source: One Euodias Bidwell, whose house stood on the point between the Tolland turnpike and Burnside avenue, was not a man of redoubtable courage. Abroad one day in the woods with his gun, he caught sight of an Indian crouching in the bushes. He held his gun at arm's length above his head, and faltered: "I am Euodias Bidwell. I won't shoot if you won't." Getting no reply, he gathered courage, and found the Indian had been dead many days. These stories, more or less credible, belong to the remnant of the Podunk tribe, which, DeForest says, was living on the Hockanum river in 1745, but in 1760 had entirely disappeared, merging into the tribes in the western part of the State, and losing their nationality. Barber (Hist. Coll.) says some of them joined the Pequots at New London. However this may be, there were Indians living in Scotland (now Burnside) within the memory of some of our older citizens.* They had a chief named Tobias, or Toby. In a fit of jealousy he killed his wife and another Indian with a pitchfork in Mr. Ozias Bidwell's barn, they having lain down there in a drunken sleep. By a town vote in 1793, Dr. George Griswold was paid for visiting an Indian woman there and dressing her wounds; and Mr. Deodat Woodbridge was paid for articles furnished her.

And this is the end of a tribe originally possessed of a certain savage health and nobility, a people adequate to themselves in their rude systems of government and of social life, —a people native to the wilderness, and as much a part of it as were the wolf and the deer, and as irreconcilable to the neighborhood of civilization. No attempt has been made here to make a pathetic tale of their story; and yet we hope that no one who reads these pages, and afterwards wanders afield or in the woods in our town in the beautiful Indian summer of the year, will escape a subtle, hazy sense of an earlier and freer occupancy by a color-loving race whom Nature with her gorgeous trappings seems not yet to have forgotten.

---

* A few Indians lived in a wigwam about eighty rods south of Mr. Geo. W. Pratt's house, on Silver Lane, about 1775-80.

EARLY OCCUPANCY.

CHAPTER II.

1635–1666.

THE bounds of the town of Hartford once included the territory now occupied by the towns of East Hartford, Manchester, and West Hartford. The history of East Hartford is one with that of Hartford until the year 1783, when it became a separate town. It included the territory of the present town of Manchester within its limits until 1823. The region north of the Hockanum river was generally called by the Indians and settlers Podunk; that south of the river, Hockanum; but these were no certain designations, and by some all the meadow along the Great River was called Hockanum.

The attention of the settlers of Massachusetts Bay was first called to this neighborhood in 1631 by the Indians, who wished their aid against the encroaching Pequots. They gave a flattering account of the region, and offered presents of corn and beaver if a settlement were made. But not until 1634, when the settlers on Massachusetts Bay began to feel the need of more and better land, were any sent to explore the country. These brought back favorable descriptions of the excellent cleared meadows upon both sides of the great river, and a glowing account of the profitable fur trade of the Dutch, who had a trading-house, or fort, known as the House of Hope, upon Dutch Point, now in Hartford.

In 1633 Lieut. Holmes and some Plymouth men set up a fortified trading-house, known as Plymouth House, in what is now Windsor. In 1635 a few other persons settled along the river, some at Windsor and others at Wethersfield. The first plan of a permanent settlement at Hartford was formed

EARLY OCCUPANCY.

by Thomas Hooker and his followers, who had determined to leave Newtown, now Cambridge, and plant themselves in the Connecticut Valley. A party of sixty persons, with Mr. John Steele at their head, intending to anticipate Hooker's company, made hasty preparation, and set out in October, 1635. They came across the "trackless wilderness," through swamps, over hills, and across rivers, and winter, which set in early that year, was upon them before they had prepared suitable shelter for themselves or their cattle. Storms delayed or wrecked the vessels by which they expected their furniture and provisions; the Connecticut froze over by the 25th of November, and the snow was so deep that many of their cattle could not be got across the river, and were wintered this side, browsing and starving in the woods. Some of the company struggled back to Boston, assisted on their way through the dreadful wilderness by the Indians; others journeyed down the river in hope of meeting their vessels, but, failing in this, they embarked in the Rebecca, and after tedious hardships reached Boston. Those who remained shared with the Indians a meagre diet of malt and acorns through the winter.

In the June following most of these sturdy settlers returned in company with ministers John Hooker and Samuel Stone, whose better organized party made the journey through the woods without mishap, living chiefly on the milk of their cows. The settlement was called Newtown until February, 1636-7, when its name was changed to Hartford, in honor of Mr. Stone, who came from Hartford in England.

The settlers brought with them a commission from the general court of Massachusetts, but found themselves beyond its jurisdiction. They straightway formed themselves into a voluntary association for the purpose of establishing a government, and of purchasing the land from the Indians. For the latter purpose a common fund was raised, and the lands were afterwards distributed, to each man his proportion according to the amount he had paid in. In 1636 Mr. Stone and William Goodwin received a deed of the land for the new settlement from Sequassen, sachem of the Suckiaug tribe.

This deed was lost, but a renewal deed was given by his surviving representatives to Mr. Samuel Willys "and the rest of the proprietors of the undivided lands within the bounds of the township of Hartford," July 5, 1670. This deed conveyed land now covered by the towns of Hartford and West Hartford only,—" the whole bredth of land from Wethersfield to Windsor bounds, from the great river on the east to run into the wilderness westward full six miles, which is to the place where Hartford and Farmington bounds meet." It is signed by "Masseeckcup his mark," and by eight other Indians, and is witnessed by "Arramatt his mark" (chief of the Podunks), and by four other Indians.

No deed has been found of the land covered by our town, although such a deed was, without doubt, given by the Indians, the territory having been held in common by the proprietors, and finally divided, as were their other purchases. Such a deed, if existing, would be merely a curious old document, and not in the least essential to confirm the titles to any of our lands. The reason for this is that the English law has never recognized the rights of the Indians to the fee of the territory they occupied in common with the beasts of the forest. The right of discovery and the formal act of taking possession by the representatives of the potentates of Europe was held to be a stronger claim than that of years of possession by the red men. Still the charter of 1662, which gives, grants, and confirms, unto John Winthrop and eighteen others, " and all others as are now or hereafter shall be made free of the Company and Society of our Colony of Connecticut in America," known by the name of " Governour and Company of the English Collony of Connecticut in New England in America," all lands from Narragansett Bay to the Pacific Ocean, recognizes the fact that the greatest part thereof was obtained for great and valuable considerations, or gained by conquest, and with much difficulty. On this charter, which healed all disputes and confirmed all prior acts of the colony, our land titles are impregnably based.

The names of the proprietors of the purchases from the Indians were arranged in a list, with their proportion of interest affixed to their names, and in this ratio they shared in any expense that arose, or in any division that was made. In this list Mr. John Haynes, the governor, stands at 200, Wm. Pantry 85 or 80, John Crow 40 or 20, Joseph Easton 10, Richard Risley 8, and others at intermediate ratios.

Later settlers, who were by a formal vote admitted inhabitants of the town, were given shares in the undivided lands, and a list of them was also kept. The interest in the partnership of this class ranges from 3 to 12. Another class had lots, "granted to such inhabitants only at town's courtesy, with liberty to fetch wood and keep swine and cows by proportion on the common."

Those grantees who did not settle here and improve their land within twelve months forfeited it to the company again; and any settler removing within four years from the commencement of his occupancy forfeited his land also to the company, which paid him for his improvements thereon.

Some who applied to be admitted inhabitants were so unfortunate as not to be received; care was taken to exclude objectionable persons. Sept. 1, 1665, the townsmen were ordered to "present 50 shillings to Robert Bartlett of Northampton for a certain parcel of land," or if he does not accept, they are to require security of him to free them from any damage "that shall happen to yᵉ town by reason of any inhabitant to whom he shall sell it."

The original north and south boundaries of the town on this side of the Great River were originally declared as follows:

"Samuel Wakeman & Ancient Stoughton doe thinke meete that the bounds of Wethersfield shalbe . . . . bettween them and Hartford . . . . and over the great River the said Wethersfield to begin att the mouth of Pewter pott Brooke, att the lower side of Hoccanō, and there to run due east into the Country 3 miles . . . . which is ordered accordingly." "The boundes between Harteford & Windsor is agreed to be," etc. "And over the said great River the saide Plantaͨon of Windsor is to come to the Riveretts mouth that falls into the said greate River of Connectecott, and then the said Hartford is to runn east into the Country, wch is ordered accordingly." A note in the margin says, "The Riverett on the other side by the Indians is called Podanke."

The lands on the east side of the Great River were early divided among the proprietors. A division of our rich meadows was made about the year 1640, for meadow and plow lots; the hay and grain being drawn across the river at times of low water, just north of the present carriage bridge. No record remains of this distribution, and the uncertainties of the early records make it impossible to prepare anything like a true plot of the first grantees. Previous to its distribution the land was divided by an east and west line, supposed to have been drawn near the site of the present Hockanum bridge,* into two parts, which were known respectively as the north and the south sides. This division corresponded with a similar one that existed in Hartford, on the west side of the river, the line there being the Little River. By a vote of the proprietors, those who had land on the north side of this line were to have 105 acres for every 100, while those on the south side were to have only 100 acres for every 100. A committee was to appoint "which of those men that live on the south side [in Hartford] that have no meadow in Hockanum shall take their division on the north side, and to hear the complaints of those who complain," etc.

These lots were bounded east by the "bog wall," or the western side of the swamp land near the meadow hill. Bounds were ordered set in them July 28, 1640.

March 24, 1640-1, it was ordered by the committee chosen to divide the ground on the east side, that "twenty acres of the land that lieth between the Great River and the line that runneth from the south to the north [bog wall?], and on the south side of the east line near Hockanum pound shall be reserved for the accommodating of several pore men that the town shall think meete to accommodate there, and then the middle line to the east shall be the dividing line between the peopell on the north and south sides, when the reserves be made even."

---

* This was the line of division when two schools were established in 1720.

EARLY OCCUPANCY. 43

Several grants of the above land were made, but not always to poor men. Thomas Case was given two acres. Wm. Blumfield was given "the ground whereon the pound now stands, and to be made up of ground about it four acres." John Willcock was given four acres; Henry Waclie, two acres: James Waclie, two acres; Thos. Blise, Sr., two acres; Thos. Blise, Jr., two acres; William Watse, two acres. "It is furdermore ordered y^t theare bee sequestered 2 two acres of that ground that shall be for the use of John Latymore if the town shall think meet to admit him an inhabitant." Jeruise Mudg had six acres on the same condition. Some of these persons receeived land in the distribution of Hockanum lands, as will be shown.

In 1642 Edward Elmer was given two acres of swamp on this side the great river, in exchange for a small piece of ground taken from his house-lot in Hartford.

Large grants of timber land were made to men of means to encourage the erection of mills on the Hockanum River and on other streams, as will be seen in the chapter on industries.

Hogs and swine were early restricted on this side. In 1641, "to preserve corn and meadow no hoggs or swine" were to be put over on the east side for one year, and all at present there were to be removed. The meadows were afterwards fenced to protect them from the swine and cattle which were allowed in the "wilderness" east of them. In 1644 a committee was chosen to view the land and appoint a fence along the swamp up to Podunk. Six years later a fence was ordered "abought" the Indian lands at Podunk, from the river to the upland, at the charge of the owners of the land within (south of) the fence. Those that had swamp were to fence across their lots next to the woodland (upland), and those that had meadow were to carry on the fence in a straight line. In 1665 the inhabitants of the east side were freed from fencing their lands; in 1669 all improved and improvable land was to be fenced according to law, and the selectmen were to have oversight of the matter.

A meeting of the proprietors of the swamp and meadow in Jan. 1683, voted that a fence be maintained so far northward as the Indians' land; Wm. Williams, Joseph Easton, and William Pitkin were to adjust the matter.

An apportionment of Hockanum meadow fence was made in 1686, a list of the names of proprietors and the number of rods set to each is preserved (Town and Lands, vol. 1, p. 225.) Mention is made in it of the "town farm," meaning probably land used by the town for farming purposes on this side of the river.

Fence viewers for both the Hockanum meadow and the Podunk meadows were chosen in 1687, and regularly thereafter.

Mr. W. S. Porter (Historical Notices, 1842,) says of our meadow that it was sometimes called Hockanum, from the southern to the northern boundary of the town. If this is true, the designation prevailed but a short time; probably until about 1660, when it appears that the boggy land, next the meadow hill, had not been divided with the meadow lots, and a petition respecting "Hockanum waste land" was before the General Court. It was ordered that the proprietors appoint a time to lay this land out according to the grants as they had in court agreed to do. But it was not divided until the upland was distributed in 1666.

The upland had been ordered divided in 1640-1, when it was voted that "ye upland of ye East side of ye Greatte River from Potuncke River to Pewter Pot River, shal be divided to ye thre miles end: y^t is to saye, half a mile of it messered & staked & e^{ch} mannes proportion to rune up ye Cunttry to ye 3 miles end." A committee was appointed to "survey ye ground of ye east side of the Greate River & estimate ye ground for ye goodness & ye equalittye, and if they can accord to set out the division betwixt the two sides, otherwise report how they judge the sides may be best suted." But no division was made until June 12, 1666. Then the order of the division was determined by lot, it having been agreed that "the first lots drawn should ly next Windsor [South Windsor] bounds, and so successivelye; and that the wast land [meadow bogs] shall belong to those lotts of upland against home it doth lye." It had also been agreed that the line between the north and the south sides should be in

EARLY OCCUPANCY. 45

the midst of the ground to be set out; those on the north to have all the waste land that fell in their division without the line, as the inhabitants of the south side were to have theirs, "they having already given 24 acres near Hockanum pound because their division is so much more." The extra five acres in every hundred was allowed those on the north side, as had been voted.

"The upland on the east side ye River. The Lotts Fell in this order:

	Acres		Acres		Acres
"Caleb Stanley,	108	Steven Post,	90	Benja: Burr,	18
(Cold T. Barnam.)*		(Recorded to the Bunces.)		Richard Olmsted,	30
John Marsh,	72	Rich'd Webb &	} 136	Wm. Pitkin *jor*	
Tho: Blachley,	12	John Higginson,		Wid. Spencer &	} 114
(Sold T. Burnam.)		(To J arth. Barnard.)		Tho: Root,	
Wm. Hide,	60	Wm. Hayden,	42	(Sold Widow Spencer's 90
(Sold S. Gaynes.)		(Recorded to Mr. Olcott.)		acres to Rich'd Case; 24 acres
Tho: Spencer,	45	Wid. Betts,	12	of this sold to John Bidoll.)
(Sold M. W——.)		John Purcas,	18	Nath' Ely,	60
John Warner,	18	John Skinner,	66	(Sold to Bidoll.)
Rob't Wade,	18	John Barnard,	72	John Biddoll *for*	
Rich'd Church,	60	John Olmsted,	12	John Clark,	} 126
Wm. Pratt,	24	Dan'l Garrad,	18	Tho: Woodford,	
Tho: Standley,	126	Mr.† Stone,	120	John Genings,	
(Sold Caleb Standley.)		Nich: Clarke,	39	Nich: Disbroe,	18
Mr. Alcott,	96	Wm. Phillips,	24	(Sold John Meekins.)
(Sold 30 acres.)		Wm. Callsey,	18	Wm. Cornwell,	24
Tho: Stanton,	48	(Sold to Mr. Philips.)		Wm. Ruscoe,	105
(Sold 30 acres.)		John Maynard,	42	Nath' Barding,	18
John Allyn,	200	Wm. Wadsworth,	156	(Sold John Meekins.)
(Recorded.)		(Recorded.)		Tho: Birchwood,	78
Mr.† John Crowe,	590	Rich'd Goodman,	} 120	John Pratt,	84
(Recorded.)		Edward Elmer,		Mr.† Wm. Westwood,	240
Tho: Barnes,	18	(60 acres sold to Jos. Eason.)			
Rob't Day,	42	Nath" Kelloge,	18	John Pantry,	} 375
Sam" Hall,	24	(Sold to Mr. Phillips.)		Steven Hart,	
(Sold Sara Crook.)		James Olmsteed,	} 264	Mr. Crows second division goes from that to the divident lyne between the North and south side of the river."	
Tho: Hall,	30	Thomas Bunce,			
John Hallaway,	18	Wm. Parker,	36		
Edw'd Stebbins,	} 270	Nath' Marvin,	90		
Seth Grant,		([Last two] Sold to Mr. Pitkin & Wm. Goodwin.)			
Tho: Scott‡ &					
John Bidwell,		Benja: Mann,	24		

* The notes given in parenthesis were entered afterward in the margin of the original record.
† "Mr."—a title of distinction at this time.
‡ Probably "Scott's Swamp" was named after him.

As is indicated by the number of lots almost immediately sold by the original grantees to other persons, few of those who drew lots came this side of the river to settle. Some, however, held their lands, and if they themselves did not settle upon them, their descendants did, and some of their names are prominent among those of our towns people to-day.

In regard to the division of the land south of the "divident line" no certain record exists. In the book for the record of town votes, under date of 1640, occurs the following list. It is without heading, or notes of any kind. But of its sixty-four names, fifty-one are of known residents of the south side of Hartford in 1640, and it contains also most of the names of those granted land about Hockanum pound in that year.

Whether it is a list of the proprietor's proportions, or a record of an actual distribution, we do not undertake to say.

In any event, some of the persons named were actual settlers on these lands, where their descendants are living to-day. The list is in two columns, and is as follows:

Mr. Haynes,	200	Richard Butler,†	16
Mr. Wyllys,	200	Arthur Smith,	14
Mr. Hopkins,	130	John Base,	14
Mr. Wells,*	100	Thomas Richards,	8
Mr. Webster,	100	Thomas Blysse, sr.,	6
Mr. Whiting,	100	Thomas Blysse, jr.,	6
Andrew Warner,	84	John Hall,	6
Mr. Hooker,	80	George Hubbard,	6
Thomas Osmer,	58	Edward Lay [Leary?],	6
Nathaniel Warde,	56	Thomas Gridley,	6
John Hopkins,	26	John Sables lott,	6
George Grave,	24	Richard Watts,*	8
William Gibbons,	22	Wm. Wesley,	8
Thomas Judd,†	25	Henry Wakley,	6
Wm. Hill,	20	John White,	50
Geo. Stockinge,	20	Mr. Cullet [Culick?],	58
Joseph Magatt,	20	Wm. Andrews,	58
John Arnold,	16	Samuel Wakman,	35
Wm. Blumfield,	16	Jeremy Addams,	30

---

*These, and others sold to Edward Andrews, who lived near Dowd's grove prior to 1678.

† "Sold to T. Hosmer,"—marginal note in original.

EARLY OCCUPANCY. 47

Richard Lyman, dec'd,	30	[Paul Peck,]	8
Gregory Wilterton,	28	[Gyles Smith,]	8
Andrew Bacon,	28	†	–
George Steele,	26	James Wakley,	4
James Ensigne,	24	Richard Billinge,	6
John Wilcox,	36	Thomas Porter,	4
Thos. Bull,	14	John Perce lott,	4
Wm. Holton,	12	John Latimer,	4
Francis Andrews,	20	Wm. Watts,	4
Mr. Coale,	12	James Bridgman,	8
Joseph Esson [Easton],	10	Mr. John Moody,	40
Richard Risley,	8	Samuel Gardner,	4
[Rob. Ba]rtlett,*	8	Ralph Keeler,	66
[Thomas] Selden,	6		

* These, and others sold to Edward Andrews, who lived near Dowd's grove prior to 1678.
† "Sold to T. Hosmer,"—marginal note in original.

SETTLERS AND INHABITANTS.

CHAPTER III.

1648-1800.

THE growth of the town of Hartford was, from the first, steady and sure. It received important accessions to the number of its inhabitants, families of education and means; and the work of building houses—new homes for souls at last free to order their lives as they would,—of clearing lands, making roads and bridges, went rapidly on. They broke up the fat soil of the meadows for their crops, and built mills with which to prepare lumber for their buildings, and to grind their grain for food. Amidst all their toil they had to be constantly watchful against the wily and treacherous Indians; and the momentous questions involved in the establishment of a new church and a new state had to be discussed and acted upon. It is not surprising that idleness and vagabondage were not encouraged at that time.

With the increase of population came a demand for more territory, and houses were soon built upon this side the Great River. It is impossible to ascertain the names of all the early settlers upon this side, or the exact date of their building here. In May, 1653, the inhabitants were exempted from training with the west side towns, and ordered to meet on the east side, as Will: Hill shall appoint, and train there together, and so continue. This indicates a permanent population here at that time. From among the names upon the monument erected to the first settlers of Hartford in the old Center Burying Ground in that city, we take the following of those who either settled on this side the Great River, or who were associated with the early history of our territory:

SETTLERS AND INHABITANTS.

JOHN CROW was one of the first settlers and one of the original proprietors of our soil. He was a large land-owner and lived near the site of the late Ozias Roberts homestead,—an old unused well remaining there to-day. He owned a tract of land extending from near the present Hockanum bridge north to the neighborhood of "Smith's lane," and running eastward to the end of the three-mile lots. Crow Hill, in the river swamp, still retains his name. He married Elizabeth Goodwin, only daughter of William Goodwin. With his father-in-law he bought 776 acres of land on this side of the river in 1639, a tract bounded west by the boggy meadow " and continueth east unto the east end of the Hartford bounds,"—three miles. William Goodwin also bought adjacent lands, with mill privileges, still used for manufacturing purposes, at Burnside. Mr. Crow and William Pitkin were the committee who laid out the four-rod highway ordered near the meadow hill, through all the lots from Windsor to Wethersfield (now Glastonbury) in 1640. A servant of his was fined for drunkenness in 1639. Mr. Crow served on a jury in 1647. His house was one of those garrisoned for safety from the Indians in 1675. He sold out his interest (one-third) in a corn and grist mill near the site of the present Hamner & Forbes mill in 1686, and went with William Goodwin to Hadley to live. His sons subsequently returned, and John Crow was appointed hayward of Podunk meadow in 1711, and Nathaniel Crow, Jr., was collector of the Ecclesiastical Society in 1761. They afterwards sold their lands. John Crow was an ancestor of Elisha Pitkin, Esq., whose house is still standing a few rods northeast of the site of Mr. Crow's early homestead. He died in 1685.

JOHN BIDWELL, one of the first settlers of Hartford, had a tan yard on an island in what is now Bushnell Park in Hartford. His house-lot was on the east side of Trumbull street, near Pearl, in that city, in 1640. With Joseph Bull he built a saw mill on "Saw Mill River" (now Hockanum river), in 1669. They were granted 240 acres in the next commons for timber for their mill in 1671. He shared with three others in a tract of 270 acres in the distribution of 1666,—probably lying along Burnside avenue (once Bidwell's lane), upon which his descendants settled,—and he bought 24 acres of widow Spencer and Thomas Root. He is set down as a freeman in the list of 1669.

RICHARD RISLEY was one of the first settlers of Hartford, and an original proprietor. He had a house and lot near the north end of Washington street in 1640. He afterwards came to Hockanum and settled near Willow Brook. He died about the year 1648. A copy of the inventory of his estate was recorded in Volume 1 of the Colonial Records, and is of such interest as an index to the possessions of our ancestors that we give it entire.

"A true and perfect Inventory of the goods and chattells of RICHARD RISSLEY, late of Hockanum, deceased.

	£.	s.	d.
In the yarde, Imp^r. two milch cows and a heifer,	14.	0.	0.
Item, 3 heifers, 9*l.*, and one steare, 3*l.*,	12.	0.	0.
Item, one Bull and two young Bullocks, 6*l.*, one calfe, 20*s.*,	7.	0.	0.
Item, one steare, 5*l.*, one spotted hogg, 50*s.*,	7.	10.	0.
Item, 2 sowes, 4*l.*, younge hoggs, 9*l.*, 6 stores, 4*l.*, and 6 shotes, 3*l.*,	20.	0.	0.
In the Hall: Item, 1 muskitt, 15*s.*, and one sword, 7*s.*,	1.	2.	0.
	1.	2.	0.
Item, 2 frying pans, 6*s.*, and one kettle, 16*s.*,	1.	2.	0.
Item, 1 kettle, 13*s.* 4*d.*, and one small kettle, 3*s.*,	0.	16.	4.
Item, 1 posnett, 2*s.* 6*d.*; one iron pott, 7*s.*,	0.	9.	6.
Item, one small iron pot, 3*s.*; pot hook and trammells, 4*s.*,	0.	7.	0.
Item, 3 platters and a plate, 8*s.*, one pewter pott, 3*s.*,	0.	11.	0.
Item, 1 pewter cupp, 12*d.*; six spoones, 12*d.*, earthen-ware, 7*s.*,	0	9.	0.
Item, 2 payles, 2*s.* 6*d.*; 2 old payles, 12*d.*,	3.	6.	0.
Item, 2 Indian trayes, 4*s.*; 2 platters, 2 bowles and dishes, 3*s.*,	0.	7.	0.
Item, 1 great wooden platter, 2*s.*, 1 lattin dripping pann, 18*d.*,	0.	3.	6.
Item, 1 paire of bellowes, 2*s.*; one joined table and formes, 10*s.*,	0.	12.	0.
Item, 2 chaires, 3*s.*; 1 childes chaire, 18*d.*, a forme, 6*d.*,	0.	5.	0.

SETTLERS AND INHABITANTS. 51

	£.	s.	d
Item, 6 trenchers, a scummer, a cleansing dish, & chaffing dish,	0.	1.	6.
Item, 1 smoothing iron, 12d.; 1 great Bible, 13s. 4d.; 1 small Bible, 2s.,	0.	16	4.
Item, 1 narrow axe, 3s.; a broad axe, 2s.; a hatchett, 12d.,	0.	6	0.
Item, 1 handsaw, 12d.; 1 hammer, 8d.; 2 augurs and a beetle ring, 2s.,	0.	3.	8.
Item, 1 charne, 3s., 1 coule, 3s.; 1 keeler, 2s.; 1 powdering tubb, [3s.],	0.	12	0.
Item, 2 beare barrills, 5s.; 1 powdering trough, 4s.; 2 payles, 12d.,	0.	10.	0.
In the parlour: Item, 1 bedsted, 10s.; a featherbed, strawbed & 2 boulsters, 5l.,	5.	10.	0.
Item, 1 pillow, 5s.; 1 paire blanketts, 30s.,	1	15.	0.
Item, curtaines, 20s.; 3 paire new sheets, 3l.,	4.	0.	0.
Item, 6 yards of lynsy woollsy, 12s.; a flock bed and boulster, 30s.,	2.	2.	0.
Item, 1 paire of blanketts, 15s.; 1 cradle, 2s.; 3 pillows, 3s.,	1	5.	0.
Item, 3 pillow beeres, and a warming pann,	0.	15.	0.
Item, wearing clothes, and mony in his purse,	3	0	0.
Item, 3 chests and a box, 12s.; a hogshead & meate tubbs, 6s.,	0	18.	0.
Item, 1 peece of sole leather,	0	3	0.
In the chamber: Item, one fann, 6s.; one great Indian bagg, 4s.,	0.	10.	0.
Item, 6[lb] of hopps, 4s. 6d.; rough hemp, 10s.,	0.	14.	6.
Item, 3 baggs, 3s., & 1 spade, 2s.; a corne baskitt, 12d.,	0.	6.	0.
Item, 1 saw, 1 old sithe, 7s.; 1 iron bayle & old how, 12d.,	0.	8.	0.
Item, halfe a bushel,	0.	2.	0.
In the Barne: Item, 55 bush: wheate,	11.	0.	0.
Item, 40 bush: of pease and rye,	6.	0.	0.
Item, 15 bush: of Indian corne,	1.	10.	0.
Item, a Howse at Hartford, with the homelott, 4 akers of swamp, and 2 of woodland,	26.	0.	0.
"John Cullick, "Totall sum is	135.	5.	10.
"Will: Gibbens.			

"There are 3 children, viz.: one daughter, by name Sarah Rissly, betweene 7 and 8 yeares old; one sonne, by name Samuell Rissly, about 2 yeares old; and one sonn, by name Rich: Rissly, about 3 months old.

"The distribution of the estate by the Courte, the 7th of Decembr, 1648, is: To the 3 children, 16l. a peece, to bee pd to the daughter at the age of 18 yeares, and to the sonns at the age of 21 years. William Hill bringing of ym vpp to write and read, and giuing security to the Courte for the payment of the seuerall childrens portions."

Richard Risley, Jr., was made a freeman in 1669. An agreement about a division line between him and Samuel Wells was signed in 1705.

WILLIAM HILLS had a house and lot in Hartford near the corner of Front and Sheldon streets in 1640. He early came to Hockanum to live. He was captain of the first train band this side the river in 1653; was nominated for a freeman in 1661; was shot by the Indians in 1675; and was listed among the south side freemen in 1669. He is supposed to have lived east of Main street, and south of Willow Brook, about 80 rods south of Mr. D. Overton's; although one tradition claims that he first settled north of the old Hockanum school-house. He died, 1683.

The foregoing names are upon the monument to the first settlers of Hartford. Possibly to them should be added the name of Thomas Spencer, who died in 1687. He is included in a list of first settlers arranged by Capt. Charles H. Olmsted. Other names of settlers who came later, or of the descendants of the first settlers, taken from the early records of the town and colony, or given on the authority of Mr. W. S. Porter, (Historical Notices,) are as follows:

EDWARD ANDREWS was made a freeman in 1657. He settled near Dowd's Grove. He bought land of John Crow, adjoining his own on the north; also of Thomas Wells, Richard Watts, Robert Bartlett and others, original proprietors in the south side lands. He was an ancestor of the Treat, Warren, Williams families, and the land bought by him is still owned by his descendants.* Traces of habitations still

---

*Edward Andrews died in 1673. His daughter, Sarah, married Henry Treat; his other daughter, Mary, married Wm. Warren. His son, Solomon, had one daughter, who married Timothy Williams.

remain on "Pigeon Hill," just east of the grove. A road was ordered laid out from the mouth of the Hockanum River, southerly and then easterly, over a bridge (on Willow Brook?) "that was made by Edward Andrews," along the north side of widow Andrews' orchard, and finally to run to the end of Hartford bounds. This was in 1679. The course of the road cannot certainly be determined, but is supposed to have passed easterly, south of Willow Brook, coming upon Main street just north of the house of Mr. Ralph Ensign.

THOMAS BURNHAM, a sturdy character in our early annals, went first to the Barbadoes, but came to Hartford before 1656. He was elected a constable that year, and made a freeman in 1657. He practised before the courts as an attorney the following year. About the year 1659, with Jacob Mygatt, he bought a large tract of land of Tantinomo, the "one-eyed" sachem of the Podunks. No record appears of this purchase, and it was treated as a mere lease of the land by the courts. Much trouble arose because of the differences about it, and Burnham had finally to buy out the rights of those who derived title from the distribution of 1666. This matter is treated more fully in the chapter on the Indians.

In 1662 Burnham fearlessly undertook to defend Abigail Betts, a school mistress of Hartford, who was accused of blasphemy. She was found guilty, and sentenced to ascend the ladder to the gallows with a rope about her neck, "to the open view of spectators that all Israell may hear and fear." Burnham, for his temerity in defending so heinous an offence, was sternly reprimanded by the court; and, although he cleverly defended himself, lost his freedom for three years, as well as his privilege of pleading before the courts. Thomas Burnham's house is said to have stood on the land now owned by Mr. John A. Burnham, and nearly opposite the house of Mr. Julius Burnham. In 1675 this house was garrisoned against the Indians. Thomas Burnham's large tracts of land were increased in 1684, when Joshua, by his will gave him and fourteen others a large tract of land reaching from the

Bolton hills on the west to Willimantic River on the east. He died in 1688, and his descendants still occupy a good part of his lands in this town.

WILLIAM PITKIN, the progenitor of the Pitkin family in our town, was one of the most prominent of our early settlers. A man of education, intelligence, and sagacity, he was of use not only to our neighborhood, but to the colony at large. He is said to have settled here in 1659. In 1660 liberty was given him to teach school in Hartford, and a house was hired, and eight pounds were voted to him by the town to encourage him in the work. Each scholar, also was to send a load of wood within a month after "Michimas," or pay three shillings for procuring wood. Mr. Pitkin was made a freeman in 1662, and appointed attorney for the court to prosecute certain persons. In 1664 he was made attorney to implead any delinquents in the colony. With Bartholomew Barnard he bought out Jacob Mygatt's interest in the Podunk lands in 1666, about which a dispute arose with Thomas Burnham, Mygatt's partner, in which the court decided in his favor. Pitkin also, in company with William Goodwin, bought out the shares of William Parker and Nathaniel Marvin, 126 acres, in the original distribution of lands here. In 1667 he petitioned with Thomas Wells that the people this side might be freed from fencing their meadows. He was one of the deputies to the General Court from Hartford in 1675; was treasurer of the Colony in 1676, and also in 1677. In April, 1676, he was appointed with Mr. Samuel Willys "to go to New York and to present the governor with .... a letter from the Council, a copy whereof is on file; and also, sundry instructions were given them to desire Gov' Andross to engage the Mohawks against our Indian enemies, and to grant them leave to go up to Albany to speak with the Mohawks, &c., as per the instructions on file will appear." This errand brought no satisfactory result, because Governor Andross in a rather unneighborly communication did not recognize the agents as sufficiently "authorized or empowered to treat or conclude, by said Council's letter or otherwise that appears."

SETTLERS AND INHABITANTS. 55

Mr. William Pitkin came to live upon this side of the great river between the years 1659 and 1666. He built his house on the meadow hill, a few rods north of the present New York & New England Railroad. In 1683 he was chosen hayward of the east side meadow, with power to appoint a substitute.

STEPHEN DAVIS is put down as a resident here in Porter's Notices. His first appearance on the records, in 1646, indicates a lawless spirit. With others he was fined five pounds for "breaking into Will' Gybbins his howse drynking wyne," and was put under bonds for further good behavior. He was made a freeman in 1658.

WILLIAM WARREN early came to Hartford and was made free in 1665. He afterwards settled this side of the Great River, a little south of the Hockanum, on Main street.

SAMUEL GAINES appears on the records in 1667. He bought William Hide's grant of 60 acres. He was collector of the Ecclesiastical Society in 1702; and was called Sergeant in 1751, when a school was to be kept between his house and Alexander Keeney's.

LIEUT. JOHN MEAKINS was a freeman (north side) in 1669; was collector of the Ecclesiastical Society in 1708; and one of the committee who were appointed to ask for town privileges for the east side people in 1720. The Meakin apple was named from some of his family. He bought land of original grantees—of Nich: Disbroe 18 acres; of Nath¹ Barding 18 acres.

RICHARD CASE was made a freeman in 1671. He bought land of widow Spencer and Thomas Root, who were original distributees—114 acres. He was hayward of Hockanum meadow in 1715. His wife was Elizabeth Purcase, daughter of John.

THOMAS TRILL was a soldier in the Narragansett war. Tradition says that his was the first grave made in our Center

Burying Ground. He was drowned while crossing the Hockanum river during a freshet. His grave is unmarked and unknown. In 1675, during the Indian alarms, for "unseasonable shooting of his gun," he was fined five shillings. In May, 1676, he was allowed 50 shillings, "for damages he suffered in his corn by creatures when he went forth in the country's service." He owned land next north of William Roberts' tract.

OBADIAH WOOD was also a soldier in the Narragansett war. His grave-stone in the Center Burying Ground bears the oldest date of any there—April 17, 1712. At a meeting of the Council, Jan. 22, 1676, it was voted: "Obadiah Wood is granted fower pownds and his cure, (and Goodwife Sandford twenty shillings for what he did for her,) of his wound he rece^d."

WILLIAM BUCKLAND lived here in 1679, on the site of the present Buckland homestead on the meadow hill on the corner of Mill and Prospect streets. His lot is mentioned in the lay-out of the North Meadow Road in that year. He was collector of the Ecclesiastical Society in 1711, and afterwards school committee, etc.

JOHN DIX owned land in Hockanum in 1679, on the proposed lay-out of the road from the mouth of the Hockanum to the end of Hartford bounds. He was collector of the Ecclesiastical Society, 1703.

JOHN EASTON lived in the meadow. In 1684 he sold land for the west end of the North Meadow Road to the town; his house is mentioned in connection with the road in 1702. He afterwards exchanged meadow for upland with Richard Burnham, without giving deeds; and in 1726 his administrators were empowered by the General Assembly to draw the requisite papers, it being stated that Easton had in his lifetime built a house and barn on said upland,—probably in Burnside. John Easton was son of Joseph Easton, one of the original settlers of Hartford, who lived on or near Elm street in 1640, and who bought land on this side of one of the original grantees—Richard Goodman,—and was one of the committee on fencing the meadow in 1683.

JAMES FORBES joined in an agreement in regard to the road south and east from the "fulling mills" (now Burnside), through his land toward Bolton line, in 1726. He gave his daughter, Dorothy, and her husband, William Roberts, six acres of land adjoining his own in 1688.

WILLIAM ROBERTS was an early settler. With his wife, Dorothy Forbes, he bought land, adjoining his own, of Nathaniel Crow, in 1688. He lived on the Meadow hill, south of the present Bridge Road, and near the foot of "Smith's lane," now so called; his cellar hollow is still to be seen there. He deeded all his land to his son, Benjamin Roberts, in 1729.

TIMOTHY COWLES appears in the records in 1695. He owned a three-mile lot, part of which was taken in the highway laid out from Richard Gilman's (north of Gilman's Brook) easterly in 1734. He was collector of the Ecclesiastical Society, in 1701, and a deacon in 1718. His wife was Hannah Pitkin.

The following are also named among the earlier settlers upon this side by W. S. Porter (Historical Notices). The date appended is that of their first appearance upon the records: Thomas Atkins, 1682 * (there were two persons of the name of Atkins here in 1708); George Ash, 1682; Richard Blanchard, 1682; Thomas Blachley, 1650; Benjamin Beven, 1689; Josiah Dibble, 1693; Richard Keeney, 1673; Sarah Crook, 1672 (bought Samuel Hall's original grant of 24 acres); Philip More, 1693 (owned land in Hockanum).

JOHN HILLS was son of William Hills, the first settler, who, in 1676, gave him 31 acres and four rods of land in Hockanum. He was surveyor for Hockanum in 1687.

---
* He married Jane Williams, daughter of William, about 1670.

NATHANIEL GOODWIN bought land of John Crow in 1684,— a tract 34 rods wide, and one of the three-mile "long lots"; also, two acres of meadow land. He did not live this side. His son,

JOHN GOODWIN (afterwards deacon), bought six acres of meadow in 1703 of John Pantry, and upland of his own brother, Nathaniel Goodwin, Jr. John was the first Goodwin who came here to live, and settled on Main street near the present Center Burying-Ground. He joined in a deed of the road north of Gilman's Brook, toward Bolton, in 1744. He was grandson of Ozias Goodwin, ancestor of the Goodwin family, and one of the first settlers of Hartford.

THOMAS CADWELL took a lease of the ferry across the Great River in 1681, and was to "keepe the ferry for seven years." It was leased to him again in 1687, for seven years longer, and after his death it was carried on by his widow. John Cadwell was a resident here in 1729, and was one of those who joined in deeding Silver Lane to the town in 1731.

JOSEPH BULL, who took the freeman's oath in 1667, probably did not settle on this side. With John Bidwell he owned a saw-mill in what is now Burnside, with a large grant of land for timber for their mill. Thomas Bull had 200 acres granted him "on the east of the great river near the cedar swamp," in 1684, probably for the same purpose. He was a fence viewer for Hockanum meadow in 1699.

THOMAS OLCOTT, Jr., grandson of one of the original settlers of Hartford, settled on Hop Brook in the "Five Miles" (now Manchester). [A Mr. Olcott had bought 42 acres of land of William Hayden, an original distributee of the three-mile tract, now East Hartford, sometime subsequent to the year 1666.] Thomas Olcott was auditor of the Ecclesiastical Society in 1703. He was appointed to keep a house of entertainment by the General Court in 1711; was a lieutenant in 1718; and, in 1720, was chosen with Capt. Roger Pitkin to manage the first schools instituted this side of the Great River in Hartford. His descendants live at Hop Brook to-day.

SETTLERS AND INHABITANTS.   59

WILLIAM WILLIAMS was made free in 1654. He was a cooper, and lived in Hartford. In 1658 he was permitted "to dispose of his servant youth, Math: Young, to another sutable master"; and said Matthew did discharge him from his engagement to teach him the trade of a cooper. Mr. Williams owned a large tract of land on this side the Great River, next to Windsor bounds. This boundary was a long time in dispute, and was finally so altered by the Court as to cut off a large tract of land from Thomas Burnham's and William Williams' possessions, and to give it to the Windsor settlers. This loss was made up to their heirs in 1730, by a grant of 300 acres in the Five Miles, a tract 160 rods wide and running along Windsor bounds 300 rods. He married Jane Westover in 1647.

WILLIAM WARREN, who married Mary Andrews, is said to have settled in Hockanum in 1664.

Thus far we have treated only those settlers who appear upon the records prior to the formation of the Third Ecclesiastical Society of Hartford, on this side of the river, in 1694. The records of this society, after the year 1699, are full and complete, affording a comparatively firm footing to the seeker who has been groping with baffled curiosity in the general records of the town of Hartford and of the Colony. By this path we enter the domain of the certain, the Society, though ecclesiastical in designation, having had a breadth of jurisdiction that included the management of schools, roads, bridges, burying-grounds, ministers, meeting-houses, and all the close-at-home affairs of our people. We have thought best to copy from the records all of the names which prominently appear upon them prior to 1800, giving the date of their first appearance, and signifying by abbreviations or otherwise the most important connection in which they are mentioned, and sometimes introducing facts from other sources:

Abbey, John,[*] 1710, joined in deed of Silver Lane, 1731.—John, Jr., collector, 1748.—Stephen, collector, 1755.—Nehemiah, collector, 1768.—Eleazer.—Eliphalet.—Jedathan.

---

[*] He bought eight acres of Benjamin Hills in 1718. He died Oct. 30, 1790, aged 109 years!

Adams, William, preached 1742.
Adkins, Charles, 1708.—B., 1711.
Andross, Widow Elizabeth, 1714.
Anderson, Ashbel, 1773.—Asahel, 1785.
Arnold, Henry, Jr., coll., 1707.—John, 1715.—Henry, coll., 1745.—Samuel, school com., 1781.
Atherton, Samuel, 1744.
Burnham, Thomas, 1714.—John, 1714.—Jonathan, coll., 1723.—John, 2d, coll., 1726.—Ensign Samuel, com. to seat meeting-house, 1726.—Richard, Soc'y com., 1728.—Jabez, coll., 1738.—Elisha, coll., 1748.—Cornelius, coll., 1759.—Silas, coll., 1763.—Charles, seating com. for meeting-house, 1764.—Moses, 1767.—David, 1769.—Ezra, 1776.—Gurdon, 1781.—Samuel, school com., 1781.—Nathaniel, 1781.—Eleazer, school com., 1785.—Roderick, 1791.—William, 1792.—Zenas, school com., 1793.
Bemont, Meakins, coll., 1776.
Blanchard, Timothy, 1773.
Benton, Elisha, coll., 1775. (Author of seating rhymes.)
Baxter, Alvin, 1740.
Belden, Stephen, 1768; Nathan, Soc'y com., 1774; James, school com., 1795.
Bowles, James, 1764.
Bigelow, Daniel, coll., 1725 (deeded part of Burnside avenue, once Biglow's Lane, in 1725); William, 1773.
Benjamin, Serg't John, coll., school com., 1714; Gideon, coll., 1756; Caleb, 1768; James, chorister to assist in tuning the psalms, 1784; Jonathan, school com., 1785. (Orchard street was once called Benjamin's Lane.)
Bidwell, Daniel, constable, 1699; com. on forts, 1704; com. to call Mr. Woodbridge, 1704, etc.; John, seating com., etc., 1709; William, coll., 1734; John, Jr., Soc'y com., 1739; James, ratemaker, 1744; Daniel, Jr., coll., 1745; Dr. Joseph, 1746; Roger, coll., 1754; Zebulon, coll., 1769 (killed in army, 1777); Jonathan, coll., 1770; Elisha, school com., 1783; Rodolphus, school com., 1787; Samuel, 1787; Simeon, 1787; Eudias, 1791.
Birt, Joseph, 1745.

SETTLERS AND INHABITANTS. 61

Bills, John, 1786.
Buckland, William, school com., 1711; Charles, coll., 1712; Daniel, 1791.
Boardman, Daniel, school com., 1784.
Butler, Moses, 1783.
Burr, Jonathan, school com., 1777.
Case, Thomas, school com., 1787.
Cadwell, John, 1729.
Clark, Daniel, 1741; Doctor, school near house, 1751; Abraham, school com., 1789.
Chandler, Samuel, 1788; Jonathan, school com., 1791.
Cheeney, Benjamin, deeded land for Burnside avenue, 1726, coll. 1732; Timothy, coll., 1756.
Church, Samuel, school com., 1792.
Collins, Mr. Nathaniel, paid for preaching, 1736.
Cowles, Dea. Timothy, coll., 1701; Orrin, ratemaker, 1712; Dea. William, coll., 1722; Joseph, coll., 1728; William, Jr., school com., 1761; Eleazer, coll., 1758; Timothy, 1779; John, coll., 1779; Abijah, school com., 1776; Stephen, chorister, 1791.
Cotton, David, 1793.
Crosby, David, 1777 (wrote Dr. Williams a caustic letter).
Crow, Nathaniel, Jr., coll., 1761.
Colt, Jonathan, 1709.
Damon, Benjamin, school com., 1748; Benjamin, Jr., coll., 1748.
Dart, Jabez, coll., 1760.
Deming, Timothy, 1764; Lemuel, 1781; Israel, school com., 1792; Lemuel, Jr., 1794.
Deliber, Samuel, school com., 1793.
Dix, John, coll., 1703; John, Jr., 1703.
Dickerson, Daniel, owned meeting-house site, 1720; John, com. on Sunday ferry, 1730.
Dike, John, 1729.
Easton, Joseph, draft of votes by, 1701; James, school com., 1705; Timothy, 1746; Silas, school near house, 1751; Abel, coll., 1769; Samuel, 1770; Abijah, 1777.
Evans, Benoni, school com., 1795.

Flagg, Dr. Samuel, Soc'y com., 1770 ; Samuel, Jr., 1791.
Forbes, Daniel, coll., 1699 ; David, com. on meeting-house, 1703 ; William, Soc'y com., etc., 1744 ; Timothy, coll., 1762 ; Ensign Moses, Soc'y com., etc., 1763 ; Moses, 1784 : Edward, coll., 1769; Timothy, Jr., school com., 1775 ; Asa, 1774 ; Elijah, school com., 1786 ; Aaron, school com., 1789 ; David, 1792 ; Ichabod, 1793.
Fox, Jeremiah, 1744; Zeniah, 1770 ; Nicholas, school com., 1795.
Gains, Serg't Samuel, coll., 1702 ; Simon, coll., 1761.
Gardiner, Samuel, 1745.
Gilman, Richard, coll., 1706 ; Solomon, coll., 1706 ; John, school com., 1741 ; Richard, Jr., coll., 1742 ; Elias, coll., 1751 ; Charles, school com., 1770 ; Eliphalet, 1773 ; George, school com., 1791 ; David, 1794 ; Ashbel, school com., 1795.
Gills, John, 1773.
Goodwin, Dea. John, Soc'y com., etc., 1705 ; Caleb, coll., 1748; Dea. John, 2d, seating com., 1781 ; Richard, coll., 1784 ; Levi, school com., 1789.
Griswold, Shubael, coll., 1790.
Grubb, Edward, 1784.
Hazentine, John, sold land for Silver Lane, 1731 ; arbitrator, 1724.
Hale, Benoni, cords minister's wood, 1769.
Hall, Timothy, school com., 1788.
Hills, Lieut. Jonathan, com. on minister's house, 1699 ; com. on forts, 1704 ; Ebenezer, coll., 1706 ; Benjamin, 1715, sold land for Silver Lane, 1731 ; Lieut. John, school between his house and Samuel Wells's, 1738 ; Jonathan, Jr., coll., 1720 ; Capt. David, coll., 1724 ; David, 2d, coll., 1750 ; David, 3d, coll., 1746 ; Jonathan, 3d, school com., 1764 ; Jonathan, 2d, coll., 1764 ; Ebenezer, school com., 1768 ; Ebenezer, Jr., school com., 1770 ; Ashbel, coll., 1779 ; Elisha, school com., 1777 ; William, school com., 1782; Stephen, 1788 ; Daniel, 1788 ; Russell, 2d, 1791 ; Amos, school com., 1794 ; Asa, to settle with Dr. Williams about his salary, 1795 ; Abraham, school near his house, 1751.
Holbert, John, coll., 1740.

SETTLERS AND INHABITANTS.   63

Hurlburt, Lieut. John, school house, on line between his land and R. Woodbridge's, 1751; Samuel, school com., 1788.
Jones, John P., 1774; David, 1774.
Judson, Jonathan, 1768; Russell, school com., 1770.
Keeney, Serg't Joseph, coll., 1699; Richard, 1715; Alexander, school between his house and Serg't Samuel Gaines, 1751; Benjamin, 1764; Joseph, 1790; Joseph, 2d, 1791.
Kilbourn, Serg't, com. on minister's house, 1699; John, deeds land for Silver Lane, 1731; Thomas, coll., 1741; Russell, 1766, com. on Sunday ferry; Stephen, 1791.
Kennedy, Samuel, Soc'y com., 1782; John, com. on ferry, 1795.
Leffingwell, Hart, use of boat Sundays, 1765.
Little, Lieut. David, school com., 1779; Deodat, school com., 1784.
Lester, Isaac, presents certificate that he is a Baptist, 1795.
Loomis, Josiah, 1769.
Marsh, Daniel, com. on dividing schools, 1766.
McKee, Robert, coll., 1752; Nathaniel, coll., 1756.
Meakin, Lieut. John, school com., etc., 1708; Lieut. Samuel, seating com., 1713; Joseph, to "fort burying place," 1713.
Miller, Amariah, school com., 1790.
Merrow, John, 1783; Elisha, 1784; Nathan, coll., 1787.
Morton, Samuel, 1748.
Mygatt, Jonathan, 1754.
Newell, Rev. Mr., Jos. Pitkin paid 25 lbs. for his board, 1741.
Norton, Job, coll., 1764; Capt. Selah, com. to procure singing master, 1772; Jabez, 1792.
Olcott, Lieut. Thomas, Jr., com. on schools, etc., 1703 (see *ante*); John, com. to call Mr. Woodbridge, 1704; Lieut. Nathaniel, Soc'y com., 1743; Josiah, coll., 1744; Capt. Joshua, school com., 1761.
Olmsted, Dea. Joseph, com. on meeting house, on forts, etc., 1699–1704 (was a deacon of the First Society in Hartford, earlier). His wife was Elizabeth Butler; they were married about 1700. He was a grandson of James Olmsted, one of the first settlers of Hartford. Richard, ratemaker, 1706; Nehe-

miah, school com., 1721; James, school com., 1732; Jonathan, coll., 1733; Ashbel, coll., 1742; William, coll., 1744; Thaddeus, coll., 1745; Stephen, seating com., 1741; Nathaniel, coll., 1753; Ashbel, school com., 1772; Isaac, school com., 1779; George, school com., 1781; William, Jr., Soc'y com., 1774; Aaron, coll., 1782; Benjamin, school com., 1782; Timothy, assistant chorister, 1781; Asahel, coll., 1782; Nathanel, Jr., Soc'y com., 1784.

Pratt, Jonathan, Soc'y meeting adjourned to his house in cold weather, 1730. He died in 1755, aged 72. Eliab, school com., 1763; Nathaniel, coll., 1785; Moses, 1781; Eli, 1789.

Polot, Samuel, 1715.

Patterson, James, 1777.

Philips, Peter, 1787; John, school com., 1794.

Porter, Hezekiah, Sr., east side selectman, 1707; Hezekiah, com. on Hockanum school house, 1720; Isaac, coll., 1740; Timothy, Soc'y com., 1731; Timothy, Jr., school com., 1742; James, coll., 1733; Joseph, coll., 1732; David, coll., 1744; Benjamin, coll., 1767; Stephen, school com., 1779; William, school com., 1781; John, coll., 1788; James, coll., 1777; Job, coll., 1778.

Pitkin, William, 2d, com. on minister's house, 1699; Capt. Roger, recorder, 1700; John, auditor, 1703; Capt. Ozias, com. on school-house, 1714; Joseph, ratemaker, 1717; Nathaniel, school com., 1721; Gov'r William, 3d, clerk, 1718–1748; com. to reseat meeting house, 1754; Caleb, school com., 1731; Samuel, repaired school house, 1736; Roger, Jr., coll., 1736; Elisha, ratemaker, 1754; Epaphras, school com., 1784; John, clerk, 1758; Isaac, ratemaker, 1759; Joshua, coll., 1760; Colonel William, com., 1761; William, Jr., coll., 1783; George, coll., 1750; Daniel, ratemaker, 1767; George, Jr., coll., 1779; Ashbel, clerk, 1783; Timothy, coll., 1793; David, school com., 1795; Daniel, Jr., school com., 1795.

Rappanier, Asahel, 1785.

Ritter, Thomas, 1748; Daniel, school com., 1792.

Risley, John, 1701; Thomas, coll., 1706; Charles, 1710; Richard, Sr., 1712; Samuel, 1714; John, 3d, boat in flood time, 1754; John, Jr., coll., 1756; Moses, school com., 1770; Job, school com., 1776; Elijah, school com., 1781; Jonathan,

SETTLERS AND INHABITANTS. 65

school com., 1785; Nathaniel, school com., 1789; George, 2d, coll., 1792.

Roberts, William, com. on minister's house, 1703; Benjamin, coll., 1721, deeded land for Silver Lane, 1731; Joseph, coll., 1739; Samuel, Jr., coll., 1760; Timothy, school com., 1781; Benjamin, Jr., coll., 1770; Eliphalet, school com., 1775; Jonathan, school com., chorister, 1774; Thomas, school com., 1775; Stephen, Soc'y com., 1774; Elias, school com., 1785; William, 1788; George, school com., 1790; Ashbel, coll., 1791; Ephraim, 1791; John, 1792; Daniel, 1793; Eli, com. on psalmody, 1795.

Robinson, John, 1708.

Rood, Rev. John, preaches here, 1699.

Stanley, Nathaniel, com. on school sites, 1720; Jonathan,* made a bier, 1737; William, died 1767, aged 56—his wife was Clemence Olmsted—coll., 1741; Elisha, Soc'y com., 1779; Jonathan, Jr.,† to cord wood for Dr. Williams, 1783; Theodore, school com., 1783; Ashbel, Soc'y com., 1787.

Sage, Ozias, 1789; John, school com., 1793.

Stedman, Joseph, 1708; Philemon, 1789.

Spencer, John, coll., 1702; Serg't Thomas, constable, 1723; Joseph, coll., 1740; Timothy, school near, 1751; Jedediah, coll., 1764; Silas, to fix price of grain for minister's salary, 1767; John, school com., 1780; Gideon, school com., 1776; Gideon, Jr., school com., 1777; John, "son of Gideon," coll., 1791.

Sheeney, Joseph, 1789.

Saunders, Samuel, 1790.

Smith, Philip, com. on meeting house, 1704 (died, 1725); David, fenced burying ground, 1733; Dea. Samuel, deeded land for Silver Lane, 1731, coll., 1734; Joseph, repaired school house, 1736; Samuel, Jr., coll., 1753; Dea. Moses, school com., 1772; John, school com., 1780; Epaphras, 1778; Silas, 1773; Gideon, 1773; Eldad, 1785; Nehemiah, school com., 1795.

---

*He died 1788, aged 79. His wife was Mabel Olmsted, daughter of Deacon Joseph.

† 18 years Town Clerk; removed to Marcellus, N. Y.

Strickland, Joseph, 1741.
Symonds, Joseph, Jr., coll., 1714; Benjamin, coll., 1748; William, school com., 1787.
Treat, Henry, (married Sarah Andrews,) came to Hockanum in 1681; Matthias, 1710; Henry, coll., 1752; Theodore, 1780; Stephen, school com., 1779; Russell, coll., 1781; Richard, coll., 1784; Matthias, 1792.
Tinker, Reuben, 1794.
Tripp, Elijah, 1788.
Taylor, John, school com., 1781.
Tucker, Nehemiah, 1781.
Terry, Noah, 1773.
Vansant, Hannah, 1787.
Vibert, James, 1748; John, 1770; William, 1774.
Ward, Gamaliel, 1744.
Wallace, William, coll., 1759; James, 1784.
Wadsworth, Thomas, Soc'y com., 1741; William, school com., 1777; Thomas, Jr., school com., 1774; Josiah, school com., 1881; Samuel, coll., 1782.
White, Lemuel, ratemaker, 1764.
Whittlesey, Chauncey, to preach on probation, 1742.
Webster, Ezekiel, coll., 1746.
Wells, Samuel, ratemaker, 1699; Samuel, Jr., com. on new meeting house, 1730; Noah, to preach here, 1743; Joseph, com. on new meeting house, 1739; Capt. John, Soc'y com., 1758; Jonathan, school com., 1764; David, coll., 1793; Daniel, coll., 1794.
Woodbridge, Rev'd Samuel, called to preach and settled, 1704, died, 1746; Capt. Russell, ratemaker, 1750; Samuel, school com., 1763; Ward, coll., 1778; Deodat, ass't chorister, 1781.
Woodruff, Benjamin, 1779.
Wood, John, 1710.
Woods, J. W., 1790.
Warren, Andrew, coll., 1703; John, 1770; Edward, school com., 1782; Daniel, coll. South District, 1790.
Williams, John, coll., 1704; Serg't William, com. on forts, and to call Rev. Woodbridge, 1704; Gabriel, com. to

SETTLERS AND INHABITANTS.

"dignify meeting house," 1707 ; Serg't Samuel, seating com., 1714 ; Daniel, 1728 ; Timothy, warns meetings, 1729 ; Lieut. Jonathan, 1729 ; Jacob, school com., 1734; Jacob, school com., 1781 ; William, Jr., seating com., 1737 ; Stephen, to preach here, 1745 ; Dr. Eliphalet, called to preach here and settled, 1747 to 1803 ; Gabriel, Jr., school com., 1748 ; Timothy, Jr., coll., 1750 ; Solomon, school com., 1762 ; Dea. John, school com., 1767 ; Ephraim, coll., 1770 ; Moses, 1772²; Ozias, coll. South District, 1790 ; Edward, school com., 1792 ; Samuel, 1794 ; Oliver, coll. South District, 1795.

Wyllys, Thomas, school com., 1787, coll. South District, 1794.

Wiles, or *Wyles*, Capt. John, school com., 1777, and com. on Sunday boats, 1788 ; David, 1789.

Witter, Thomas, 1743.

We have chosen in this chapter to give little beyond a mere hint of the value of the old records of the First Ecclesiastical Society of our town, as a store house of family names and genealogies. Elsewhere we have made larger use of the records, and in the chapter on Houses and Lands we have tried to indicate as nearly as possible the habitations of all whose names we have copied above, upon which any definite information was to be had.

EARLY HISTORY,—CONTINUED.

CHAPTER IV.

1670-1774.

MAIN STREET in our town was laid out in 1670. The selectmen in the respective plantations were ordered to "lay out a highway six rod wide upon the upland on the east side of the Great River, that men may pass to their lots there as occasion shall require;" it was to extend from plantation to plantation, and was called the King's Highway. The selectmen were also to order "the fence sett up in the place where they shall order the highway to be sett out;" and the bounds of the several plantations were extended "eastward twenty rod farther than their three miles formerly granted in consideration thereof."

The bounds of the town of Hartford were extended eastward five miles in 1672, for the encouragement of people to plant there. This new tract was known as the Five Miles until 1773. The deed of this land from "Joshua Sachem," was not procured until ten years later, but probably the land had been bargained for before this time, for the town of Hartford in 1681 voted to pay to the administrators of Joshua's will the money agreed by Major Talcott with Joshua, provided sufficient deeds were given. The deed was given in May, 1682, by James Fitch, Jr., and Thomas Buckingham, Joshua's administrators. The tract is bounded as follows: "The western side three miles from Connecticut River, and is abutting on lands belonging to the towne of Hartford on the west, and the whole bredth of the towne of Hartford three miles eastward from Connecticut River and runs toward the east five miles in length and abutts on the Commons east, and on Windsor bounds on the north where it was

EARLY HISTORY—CONTINUED.

last stated by the Court, and on Wethersfield bounds on the south." It was at once voted to divide this last grant of land among the inhabitants, "according to the disbursements of etch person paid in list of 1682." But a real division was not made until 1731. (See chapter on Parish of Orford.)

In 1675 the Narragansett war broke out, and some of the enemy came into Hockanum and shot William Hill. Among the active measures was the garrisoning of four houses on this side the river—one at Bissell's ferry in Windsor, one at Thomas Burnham's in Podunk, one at John Crow's on the meadow hill, a little way north of the Hockanum river, one at Naubuc, and one also at "Mr. Wyllys his farm," still farther south. A fuller account of the troubles of this time will be found in the chapter on Indians.

A difference arose with Windsor concerning the northern boundary of the town on this side the river. An attempt to adjust the matter was made in 1675, and the loss to owners of the lots on this side was to be made good by a committee, out of an undivided triangular piece of land between Windsor bounds and Thomas Burnham's land, if it would answer the loss. But the adjustment was not final; in 1677, on petition of Joseph Fitch, of Windsor, a committee was appointed "to lay out the line between the sayd Mr. Fitch and Thomas Burnham their upland at Podunck, and to doe it according to their best judgment is agreeable to the deed of sale made to Mr. Fitch by the Country." As usual the court decided against Thomas Burnham. But the trouble was still unhealed; in 1678 the matter was again agitated. Burnham was not a man to acquiesce with the decision of any court, as the following warrant, issued in 1682, shows: " By virtue hereof you are required to give Thomas Burnham warninge to for barre any further meddling with any of the land at Podunke that lyes abov the line that was laid out by the Hartfordmen and Windsormen." (Towns and Lands, 1, 64.) And here the matter rested for awhile; but fresh and cumulative interest was manifested from time to time, and in 1719 the town of Hartford voted to defend the lots south of the line laid out from Podunk river eastward in 1636. But in a suit brought by Samuel Tudor, of Windsor, against Samuel Burnham, in 1721, the court decided that the line set by the General Court in 1636 did not pass the title of the disputed land to Hartford. The town then voted to appeal the case to the General Court, but with no better result, and the town finally made good to the heirs of Thomas Burnham, and of William Williams, " what Windsor line had cut off their upland lots," by giving them a tract of 300 acres in the Five Miles— a tract bounded north by Windsor bounds, 300 rods, and west by the three mile lots, 160 rods.

The dividing line between the towns was settled by the General Assembly in May, 1719, which accepted the report of their committee, and enacted " that the said line shall be and remain the dividing line between the said towns, and the ditches made by said committee shall be the lawful bound marks, and be so kept and renewed by said towns." The town of Hartford did not rest content with this, but in 1751, appointed a committee to settle the line with Windsor, from the Country Road (Main Street) to the river, and to agree on no other than that anciently settled. But nothing appears to have come of it. This line was again adjusted, and stones set, by the selectmen of the towns of East Hartford and South Windsor in 1874.

In 1679, the townsmen (selectmen) of Hartford were directed to appoint two yards on this side, one between Mr. Crow's and Goodman Williams', and the other in the most convenient place in Hockanum, for the pounding of cattle, and to empower the owners to be keepers of the pounds.

In 1683, William Pitkin was chosen hayward " for meadow," with power, if sick or disabled, to appoint one in his place.

In 1686, Roger Pitkin was chosen hayward for the east side, and William Hills for Hockanum.

In 1687, William Warren was chosen surveyor " from the Riveret to Potunck ;" and John Hill for " Hoccanum." Fence viewers were also appointed this year. And so our embryo town came slowly to have its special officers, albeit they were elected by a vote of all the inhabitants, and upon the other side of the river.

EARLY HISTORY—CONTINUED.

In 1699 was begun the first meeting house this side the river, and the first constable was appointed—Mr. Daniel Bidwell.

In 1707 Mr. Hezekiah Porter was appointed our first selectman; and we were allowed a brander to brand our horses in 1708. The appointment of persons to these offices on this side the river was regularly done from this time until we matured into a town.

The bridge over the Hockanum river on Main street was built in 1700; William Pitkin (2d), of the east side, and Capt. Cyprian Nichols, and John Marsh of the west side, being the committee to view the site and order the building of the same. Prior to that time the river was crossed by fording.

Our ancestors about this time must have begun to look about them with a very commendable pride. Many roads had been laid out, and bridges built; the Indians and wild beasts had been dispossessed and driven back; Main street, long known as the "Country Road," the road along the meadow hill, and the cross roads to the eastward were thinly dotted with houses; on the streams the clatter of the mills scarcely stayed night or day, while in the near forests the axes of the woodmen rang sharply all the busy week. Few stumps remained in the gardens and nearer fields; and toil to the hard-handed farmer began to take on a brighter aspect. His soil was new and deep, and apparently inexhaustible. He raised his own flax and wool, which his wife and daughters spun into durable garments for themselves and for him; he raised his own pork, beef, grain, and vegetables; took his own hides to the home tannery, and left them for an unconscionable period, that he might have them afterwards made into boots that were well-nigh indestructible. He was becoming self-contained, and might well have the complaisance of those who have begun to be forehanded in the world. Nor had he forgotten higher things. The new meeting house had been built, and stood beaming in plain, unpainted glory across the river swamp from its hill in the midst of the town. Here on Sundays, and lecture days besides, the Rev. John Rood ministered zealously to the spiritual needs of a flock over which he never became a settled pastor. And he abated no whit of his sermon though a midwinter chill was in the air, and there was no fire save in the tiny foot-stoves that half-filled the room with thin blue smoke—the rime gathering the while, perchance, on the muskets that had been brought as far as the porch, and left in charge of the sentry there.

And there was need of caution at this time. In 1704, Deerfield was assaulted and burned, and the General Court thought best to order four houses to be fortified on this side of the river, at the cost of the residents here. William Pitkin (2d), Lieut. Jonathan Hills, Dea. Joseph Olmsted, Daniel Bidwell, and Serg't William Williams were the committee to appoint the houses which were to be fortified, and to "proportion each man's share that he is to doe of said fortification."

It is not known what houses were fortified; but a well-grounded tradition exists that one of them stood in the Center District, at the foot of a new road lately laid out by Mr. Joseph Merriman on his land. Until within a few years the ditches which it is thought encompassed it were traceable. The fortifying was accomplished by enclosing the yard about the house with a stout fence of pointed posts or palisades, with a strong gate, and loop holes for the guns. Outside of this a wide ditch was dug, the earth being sloped up against the palisades, and sometimes fixed full of sharp protruding boughs. Little platforms placed in the inner angles of the palisades and reached by a ladder, or by steps, furnished an out-look for the sentinels, who, in dangerous times, were kept at post both day and night.

A writer in the *Elm Leaf* (1863), says that the site of this fortification was north of the New York & New England Railroad, at the house of William Pitkin, the first settler. As the elder William Pitkin died in 1694, this could hardly be possible. His son William, however, was one of the committee. This writer says the people were summoned to the fort at night by the ringing of a bell, and probably this was the signal also in case of an alarm by day.

Beyond giving the people a sense of security in a troubled

EARLY HISTORY—CONTINUED.

time, these forts appear to have been of no use. A list of those who, with their families and "feeble folk," sought the protection of the palisades, would show the names of the founders of our staid community, names which some of us bear with a modesty which well becomes us as we look back upon their conscientious work. The Bidwells would be there, Daniel and John, from Bidwell's lane, now Burnside avenue, and Henry Arnold; Dea. Joseph Olmsted, and Richard Olmsted, and Timothy Cowles, afterwards Deacon Cowles, from the neighborhood of the junction of Prospect street with Main street, and a half mile north; Joseph and James Easton, from the north meadow; Richard Gilman, living north of Gilman's Brook or the "old road"; John Goodwin, later deacon, from the center, close beside the plot where the burying ground was afterwards laid out; Lieut. John Meakins; and, perchance, the Olcotts—Lieut. Thomas and John—from Hop Brook in the Five Miles, unless they felt equal to their own protection there; Jonathan Pratt, tanner, from the west side of Main street, just north of the hollow by the old meeting-house site (then new); the Pitkins—William, Capt. Roger (if he was not in more active service), and John; William Roberts from the meadow hill, half a mile south of the fort, and William Buckland who lived only a few rods away; William Stanley, perhaps, although he does not appear here until later; John Spencer, who either lived at the head of Mill street, on Main street, or at Burnside; and the Williams family—John, Serg't William, Gabriel,—who lived at Willow Brook, or at Podunk and eastward, and perhaps at both places; and the Burnhams of Podunk also, unless they had a fort of their own, as Thomas Burnham had in 1675; and Philip Smith, who, in 1710, was licensed to keep a public house, and who owned much land in the meadow, and on Silver Lane, and eastward. And for the spiritual support and guide of this goodly company of men and women and children, the Rev. Samuel Woodbridge, our first settled minister, whose house stood north of the old meeting-house, on the west side of Main street.

South of the Hockanum there lived at this time John Abbey, on what was subsequently Silver Lane; Andrew Warren, between the Hockanum and Willow Brook; Samuel Wells, on site of Mr. Reuben Brewer's house; Matthias Treat, near Dowd's Grove, on the meadow hill; John Risley and Thomas Risley, near Willow Brook; Hezekiah Porter in Hockanum; Daniel and David Forbes of Willow Brook, or Burnside; Lieut. Jonathan Hills, and Ebenezer Hills, and Joseph Keeney, of Hockanum; Serg't Thomas Kilbourn, near Silver Lane; and John Dix, near Brewer Lane. These and their families were a company numerous enough to be provided with shelter in their own neighborhood from the expected assaults of the Indians, but no record appears of any means taken to that end.

Meanwhile, despite the fear of an irruption of the Eastern Indians, parties had settled in the Five Miles. But as that tract was common land, their stay there was rather precarious. In 1706 a committee was appointed to "eject any such persons who have entered upon or taken possession of any part or parcel of land," within said Five Miles. This committee was also to set out this tract as in the deed from Fitch and Buckingham, Joshua's administrators. But, if ejected, the squatters with characteristic persistency returned and squatted again. In 1719 a saw mill had been erected there without leave by some Windsor men; and as late as 1735 action was taken concerning the unlawful taking of wood and timber from these commons. The first division of them among the proprietors was made in 1731. (See chapter on Orford Parish.)

The first action in regard to a burial place this side the Great River was taken by the voters of the town of Hartford in 1709. A committee was chosen to view a convenient place for a burying yard, and, if necessary, to purchase the land. The deed of the first purchase for the Center Burying Ground was given by John Pantry to the town of Hartford, January 1, 1710. It conveyed one acre, for a consideration of four pounds. The plot was twenty rods in length east and west, and eight rods in width; and was bounded east and south by John Pantry's land; west by highway; north by land of John Goodwin.

The wants of the living also were not disregarded. Philip Smith was given liberty to keep a public house in 1710,—he attending to the rules of the law. Of this tavern, or of Smith's character as a host, we know nothing. Possibly it was kept in the meadow, near the ferry, where later public houses flourished, and where Smith owned land. This land and a large tract of 300 acres, on what was subsequently Silver Lane, he bought of the heirs of John Hamlin, who had bought it of John Crow.

The following year Thomas Olcott was licensed to keep a house of entertainment. This he did in the Five Miles, at Hop Brook,—an indication that the tide of travel and of population was drifting that way.

In 1715 a committee was appointed to run a straight line from Windsor to "Glassenbury bounds, between the three mile lots and said five miles of land."

The line between the towns of Hartford and Bolton was ordered run out, between the town's land and lands of the legatees of Joshua, an Indian sachem. This was in 1718. In 1724 the line was again ordered to be run out and monuments set. But not until 1726 was the line established and fixed.

An order in regard to draining certain lands in our meadows was passed at a meeting of the Governor and Council, in New Haven, Oct. 19, 1719, William Pitkin (2d), of Hartford, being one of the assistants: "On petition of the proprietors of a certain piece of low-land or hollow (commonly called Eason's Hollow), in Hartford meadow on the east side of the Connecticut River: Ordered, that a commission of sewers, for draining of the said low-land or hollow, be granted to Capt. Ozias Pitkin, Mr. Nath¹ Stanley, and Mr. John Meakins of said Hartford."

We have already seen something of the troubles that arose from the indefiniteness of the early land boundaries. In the early days, when land was abundant, good men were given large tracts, to be taken up anywhere, so that it prejudiced no earlier grant. But soon the settlers began to elbow each other, and a more orderly state of things was absolutely necessary. Then the General Court found plenty of business in rectifying the errors of its own generous youth. Differences early arose in regard to the east and west "diffident lines," of the three mile lots, from Windsor to Glastonbury. A committee was appointed to inquire into the matter in 1729. The following year the Court empowered a commission to run out the dividing lines between the lots, parallel to the line of the north side of Glastonbury, as it runs the first three miles from the Great River, from the Country Road (Main street) leading from Windsor to Glastonbury, to the eastern end of said lots. The work was to be paid for by such as had their lines run out. The nearly east and west courses of these lines govern the boundaries of our lots to-day, and account for the awkward angles at which the lines of many of our house-lots intersect Main street. Most of the roads running eastward are laid out parallel to these lines. That next north of Gilman's Brook, when surveyed in 1734, was run parallel to the dividing line between Hartford and Glastonbury, although five miles distant from it.

In 1749 the lister for this side, who assessed the property here, became a salaried officer and received five pounds for his pains.

The same year sign-posts were ordered in the towns on both sides the river, for the posting of public notices. And tradition says they were used for purposes less gentle also. The old one in our street knew no softer name than " the whipping post." It was a stout oaken post, about ten inches square, with a rough neck and head, hewed squarely to a point at the top. It was studded with rusty tacks and nails, and nothing but the obduracy of its oaken head and heart had kept it intact for so many years. Several times it rotted off at the surface of the ground, but was set down afresh, its loss of stature giving it an aspect of fresh devotion to the cause of punitive justice in our borders—a sort of new consecration, as though it had just bethought itself to go down on its knees in behalf of society. It stood on the east side of Main street, nearly opposite our present sign-post, in front of the house of the writer. Some among us, who are not yet old, remember when the constable laid the lash across the bare shoulders of offenders bending before this stern but salutary shrine. The progress of the old time "tramp," if he were a vagabond indeed,

EARLY HISTORY—CONTINUED.   77

between these wayside shrines, was no festive march, and he did not linger long in their neighborhood. The remains of the old whipping-post I have described are still preserved by Mr. S. G. Phelps.

The French and Indian war drew from among our citizens a goodly number of martial spirits, who enlisted in Lieut.-Col. John Pitkin's company, of which the muster roll has been found among the papers of Gen. S. L. Pitkin. It is as follows:

"A Muster Roll of Lieut.-Colonel John Pitkin's company, being the second company in the First Regiment raised for the reduction of Crown Point, April, 1755 (in service 28 weeks).

John Pitkin, *Col. & Capt.*
Lemuel Hull, *Lieut.*   James Jones, *Lieut.*
William Stanton, *Clerk,*   Reuben Chittenden, *Drummer.*

Sergeants:

John Keeney,   Isaac Turner,
Daniel Cone,   Charles Buckland.

Corporals:

Jonathan Avery,   Peleg Redfield,
Alexander Keeney,   Jeremiah Stevens.

Privates:

Amos Raiment,   Aaron Pratt,
Benj. Keeney,   Samuel Evens,
Nath'l Dewey,   Josiah Standift,
Abner Elger,   William Brown,
Asa Burnham,   Benj. Brewer, Jr.,
Benoni Evens,   Benoni Loomis,
Moses Evens,   Elisha Parker,
Samuel Evens, Jr.,   Gideon King,
Joseph Keeney,   Daniel Brewer,
Ozias Bissell,   Samuel Chandler,
William Ross,   Simon Gains,
Thos. Brewer, Jr.,   John Benjamin,

Giles Wilcocks,   James Redfield,
Israel Harding,   Ichabod French,
Thomas Stevens,   Reuben Turner,
Thomas Rooly,   Jonathan Shephard,
Joseph Daton,   Aaron Stevens,
Moses Wright,   Ebenezer Belding,
Abraham Brooker,   Ezekiel Hull,
Abraham Stevens,   Miles Wright,
Ezra Crain,   Reuben Kelsey,
John Nichols,   Joseph Carter,
Edward Hutchins,   Jesse Chatfield,
Daniel Franklin,   Ezra Ephraims,
Gideon Fox,   Samuel Wells,*
Simeon Mentor,   Benj. Bragg,
John Ryant,   Lebbeus Tubbus,
Jedediah Fox,   Benajah Tubbus,
Israel Rowley,   Amos Jones,
William Dodge, Jr.,   James Webb,
Andrew Clark,   Elijah Thomas,
Judah Spencer,   Abner Scovill,
Peter Homan,   Daniel Shields,
Suckheiom,   John Abbey, Jr.,
Thomas Keeney,   Aaron Kelsey.

"Hartford, 22d May, 1755. Then mustered ye above company, ye Colonel and Lieut^s. being present and find them all able bodied, effective men. Joseph Pitkin, Esq., one of his Majesties Justices of ye peace, being also present. 79 in number.

"*Teste,*   Elihu Lyman, Com'y of ye Masters."

"The expedition against Crown Point," says Goodrich, "was conducted by Gen. William Johnson, a member of the Council of New York; and although it failed as to its main object, yet its results diffused exultation through the American Colonies, and dispelled the gloom that followed Braddock's defeat." It accomplished the defeat of Baron Dieskau and two thousand of the enemy in the battle of Lake George.

An incident of this war was the settlement of the neutral

---

* Was a First Lieutenant in 1757.

French inhabitants of Nova Scotia among the towns in the Colonies. The French force in that province "being subdued, a difficult question occurred, respecting the disposal of the inhabitants. Fearing that they might join the French in Canada, whom they had before" aided, "it was determined to disperse them among the English Colonies. Under this order nearly 2,000 miserable occupants of a sterile soil, ... and yet attached to it, and so loyal as to refuse to take the oath of allegiance to the King of England, were driven on board the British shipping, and dispersed among the English Colonies." (Goodrich.) On this dispersal is based Longfellow's poem, "Evangeline."

A vote of the General Assembly of this State indicates that about 400 were expected to be provided for here, and allots the number each town was to receive. Families were not to be broken up in the distribution. The selectmen of the towns were ordered to receive the number assigned to their respective towns, and, with the advice of the civil authority, to take care of, manage, and support them as though they were inhabitants. And these people were not to leave the towns to which they were allotted without a writing under the hand of some of the civil authority; otherwise they were to suffer arrest and be conveyed back from constable to constable, through the different towns, until they were delivered into proper custody again. The town of Hartford was allotted fifteen of these people, and voted in 1756 to build a house for their accommodation.

The line between the towns of Hartford and Wethersfield and Glastonbury was adjusted in 1769. The town agents were directed to appear before the committee appointed by the General Assembly to fix the same.

As early as 1748, the inhabitants of the Five Miles were allowed to have preaching there three months in the year, when the roads were in bad condition, with which they were a long time content. But in 1763 they petitioned to be made a separate society. Partly through a lack of unanimity among themselves they did not attain their object until 1773. In June of that year they were incorporated into an ecclesiastical society, under the name of the Parish of Orford. The site of their meeting house was determined in May, 1774.

Their petition was from the first opposed by the old society, especially because they asked to have their bounds include not only the Five Miles, but a good half mile west of the ditches between it and the three mile lots. This opposition however, was of no avail. The line between the societies was defined as five and one-half miles from Bolton line. The old society tried to contest it, but without result. Still it kept alive the memory of its wrong until the growing parish wished to become a town, and then a vote was passed in town meeting to oppose the petitioners before the General Assembly, unless they would consent to have for their western boundary the old line between the three and five mile lots. In this, however, it finally failed, and the line between the towns is about one hundred rods west of the old line of the lots. Keeney street, in Manchester, is laid along the old line between the Five Miles and the three mile lots.

DURING THE REVOLUTION.

CHAPTER V.

1770-1783.

WE may reasonably claim for our people a large share in the part which Hartford took in the Revolutionary War. The disparity between the wealth and population of the two sides of the river was not so great in 1774 as it now is. Our present town was at that time no mere suburb of Hartford, but an important factor in its activities and its councils. A computation of the entire population of Hartford, Dec. 13, 1761, gives but 3,938 people, black and white; of this number 1,588 are put down as living on the east side of the river. A census taken in 1774 gives Hartford a total population of 5,031. The same year the inhabitants of the east side, in their petition to be allowed separate town privileges, claim to number 2,000 souls, with a property list of 19,000 pounds. From about the year 1707, one selectmen at least was elected annually from this side, and we had our constable, haywards, fence viewers, etc., as has been shown. In the affairs of the Colony, civil, military, and judicial, our people had a prominent representation through the influential Pitkin family, and others, many of whose names live prominently among us to-day. And when the crisis came, in which the young colonies were to take their stand against one of the most powerful nations on the earth, our people responded with such alacrity and in such numbers as to prove that their previous part in the growing determination of resistance had not been that of idle or doubtful lookers-on.

Every vote recorded in the records of the town of Hartford at this time has a vital interest for us, bringing as it does to our very firesides the history of those resolute years. There is in none of them a doubtful tone.

The first mutterings of dissatisfaction were manifested in 1770, when John Ledyard, Esqr., Col. John Pitkin, Capt. John Lawrence, and Mr. Elisha Pitkin were appointed a committee to represent the town of Hartford at New Haven, and directed to use their endeavors in the support of measures designed to prevent the importation of English goods, and in the promotion of the use of American manufactures, " at this critical juncture .... in the common cause."

In 1774, six resolutions of sympathy were passed, expressing sympathy with embargoed Boston, and approving the association entered into by the late Continental Congress. A committee of "correspondence and observation" was appointed.

There was something in these resolves besides their rhetorical flourish. When, in April, 1775, came the news of the Concord and Lexington fight, announced by couriers through all the land, there was no hesitation. A paper, written by General S. L. Pitkin, has been found, which shows that "Old Put" was not alone in leaving his plow in the furrow at this eventful time:

"The following named persons marched from Hartford for the relief of Boston in the Lexington alarm, April, 1775.

"George Pitkin, Esqr., *Lieut. Colonel.*
Selah Norton, *Ensign.* Daniel Marsh, *Sergeant.*
John Hurlburt, *Sergeant.* Timothy Olmsted, *Fifer.*
Gurdon Burnham, *Drummer.*

Privates:

Job Norton, Samuel Woodbridge,
Stephen Rogers, James Kilbourn,
George Clark, John Reynolds,
William Olmsted, Nathaniel Olmsted,
Theodore Stanley, Joseph Pitkin,
John Taylor, Moses Butler,
Asahel Olmsted, Epaphras Olmsted,*

---

* Was a cavalry man later in the war.

Gideon Olmsted,*	Thomas Wyllis,
William Roberts,	Benoni Evens,
Epaphras Gilman,	Samuel Hurlburt,
Augustus Burnham,	Jacob Williams,
Joshua Williams,	Daniel Williams,
Epaphras Bidwell,	John Roberts,

* He had a subsequent history which must here be told. In 1778 he was captain of a French privateer, and was captured by the English sloop Ostrich and taken to Jamaica. Here, with three compatriots,—Artemas White, Aquila Rumsdale, and David Clark,—he was put upon the sloop Active, Captain John Underwood, bound for New York, with a cargo of rum, coffee, pimento, etc., for the British army and navy. After assisting to work the vessel to New York, the prisoners were to be transferred to the infamous prison ships at that port. Besides these, Capt. Underwood's crew consisted of his mate and two sailors, and there were three male passengers with a negro servant on board. They left Montego Bay Aug. 1, 1778, under convoy of the Glasgow, man-of-war, for twenty-seven days. Sept. 4th they made Cape Charles and met the brig Tryon, and were warned to keep away from the coast on account of privateers. Sunday night, about 12 o'clock, Olmsted, White, and Rumsdale were on deck, an old sailor being at the wheel. Rumsdale called the watch, and Clark and the other sailor, a young colored man, came on deck. Capt. Underwood and the mate were about to follow, when Olmsted and Clark drew up the ladder and told them they were prisoners, and swore they would kill them if they came on deck. They ordered the sailor back to the wheel, and coiled a cable around the companion-way, Olmsted being wounded by a pistol ball from below while doing so. The course of the vessel was changed toward Egg Harbor, New Jersey. Toward daylight those below began to fire their pistols through the chinks of the cabin. Capt. Olmsted told them to desist or he would fire a four-pounder into the cabin. Capt. Underwood retorted, "Fire and be d——d!" And they did, damaging, however, only a puncheon of rum and a barrel of coffee. Underwood, in a rage, cried out that he would blow up the vessel. Olmsted told him he might do it and be d——d, he was no more afraid of going to the bottom than they. Underwood was about to fire his pistol into the powder barrel, when the mate stopped him, and one of the passengers offered to pay all their losses if they would cease firing their pistols. But they did not, and another four-pounder was sent through the bulkhead.

The foresail was then unbent and lashed around the companion to screen those on deck; but, finding that the rudder had been wedged, they cut a hole in it and fired a swivel, loaded with thirty musket balls, into the cabin. This was the last shot fired. Capt. Olmsted and his comrades now began to tear up the deck to get at the rudder, when those below gave up the contest, hoping the Yankees would take a boat and leave when near the shore, or that an English cruiser might relieve them. They

Aaron Burnham,	John Spencer,
Timothy Mawley,	William Griffin,
Benjamin Gilman,	Samuel Kennedy,
Aaron Olmsted,	Levi Goodwin,
Thomas Spencer,	Silas Easton,
Abraham Clark,	Russell Woodbridge, Jr.,
John Pitkin, Jr.,	Elijah Roberts,
William Chandler,	—— Jones,
Daniel Call,	Benjamin Woodruff.

Of the deeds of these ready volunteers in the field we have no record. Many of them probably served later in the war;

---

unwedged the rudder in this hope, and things became more "friendly," as a narrator quaintly says, and a quarter of mutton was passed into the cabin. Early Tuesday morning the captors made Cape May and hauled down their sails to avoid discovery by any chance cruiser. They were discovered, however, by the American brig Convention, which showed British colors, and fired upon them. Capt. Olmsted then asked Capt. Underwood to give him the sloop's papers; but he would not give them up, and hung his English colors out of the cabin window. The sloop was taken in charge by the Convention and her consort, the Girard, and taken to Philadelphia.

The Active's cargo sold for $98,800. An interest in the prize money was claimed by the Convention, and by her consort, the Girard, and by Gideon Olmsted and his companions. The admiralty court of Pennsylvania awarded to the captain of the Convention one-fourth of the amount; to her owners (the State of Pennsylvania), one-fourth; to the Girard, one-fourth; and to Gideon Olmsted and associates, one-fourth.

Olmsted and his associates appealed to the United States commissioners of appeals, and they set aside the decision of the admiralty court and awarded the entire amount to Gideon Olmsted and his associates. Olmsted bought out the claims of his companions, but as the case was a complicated one, and involved a conflict of authority between the State courts and the United States courts, the matter did not come to a final adjustment until November, 1809; and, even then, the State declined giving up the amount originally deposited in its treasury for the captain of the Convention ($24,700).—*Sundry Documents relative to the Claim of Gideon Olmsted, etc.* Phila., 1811.

Another incident in regard to Capt. Gideon Olmsted's privateering has just come to the writer's knowledge. He fell in with a rich merchantman disguised as a man-of-war, and cruised near it for a while, uncertain whether to attack it or not. His crew urged him to do so, but Capt. Olmsted declared that it looked too wicked; those silent port-holes might be only waiting to blow him out of the water; and he allowed her to slip away, much to the after chagrin of his intrepid nature.

and most returned finally to their homes, to die in peace, and are buried in our town.

The few names we have gathered of others who served in the war may be given here:

Stephen Olmsted died in Westchester County, New York, Sept. 9, 1776. A long elegy, addressed to his widow, was written by Mr. Elisha Benton, a fellow-soldier of his, and shows him to have been a man of worth. This elegy has been printed in the *Elm Leaf* (1863).

Mr. Elisha Benton was our local poet; he came home in safety, and died in 1818.

Captain Zebulon Bidwell was killed at (or after) the battle of Stillwater, in New York, in 1777. The following quaint record is from the gravestone of his son: "In memory of an Infant son of the late Capt. Zebulon and Mrs. Mary Bidwell, who was still-born soon after his Father's Death (and perhaps quited Life at ye news thereof) who was killed in ye Northern Army, Sept. 20th, 1777, in his 34th year.

> "Abroad from home in Earth's cold womb,
> His body sleeping lies;
> May we prepare to meet him where
> Are everlasting joys."

Capt. Stephen Buckland died in the prison-ship Jersey, at New York, May 7, 1782.

Capt. Lemuel White was also confined on board the prison-ship at New York. He declared that the fare was so abominable that the swarming vermin actually gave it a relish! An account of the horrors of the prison-ships may be found in Barber's Historical Collections of Connecticut, p. 286. Three hundred and fifty persons were confined in the hold of one vessel, and the air was so foul that a lamp would not burn there. Some lay ten days dead before they were discovered and taken out.

Col. Jonathan Wells, of Hockanum, was also an officer in the Revolutionary army. He lived in the house lately owned by Mr. Abial Pease. He died in 1816. Upon the grave-stone of Levi Risley, who died in 1834, at the age of seventy-four, are the words, "A Patriot of the Revolution."

In 1777, eight battalions were to be raised, and one of them, commanded by Col. Samuel Wyllys, was quartered in Hartford for the winter, for the purpose of filling up its ranks, and for military exercise. The town instructed the selectmen to assist in procuring barracks, provided no expense was made to the town.

A committee was appointed to procure necessaries for the families of soldiers at prices affixed by law; and the same was subsequently renewed from time to time.

The same year a bounty of twenty pounds was voted to each soldier who enlisted to fill the quota of the town in the eight battalions, and a tax was laid to raise the necessary money. Clothing was to be furnished them, the quota of salt allowed the town by the State being appropriated toward paying for the same.

About this time the Colonies began to distribute their prisoners of war among the towns for safe keeping. A number were quartered in South Windsor; among them William Franklin (son of Dr. Benjamin Franklin), the royal governor of New Jersey, and Generals Hamilton and Prescott. But although they occupied houses close upon our borders, none were quartered within our town. This probably was the result of a vote passed in 1777, instructing the selectmen to apply to the General Assembly to remove all prisoners of war that are or may be sent to this town, and for other relief as may be required.

In 1777, also, William Pitkin (4th), and six others were appointed " to consider the articles of confederation drawn up and proposed by Congress for a Plan of Union to be adopted and come into by the United States of America;"—the town expressing its opinion that some alterations were advisable.

In 1780 a committee was chosen to stop the trade in embargoed provisions, " which they shall suspect are driving," by carrying them through the town and out of the State contrary to law.

A bounty of thirty pounds was voted by the town this year to men who had served three years, and would re-enlist to serve during the war; eighteen pounds to those who enlisted for three years; and three pounds to those who would enlist to serve till January first next (6 months). These were in addition to State bounties, and were offered in order to fill the quota of the town. They were payable in wheat at a fixed price per bushel.

The town had 86 men credited as in the service in 1781; the quota required 97. But it was thought it had sent more than were credited, and a committee was chosen to ascertain and report to the governor, if they found it so.

The same year (1781), when Forts Griswold and Trumbull were taken, and New London burned, troops had to be raised for the defence of the posts at Horseneck, and other parts of the State; they were to continue in service until March 1, 1782, unless sooner discharged. For this purpose the inhabitants were classed into as many classes as there were men to be raised, and each class was to procure one man. A like necessity in 1782 was followed by a similar classification to raise troops for the defence of the western frontiers.

The close of the war was followed by speedy efforts on the part of the town to pay off its debts, taking advantage of the cheap money then afloat.

Gratifying and full of promise as were the results of the war, there followed the difficult task of organizing the new government. It was a critical time, when the men who had guided the States through the war held in their hands the future of a nation which already owed so much to their self-sacrificing toil and care. It is not strange that there should be something of distrust and watchful suspicion. This is manifest in a vote passed by the town of Hartford in 1783, instructing its representatives "to strenuously oppose the encroachments of the American Congress upon the sovereignty of the separate States, and every assumption of power not vested in them by the Articles of Confederation."

But, thanks to the integrity of that time, the young nation passed through its early perils in safety, and we can well afford to do homage to the men who gave up their own alluring opportunities, and looked only to the future well-being of the nation.

THE FRENCH ENCAMPMENT.

CHAPTER VI.

BELONGING to the Revolutionary period are the stories of the encampment of the French troops here in 1781, when on their way from Newport to join Washington's forces near New York.

A French fleet under M. de Ternay arrived at Rhode Island in July, 1780, having on board 6,000 soldiers under command of Lieutenant-General Count de Rochambeau. These troops were welcomed with grateful enthusiasm by the Americans, and given immediate possession of the forts on Rhode Island. Rochambeau, who was subordinate only to Washington, was met by the commander-in-chief at Hartford in September, and together they conferred in regard to their future plans. They met here again * in May, 1781, when the proposal to attack New York was favorably considered. But Sir Henry Clinton becoming aware of their purpose, they changed their plan, and resolved to bring all their resources to bear against Cornwallis in Virginia. In order to deceive Clinton they kept up the show of preparation to attack New York. Washington moved his own forces down to Kingbridge, within fifteen miles of the city, and the French army, consisting of 5,000 men

---

* An Account of the Tour of General Lafayette through the United States, in 1824–25—(Hartford : Silas Andrus & Son, 1855), speaking of Lafayette's start from Bennett's Hotel, says : "On this very spot where stood his carriage, General Washington first met General Rochambeau, at the head of the French army, after their arrival from France to aid in the cause of the Revolution. Here Washington and Hamilton and several other American officers first shook hands, in the presence of Lafayette, with the officers of the French army. This place, too, was in front of the mansion [Col. Wadsworth's, now the Atheneum], where those officers convened from day to day to project and mature the seige of Yorktown, which ended in securing our independence."

THE FRENCH ENCAMPMENT.

under Rochambeau, joined him in July. They appeared to daily expect the arrival of the French fleet before New York, when suddenly they crossed the Hudson and began their rapid march across New Jersey. Clinton, deceived by misleading rumors, believed their movement only a feint, and neglected to follow them until it was too late. In October Cornwallis surrendered to the combined armies. (Williard's History.) So much for the published histories. Tradition has it that the French troops were twice encamped within our borders,—once on our meadows, when Count de Rochambeau met Washington in Hartford to confer with him ; and again, at a later time, when they encamped north of the house of the late Nathaniel Warren, on Silver Lane. The Count boarded at Esquire Elisha Pitkin's, near the old meeting-house. Others of the French officers were quartered at the public houses, and in the principal houses on Main street,—certainly at Joseph Goodwin's (senior), where the grease-spots on the chamber floor from their culinary operations were never effaced, and at the Warren house, just south of the Hockanum bridge.

Wonderful tales of their barbecues in the meadows are still told—of the huge carcasses of oxen roasted whole over pits dug in the ground—the poor beasts having been beaten almost to a jelly while yet alive, to fit them for the fastidious palates of the foreigners. An iron cattle ring, cut from near the heart of a tree in the meadow by Mr. Austin Case, is a relic of their occupancy. They also had their cattle-roasts, and made barrels of soup in 'Squire Pitkin's door-yard. The old meeting house was used for a hospital during their stay.

Their sojourn here was marked by much cordial sociability. Our grandmothers and great grandmothers came from long distances to dance with the gay and polite French officers in Mr. Ashbel Roberts' orchard, back of what is now Mr. Jason Roberts' house on Silver Lane. The French named the apples from a tree which was until lately standing in this orchard, " Belle Bonne,"—signifying good and handsome, a name which this variety of apple has borne ever since, although it is sometimes corrupted into " Belle Bound," and shortened into " Bounders."

The French officers also visited the distinguished English prisoners quartered in South Windsor, where Governor Franklin lived in princely style. He was quartered at Lieut. Diggins' house, about a mile south of the meeting house, and served sour punches under an elm tree east of the house, near Podunk Brook. This drink, in which the opposed ingredients of sweet and sour were so happily mingled, was called by the French "one grand contradiction."

The influence of the good manners and cultured tastes of the French officers remained after they had departed. It has been said that it was at their suggestion that the trees were first set along Main street, but we do not find this corroborated in any way. In South Windsor some of the elms are said to have been set by the British and Hessian prisoners who were quartered there, and this may have given rise to the report.

Silver Lane derived its name from the French, who paid their troops there,—opening, it is said, kegs of coin for that purpose. "They left much good money here," says one informant. It was a time when the home currency was so depreciated that a committee was appointed to determine at what rate it should be received when offered to pay Dr. Williams's salary, and "good money" was a delight to the eyes. The people gladly served the generous soldiers, the boys running errands for them, and the housewives doing their sewing and mending, and serving them at their houses with unwonted gingerbread and pies, for which they were well paid. The soldiers cut fagots for their camp-fires in the woods, south of Silver Lane, and brought them in bundles on their backs. One soldier died here and was buried near the hillside, north of Silver Lane. The bank afterwards caved away, but we cannot learn that anything was found. For many a day after the troops had gone the boys found stray coins on the site of the French camp on Silver Lane.

Boats were impressed at different times during the Revolution for the transportation of troops across the Connecticut river at Hartford. A copy of an order for such a purpose is still preserved by the state librarian.

THE FRENCH ENCAMPMENT.

The gratitude of our people for the assistance given them by the French in their struggle for independent life manifested itself with spontaneous ardor on the occasion of the revisit of the Marquis de Lafayette to this country in 1824. His route from one town to another was an unbroken ovation. Festooned archways, with mottoes of welcome, everywhere crossed his path, and he was greeted with fresh salvos of artillery, with ringing of bells, and martial displays as he entered town after town on his way. The Governor's Horse Guard went out fourteen miles from Hartford to meet him, and escorted him along the Tolland turnpike. He passed through our town on the forenoon of Sept. 4th. The morning was unpleasant, but many went out on the turnpike to meet him and join in his escort, some in vehicles, some on horseback, and many on foot, and a discharge of artillery announced to the people of Hartford that the distinguished Frenchman was approaching. He alighted from his carriage and passed slowly into Phelps' tavern. He walked with crutches, the result of an accident in 1803. Here he remained but a few moments, receiving our town's people. Passing again to his carriage, he was driven down the Bridge Road, and over the great bridge, to receive the splendid hospitalities of the city, which was gay with street decorations and swarming with people from all the region around.

TOWN HISTORY.

CHAPTER VII.

So early as the year 1726, the inhabitants living on the east side of the Great River in the town of Hartford petitioned the General Assembly to set them off as a separate town. The town of Hartford, by a vote at this time, appointed a committee, of which Governor Talcott was a member, to consider the effect of their petition upon the town. In 1728 the request was renewed; and again in 1737. But nothing came of it, the west side people taking prompt measures to oppose the project. In 1769 they again asked for town privileges, setting forth the territory represented as eight miles long east and west, by five and one-half miles north and south, and claiming a property list of 17,000 pounds. They also stated, "that for many years past we have been burdened with long travel to attend the public meetings in said town, and many seasons of the year the Great River in said town is impassable . . . . and although we cannot boast of our Opelance yet Encouraged by your Honors well-known and established maxims of Righteousness, as well as the recent Instances of Paternal Goodness in relieving all others in like circumstances, humbly pray your Honors to incorporate and made us a Distinct Town."

The memorial is signed by William Pitkin (4th), Jonathan Hills, and one hundred and fifty-four others. On it is the endorsement of the constable, stating that he has cited the inhabitants of Hartford to appear and show cause why the prayer of the petitioners should not be granted. (Towns and Lands, Vol. 9.)

In May, 1774, we find a fresh petition, which gives the population this side as 2,000, and the property list as 19,000 pounds. This petition was freshly opposed by the town of

Hartford, and was continued until 1780, when the property list is stated as 20,000 pounds. It says that for more than eighty years past they have found it not only inconvenient to attend public meetings in Hartford, but a grievous burden, with its six, eight, and ten miles of travel. Additional names were added to this petition in January, 1783, and in October the General Assembly, met at New Haven, passed the incorporating act, as follows :

"At a General Assembly holden at New Haven, in the State of Connecticut, on the second Thursday of October, Anno Domini, 1783.—

"Upon the memorial of John Pitkin, &c., inhabitants of the Town of Hartford on the East Side of Connecticutt River, shewing that by reason of the distance many of them live from the place of transacting public Business in said town, and the difficulty of passing the Great River at various seasons of the year, they labour under Great Burdens, and are often prevented attending and enjoying their Legal Privileges,—also that they are of Sufficient Ability and Numbers to be Constituted into a Destinct Town, and praying for the same as p^r Memorial on file :—

"Resolved by this Assembly, that all the Lands in the Town of Hartford lying East of Connecticutt River, and the Inhabitants thereof, within the following Boundaries (viz.): West on Connecticutt River ; East on Bolton Town Line ; North on East Windsor Town Line ; and South on Glastenbury Town Line, including the two Ecclesiastical Societies within said Limitts, be and the same are hereby Made, Constituted and Incorporated into a Distinct Town by the name of East Hartford: To Have, Exercise and Enjoy all the priviledges, Immunities, Franchises, and powers which other Towns in this State are by Law invested with :—And that all Monies due to the late Town of Hartford, the Stock on hand, if any, and the Debts owing by said Town, and the poor belonging to said Town, shall be divided between said late Town and the Town now constituted, according to their list, and the priviledge of keeping one-half of the Ferry accross Connecticutt River, at the place or places where the same has been usually kept in said Town of Hartford, shall belong to

East Hartford during the pleasure of this Assembly:—That all Town Officers dwelling within the limits of said East Hartford continue in their respective Offices untill new shall be appointed,—and the two Selectmen now dwelling in said East Hartford, with an Assistant, or Justice of the Peace, are hereby autherized to warn the first town meeting, to be holden at the Meeting house in the first Society in said town of East Hartford, on the second Tuesday of December next, for the purpose of chusing Town Officers and transacting other Business proper to be done in Town Meetings.

"A true Copy of Record,
Examin^d
By George Wyllys, Secret^y.

"The foregoing a true Coppy, Test, Jonathan Stanly, Junr, Reg^r."

The above is from our town records, recorded by Jonathan Stanley, Jr., our first town clerk and register.

The call for the first town meeting is as follows:

"The Inhabitants of the town of East Hartford are hereby notifyed and warned to meet and convene together at the Meeting House in the first Society in East Hartford on the Second Tuesday of December next, at ten of the clock in the morning, then and there to chufe the Town Officers by law required and to transact any other Business proper to be done in Town Meeting.

"Given under our hands the 18th day of November, 1783.

"George Pitkin, Justice of ye Peace.
"Daniel Pitkin   ⎞ Selectmen of
"Richard Pitkin ⎠   East Hartford."

"In pursuance of the foregoing warning I proceeded and warned the Inhabitants of the Town of East Hartford to conveene and meet at the Meeting House in the first Society in said Town to meet at Ten of the Clock in the Morning to chuse Town Officers by law required and transact any Other Business proper to be done in Town Meeting.

"Daniel Pitkin, Selectman for the
"East Hartford 2nd & 3rd, ⎞   Town of East Hartford.
December, 1783."   ⎠

The meeting was duly opened by the selectmen, and Wm. Pitkin, Esq. (4th), was chosen moderator.

Jonathan Stanley was chosen *town clerk* and *treasurer*, offices which he held for eighteen years, part of the time without reëlection. Other officers were elected as follows:

Selectmen.—Daniel Pitkin, Capt. Richard Pitkin, and Capt. Samuel Smith.

Constables.—Mr. John Wyles and Mr. Timothy Bryant. Mr. Wyles was excused, as were several others, and Mr. George Olmsted was appointed in his place.

Collector of Country Tax.—Mr. John Wyles, who was excused, and Mr. George Olmsted appointed, for the First Society; and Mr. Timothy Bryant for the "Eastermost Society."

Grandjurymen.—Mr. Ashbel Pitkin, Capt. Moses Forbes, Timothy Stedman.

Surveyors of Highways.—George Gilman, Theodore Stanley, Joseph Arnold, Russell Kilbourn, John Cadwell, Timothy Braynard, Elisha Buckland, Richard Pitkin, Jr.

Fence Viewers.—Capt. John Wells, Geo. Olmsted, Stephen Cone.

Listers.—Daniel Pitkin, Stephen Treet, Nathan Stedman.

Leather Sealers.—Jonathan Stanley, Benjamin Brown.

Tythingmen.—Levi Goodwin, David Pitkin, John Symonds, Ebenezer Bryant.

Packers of Tobacco.—David Hills, John Hurlburt.

Sealers of Measures.—Jonathan Olmsted; *of Weights*, Geo. Gilman.

Elisha Pitkin, Esq., Capt. John Wells, Richard Pitkin, Esq., and Capt. Samuel Smith were appointed a committee to take care of the ferry, and to lease the same.

The selectmen and Elisha Pitkin, Esq., were appointed to meet a committee appointed by the town of Hartford to adjust the accounts between the two towns, to divide the moneys, stock on hand, if any, debts, and the town poor, according to the act of incorporation. These accounts with the "ancient town of Hartford" were not finally adjusted until 1787.

The selectmen were ordered to fix a price on the guns belonging to the new town, and to sell the same, reserving only so many as were necessary to arm such number of soldiers as the law obliged the town to supply.

The first town meeting was held in the old meeting-house which stood on a hill near the north end of the Hockanum causeway until 1835; and subsequent meetings have been held in the meeting-houses ever since. In 1813 a town meeting was held in the meeting-house (at Manchester Center) in Orford Parish; and from that time until the town of Manchester was incorporated (in 1823), the meetings were held there alternately with the First Society.

After the new meeting-house was built on the corner of the Bridge Road, in January, 1836, the town gave the First Society $1,000 for the use of the basement for the purpose of holding town and electors' meetings only, permanently; and it was provided that the town be subjected to no further expense for keeping the room or building in repair. At that meeting a vote was passed that the bell be rung one hour previous to town meetings.

The freemen used to vote in the early meetings by rising from their seats when the ayes or noes were called for, whether for the choice of town or State officers; and the time was when a few sturdy Democrats faced an overwhelming majority for many years, always rising to be counted,—"the same old ten," as they came to be called. Among the number was Epaphras Olmsted, Benjamin Olmsted, Joseph Goodwin, Sr., Isaac Lester, and Theodore Stanley. Their number slowly increased until there were fourteen; after that they gained more rapidly, and about the year 1835 they were strong enough to "carry the day." On this, the occasion of their first triumph, Mr. Ira Anderson threw his hat—a tall, fuzzy "bell-crown"—high up toward the ceiling of the old meeting house, and shouted, "Glory to God! Goliah's slain!" He was promptly called to order by Dea. George Goodwin, whose quick sense of the sanctity of the place could not tolerate such an act.

Sometimes the votes were taken by a raising of hands.

After a time important officers were elected by balloting; our representatives being first balloted for in 1787. They were then voted for separately, all the electors present passing in their tickets before the count was made. When the first was chosen, the electors were asked to bring in their ballots for the second; but the choice of the first usually indicated the choice of the other, and the mounted messenger waited only for the first result, and then galloped away to Hartford to tell how the election had gone here.

Often the result was a foregone conclusion, and the story is told of a moderator who made the blunder of saying, "Gentlemen, you will now bring in your votes for General Griswold for first representative."

In 1837 both representatives were voted for on a single slip of paper. The selectmen were first chosen by ballot in 1792. In 1837 the names of electors were taken down as they voted. As population increased, and it became necessary to place greater safeguards about the ballot-boxes, our present registry system became a general law.

Our second town clerk and treasurer was Major Samuel Pitkin, who succeeded Jonathan Stanley in 1801. He held the offices thirty-five years, declining longer to serve in Nov., 1835, when he was seventy-five years old. After the first few years he was not annually elected, but held his offices by the common consent of the people. His records are remarkable for neatness and care. He was a graduate of Yale College, and represented our town in the legislature. He was a deacon twenty-six years.

His son, Gen'l Samuel L. Pitkin, succeeded him, and held office two years. His pages are handsomely written, and neat as copper-plate printing. He also represented our town for three years.

General Shubael Griswold was one of our selectmen from 1801 to 1812, and represented our town in the legislature at different times from 1805 to 1824, being elected in all thirteen times to that office. He was a merchant in East Hartford for more than twenty years. He first opened a store on the place now owned by Mr. R. A. Chapman. He afterwards removed his place of business to the corner of Orchard street, where Mr. John L. Olmsted now lives. He married for his first wife a daughter of Dr. Samuel Flagg; for his second wife a daughter of Mr. Elisha Stanley. General Griswold came from Torrington. He possessed superior natural abilities, combined with great energy of character and a fitness for leadership. In the legislature he was one of the most prominent members of the House, and exerted a large influence upon the legislation of that body. Although a Federalist, like the Pitkins, yet his flexibility and readiness as a leader enabled him to undermine their ancient prestige here, weakening their influence and lessening their share in the emoluments of the town. The fact that he had no other than a mercantile education, and yet could do this, proves him a man possessed of more than ordinary force and tact. Indeed it was said of him, by one competent to speak, after his meeting with President Monroe, at the old Wells tavern, that General Griswold would make the better president.

The Hon. Richard D. Hubbard, ex-governor of our State, was a ward of Mr. Ozias Roberts, and a pupil in our academy. He was made a voter here in 1840, and represented our town in the State legislature in 1842, and the following year, when the ferry and bridge question was again in agitation.

The following is a list of those who have filled our higher town offices from the incorporation of the town to the close of 1879. The date shows the year of their first election; the figure next following the number of times they were elected, —if elected more than once.

Representatives.

Hon. William Pitkin, 1784 to 1805.
Elisha Pitkin, Esq., 1784 to 1805.
Shubael Griswold, 1805, 13.
Samuel Pitkin, 1805, 7.
William Olmsted, 1812.
Zebulon Bidwell, 1813, 3.
Benjamin Lyman, 1815, 4.
Daniel Pitkin, 1819, 2.
Joseph Pitkin, 1819.
James Pitkin, 1820.
Daniel W. Griswold, 1820.

Ralph R. Phelps, 1821.
Lemuel White, 1824.
Ozias Williams, 1824.
Solomon Olmsted, 1825.
Selah Webster, 1825, 2.
Timothy Hall, 1826.
John Pitkin, 1826, 2.
Charles H. Olmsted, 1827, 3.
George Goodwin, 1828, 3.
Ozias Roberts, 1828, 4.
Levi Wells, 1829.

TOWN HISTORY. 99

Samuel Brewer, 1830, 4.
Timothy Ellsworth, 1831.
Ralph Pitkin, 1832, 2.
Daniel Pitkin, 1832.
Erastus Woodruff, 1834, 4.
Samuel L. Pitkin, 1836, 3.
Joseph P. Jones, 1837.
Ashbel Olmsted, 1838.
Charles Forbes, 1838, 2.
Pardon Brownell, 1839.
Austin Hall, 1839.
John Kennedy, 1840.
Luman Hurlburt, 1841.
Richard D. Hubbard, 1842, 2.
William Bigelow, 1843, 2.
James Fitch, 1844.
Daniel Winslow, 1844.
Leonard Fox, 1846.
Henry Lester, 1847.
Samuel Tripp, 1848.
George H. Olmsted, 1848.
Mahlon Forbes, 1849.
Roderick F. Fowler, 1849.
Edmund Abbey, 1850.
Stephen Marston, 1851, 2.
Elihu Smith, 1851.
Thomas Burnham, 1852, 2.
Chauncey Lester, 1853.
George Risley, 1853.
Horace Cornwall, 1854, 2.
Thomas Wyllis, 1855.
Ezra E. Smith, 1856.
Joseph Merriman, 1857.
Martin O. Hills, 1857.
Samuel E. Chapman, 1858, 2.

George P. Persons, 1858.
Francis Hanmer, 1859.
William B. Smith, 1859.
Selden Brewer, 1860.
Aaron G. Olmsted, 1861.
Thomas Dowd, 1861.
Reuben A. Chapman, 1862, 3.
Henry Fox, 1862.
William Hanmer, 1863.
Joseph O. Hurlburt, 1863.
James Hills, 1864.
Walter S. Pitkin, 1864.
Edwin Brewer, 1865.
Elijah Ackley, 1865.
John R. Beaumont, 1866.
Charles T. Marston, 1866.
L. Newton Olmsted, 1867.
George Forbes, 1867.
James F. Comstock, 1869.
Albert C. Raymond, 1869.
Moses Chandler, 1870.
John L. Olmsted, 1870.
Z. Arthur Burnham, 1871.
Henry L. Goodwin, 1871, 3.
William M. Stanley, 1873.
George W. Pratt, 1873, 2.
Lucius W. McIntosh, 1875.
Charles F. Hanmer, 1875.
Henry R. Hayden, 1876, 2.
Elizur R. Ensign, 1876.
Heman A. Tyler, 1877.
Seth Risley, 1878.
Joseph O. Goodwin, 1878.
Sterling C. Newton, 1879.
William H. Boyle, 1879.

Town Clerks.

Jonathan Stanley,* 1783, 18.
Samuel Pitkin, 1801, 35.
Samuel L. Pitkin, 1835, 2.
Ashbel Olmsted, 1837.
Salmon Phelps, 1838, 5.
Owen P. Olmsted, 1839, 2.
Edward S. Goodwin, 1845, 8.
Edward Hayden, 1848.

Joseph Hurlburt, 1854, 7.
Clarence M. Brownell, 1856, 3.
George T. Clark, 1859.
John L. Olmsted, 1865, 2.
Ephraim Rood, 1867, 4.
Edward W. Hayden, 1871, 2.
Lee H. Buckland, 1873.
Joseph O. Goodwin, 1874, 5.

*He removed to Marcellus, N. Y., about 1801. His wife was Jerusha Roberts, daughter of Benjamin.

Selectmen.

Daniel Pitkin, 1783, 13.
Richard Pitkin, 1783.
Samuel Smith, 1783, 7.
Timothy Cheeney, 1784, 3.
Moses Forbes, 1785, 10.
George Olmsted, 1786.
Samuel Flagg, 1786.
Daniel Marsh, 1786, 2.
Nathan Stedman, 1788, 4.
Deodat Woodbridge, 1792.
Richard Pitkin, Jr., 1793, 4.
Ozias Bidwell, 1793, 4.
William Olmsted, Jr., 1793, 7.
George Griswold, 1796.
William Wallace, 1796, 7.
Russell Kilbourn, 1797.
Elisha Buckland, 1797, 4.
George Pitkin, Jr., 1798, 3.
John Olds, 1800, 6.
Zebulon Bidwell, 1800, 11.
Shubael Griswold, 1800, 11.
Daniel Hills, 1802, 7.
Nathaniel Merrow, 1809, 5.
Timothy Williams, 1807, 6.
Daniel Pitkin, Jr., 1810.
Charles Bruce, 1813.
Benjamin Lyman, 1813, 2.
Elihu Olmsted, 1814.
Levi Goodwin, 1815, 2.
Josiah Hollister, 1815, 2.
Ozias Williams, 1815, 6.
Martin Stanley, 1816.
Joseph Goodwin, 1818, 2.
Ephraim Wyllis, 1818, 2.
Joseph Treat, 1818.
Dudley Woodbridge, 1818.
John Pitkin, 1819.
Samuel Brewer, 1819, 6.
Martin Keeney, 1819, 4.
Selah Webster, 1819, 4.
Aaron Buckland, 1819.
George Roberts, 1820, 2.
Solomon Olmsted, 1822, 2.
Austin Hall, 1822, 2.

Isaac Lester, 1824, 2.
Levi Wells, 1826, 5.
David Bemis, 1827, 2.
Joseph Spencer, 1829, 4.
James Stanley, 1831.
Sylvanus Wing, 1831.
Ashbel Olmsted, 1832, 5.
Orrin Forbes, 1832, 2.
George Pitkin, 1835.
Daniel Easton, 1836.
Elihu Smith, 1837, 6.
Charles Forbes, 1837, 3.
Eli Olmsted, 1839, 2.
Luman Hurlburt, 1838, 6.
Allen Brewer, 1840.
Samuel L. Pitkin,' 1841, 2.
Roderick F. Fowler, 1842, 5.
Mahlon Forbes, 1843, 12.
Selden Brewer, 1845, 5.
Julius Marble, 1845.
Jesse Judson, 1846.
Henry Olmsted, 1848.
George Brewer, 1849.
Edwin Stevens, 1849, 3.
Henry Lester, 1850.
Ransom Riley, 1850, 2.
Anson Hills, 1851.
Aaron G. Olmsted, 1851, 3.
Seth Risley, 1852, 2.
Henry Fox, 1852, 2.
William B. Smith, 1854, 2.
Ralph Pitkin, 1856, 3.
William M. Stanley, 1856, 15.
Daniel Winslow, 1859, 2.
Ira Hills, 1861.
George P. Persons, 1861, 3.
William H. Risley, 1862.
Amariah M. Hills, 1865.
John A. Burnham, 1865.
Rufus Wadsworth, 1866, 3.
Norton L. Turner, 1868.
William H. Ulrich, 1869.
Ira W. Porter, 1870, 2.
Elizur R. Ensign, 1870, 2.

TOWN HISTORY. 101

Daniel A. Tuttle, 1870, 3.
Charles W. Roberts, 1872, 6.
John H. Elmer, 1873, 2.
Ashbel Gilman, 1873.

George W. Pratt, 1874, 2.
Norman L. Anderson, 1874, 3.
Joseph Merriman, 1875.
Spencer H. Burnham, 1878.

Town Treasurers.

Jonathan Stanley, 1783, 18.
Samuel Pitkin, 1801, 35.
Ozias Roberts, 1835, 2.
Solomon Olmsted, 1837.
Horace Williams, 1838.
Pardon Brownell, 1839, 7.
Jared Ayres, 1846.
Daniel Pitkin, Jr., 1847, 4.
Ralph Pitkin, 1848.

Ransom Riley, 1852, 4.
Sidney Pitkin, 1856, 4.
George T. Clark, 1860, 3.
Ezra E. Smith, 1863, 3.
Thomas Dowd, 1865, 5.
William Hanmer, 1870.
Edward S. Goodwin, 1871.
Leonard T. Pitkin, 1872, 6.

THE TOWN'S POOR.

CHAPTER VIII.

WHEN Hartford, so soon after the close of the Revolutionary war, divided with our young town her somewhat meagre assets, she gave us also our share of the town's poor, a possession which the scriptures and our annual town reports lead us to believe will continue with us until the end of time. How they were provided for at first does not appear. It was not decided to build a house for them until 1787, when sixty square rods of ground was bought for that purpose of Mr. Daniel Pitkin. This land was bounded north and east by land of Jonathan Pitkin, west by the highway, and south by land of Samuel Pitkin. The house was to be forty by eighty feet upon the ground, and one and one-half stories high. We have been unable to determine its location. The house and land were sold in 1800, and it was voted to let out the poor to the person "that will keep them cheapest, where they will be comfortably provided for." A committee to receive proposals was appointed. This practice was probably continued until the year 1823, when steps were taken to establish a work-house in conjunction with a house for the town's poor. The committee were to obtain a temporary privilege with Hartford, or some other town, for the confinement and superintendence and management of sentenced offenders, at the town's expense. At this time our present town farm in Hockanum was purchased, and the buildings were altered to suit the uses to which they were to be put. The by-laws of the town of Hartford were adopted for its regulation.

An addition was made to the north and east sides of the alms-house, twenty by twelve feet, and two stories high in 1849, to meet the expanding necessities of the institution.

The house was wholly burned down in 1877. The fire caught in the "tramp's room" in the day-time, it is not known how. The town at once leased the Wadsworth house across the road for a temporary home for its dependent family.

Some of the early votes in regard to what are still oddly known as the "out-door poor," may prove of interest.

In 1787 the selectmen were directed to procure passage for John Abbott to Ireland,—probably an easy method of shirking prospective responsibilities in regard to him.

In 1793 Dr. George Griswold was paid for visiting an Indian woman at Mr. Ozias Bidwell's and dressing her wounds; and Mr. Deodat Woodbridge for articles supplied her. This case is further alluded to in the chapter on Indians.

In 1795 the expenses of "Jupiter Negro's" last sickness were paid by the town. He was probably a superannuated slave.

"York Negro," of Hartford, was "suffering" here in 1801, and it was voted that if that town made no provision for him, the selectmen were to "transport the said York, by a proper precept," to one of the selectmen of Hartford.

Ten dollars were voted in 1828 to assist a man and his family to the "Western world."

A question in regard to the support of "Old Flo'" arose in 1830. She was an aged negress, once the servant of Elisha Pitkin, Esq. She will appear again in the chapter on Customs and Laws.

Small offenders were sentenced to the work-house a few years ago, more generally than now. They were employed in farming operations, and, in winter, were set to picking oakum.

PEST-HOUSE AND INOCULATION.

CHAPTER IX.

A PEST-HOUSE had been built on this side the Great River in 1761 by order of the town of Hartford. It was built east of Benjamin Roberts' (now Hezekiah Roberts') house, three-fourths of a mile east of the country road leading to Glastonbury, and probably on the land of John Goodwin, who applied to the town in 1777 for satisfaction for the use of his land and wood for the pest-house. I think it was built on "Pock-House Hill," the later site of Drs. Hall and Flagg's inoculation hospital. Its use was for those who were accidentally smitten with the small-pox; while the later "hospital" was for the use of those who submitted voluntarily to the disease in the hope of escaping most of its terrible effects.

Among the earliest business upon which our young town had to act was the petition of Drs. Timothy Hall and Samuel Flagg to be allowed "to set up inoculation for the small-pox." Much doubt existed in regard to the wisdom of allowing people to subject themselves voluntarily to this so often fatal disease, and their petition was not granted.

Public opinion, however, changed in the succeeding nine years, and in September, 1791, at a special town meeting called for that purpose, liberty was given them "to set up and carry on inoculation for the small-pox in this town during the term of time the civil authority and selectmen shall judge it consistent with the welfare of the inhabitants of the town: the petitioners allowing the town the benefit of the said hospital, gratis, for the poor of the town that may have taken the small-pox the natural way."

The following April their privilege to carry on inoculation

in their hospital was extended four years, "the term of time from the 15th of May to the 15th of September in each year excepted": "Provided always that the s^d doctors erect such buildings as the [civil] authority and selectmen shall judge necessary and direct for cleansing, and abide by such rules and regulations as the s^d authority and selectmen shall judge proper and necessary for the safety and welfare of the inhabitants; and the s^d Doctors Samuel Flagg and Tim^o Hall shall give such bonds as shall be judged proper for their well and prudently managing the inoculation in the penal sum of one hundred pounds. Also, provided, that the said Doctors shall inoculate such of the inhabitants of this town as shall offer themselves at as low a lay as is or shall be done in Middletown or Haddam."

Dr. George Griswold was granted a like privilege for the Parish of Orford.

In the record of this town meeting the following appears:

"Whereas, Jonathan Stanley, Elisha Pitkin, Junr, Selah Norton, Jonathan Benjamin, Thomas Case, Samuel Hurlburt, Stephen Abbey, Junr, James Benjamin, being desirous of obtaining liberty of this town of taking the benefit of the safe and easy method discovered and pointed out by Divine Providence for carrying their families through that dreadful disorder the small-pox, by inoculation, do, in their own behalf, and in the behalf of any other inhabitants of this town who wish to join, ask liberty of this town to provide themselves a house or houses and everything else necessary for inoculation, and to inoculate their families under the same regulations and restrictions the hospital erected in this town is under. In consequence whereof" liberty was given them.

The confidence of the people in this "safe and easy method," as practiced by the good doctors, was short-lived. The liberty granted in April was taken away from all the parties the following September.

The hospital alluded to in these votes was a barn-like structure with few windows, which stood on "Pock-House Hill," a promontory extending into the swamp pasture, at the foot of "Cow lane," south of Burnside avenue. The bowl-shaped hollow, which was once its cellar, may still be seen, while bits of brick, plaster, and glass are mixed in the soil about it.

Two acres of land here were leased for the hospital to the Doctors by Mr. Joseph Hurlburt, in October, 1791. There was included in it "a privilege for the patients to walk for recreation on s^d Hurlburt's land north 20 rods; west as far as the division line between s^d Joseph and Samuel Hurlburt's land; and south .... to the river, without crossing it."

The "recreations" of the patients are said to have been of a not very luxurious kind. They were made to slide down hill in wintry weather in the thinnest of cotton garments, and subjected to other rigorous treatment. The building itself was not palatial in its appointments, and they were fed with hominy and other coarse dishes. The presiding genius of the place was "Old Ocolo," a hideously pitted negro, who cared for the patients. When the friends of those confined brought them articles of food or clothing, they set them down at the fence and hurried away. Afterwards Old Ocolo came out for them. Nothing with salt in it was allowed.

Caleb Goodwin was one of those who submitted to treatment, and Old Ocolo came one night to his father's bedroom window, with the breathless announcement: "Mr. Caleb is a-dyin',—want to see him—must come quick. He's a dyin', suah!" Mr. Caleb, however, lived through it.

But one patient is known to have died here, and that one was Mr. John Hurlburt, son of the lessor of the land. He was buried near the hospital.

The hospital is remembered by some of our older citizens, one of whom tells of hunting swallow's nests in it; and of kicking over the old clothes upon the floor. It was finally taken down, and its material removed.

PUBLIC HOUSES AND SALE OF LIQUORS.

CHAPTER X.

THE necessity of providing for the wants of travelers was early apparent to the settlers of our State. June 3, 1644, the following order was passed by the General Court:

"Whereas many strayngers & passengers that vppon occation haue recourse to these Townes, and are streightened for waint of entertainment, It is now Ordered, that these seuerall Townes shall pruide amongst thē selues in ech Towne one sufficient inhabitant to keepe an Ordinary, for pruisiō and lodgeing in some comfortable manner, that such passengers or strayngers may know where to resorte; and such inhabitants as by the seuerall Townes shall be chosen for the said searuice shall be prsented to two Magistrats, that they may be judged meet for that imployment, and this to be effected by the seuerall Townes wthin one month, under penalty of 40s. a month, ech month ether Towne shall neglect yt."

But what proved a convenience for the stranger soon became a snare to the citizen, by reason of "that great abuse wch is creeping in by excesse in wyne and strong waters;" and it was ordered that no inhabitant should continue at any common victualing house in his own town "above halfe an hower att a tyme in drinkeing wyne, bear, or hott waters, nether shall any who draweth & selleth wyne suffer any to drynke any more wyne att on tyme then after the proportion of three to a pynt of sacke." Neither was he to sell any liquor out of his house except under a writing from a master of a family; nor sell any at any time except in case of necessity, and then in moderation. To the Indians he was to sell such cider only as they drank in his presence, that drunkenness and the evil effects thereof might be prevented.

Suitable fines were provided for the punishment of drunkenness and excessive drinking, and for continuing above half an hour tippling, "and for tipling at unseasonable times, or after nine a clock at night"; and in default of payment offenders were to "be imprisoned untill they pay, or bee set in the stocks one houre or more, in some open place, as the weather will permit, not exceeding three houres at one time." Public whipping was also prescribed for drunkenness.

Innkeepers were to provide for the beasts of their guests, enclosed pastures in summer, and stable room, with hay and provender, in winter.

The constables were from time to time to make search throughout the limits of their towns, "uppon Lord's days and Lecture dayes in times of exercise, and allso at all other times," as they see cause, for offences against the laws, and the innkeepers were always to be ready to answer to the court.

The first "ordinary" or house of common entertainment on this side the river was kept by John Sadler, we think on a brook near the Connecticut River in Naubuc. Mention is made of it in 1648 as the place where two delinquents, Geo. Chappell and Matthew Williams, were likely to resort. Chappell had been fined five pounds for abusing a constable and for excessive drinking, and an execution was out against him for other offences. Williams was an old offender, had been twice whipped, and fined five pounds, and a fresh judgment had been declared against him. These worthies had fled from justice, and Sadler was warned to give notice to the magistrates in case they appeared at his house.

Sadler's ordinary is mentioned again in 1663, when the inhabitants of Hockanum were ordered to make two bridges, "one over the brook at the place called Sadler Ordinary, the other at Frog Brook." Frog Brook crosses Main street near the house of Mr. Joseph H. Porter in Hockanum.

In 1710 Philip Smith was given liberty by the town of Hartford to keep a public house on the east side of the river, he attending to all the rules of the law. We can only guess at its site, but think it was kept near the ferry over the Great

River, where the chances of crossing in all weathers would seem to indicate the necessity of a public house. Possibly it stood just north of the old ferry road, south of the present bridge, where, many years later, Daniel Pitkin kept a tavern, the well of which is still there. Mr. Smith, at any rate, owned land here, near Gilbert's Island, as well as 300 acres of upland on Silver Lane and eastward, of which he sold parcels to Benjamin Hills (1709) and Thomas Spencer (1714).

The next year Mr. Thomas Olcott was licensed to keep a house of entertainment at Hop Brook, in the Five Miles, setting up his hostelry near the site of the present homestead of Sidney Olcott in Manchester.

Benjamin's tavern stood in 1776 on the site of the house now occupied by Mr. John L. Olmsted. It is named in an almanac of that date as one of the principal public houses on the old Boston stage route. A little way down the lane in its rear stood a weaver's shop, owned also by the Benjamins.

Samuel Hurlburt kept a tavern at one time on the corner of Burnside avenue and Main street, before 1800.

Near the corner of Silver lane Dr. Epaphras Bidwell kept a public house in the house next east of Mr. Sisson's store, about 1820.

Levi Goodwin once kept a tavern on Main street on the site of the house of Mr. Ralph Olmsted, and his books show that his bar was well patronized by many of our once substantial citizens (about 1800).

In Burnside a public house was kept in the old house lately moved back from the street, and recently owned by Mr. Dudley Hills. The tavern was kept by Mr. Hills' father.

One of the older public houses, which some of us remember, was that kept by the Wells family. This tavern (still standing) was in its day one of the most resorted to in town. It was kept in 1811 by the Woodbridge family, and in 1817 by a Mr. Buckler. It has a low, spacious bar-room, with a slat-enclosed bar, until recently intact, with a large fire-place on one side. The "best chamber" was until lately complete in its ancient furnishings, with flowery-blue wall-paper, and two high-post bedsteads, canopied with large-figured blue curtains. It had curtain rests, like rosettes of brass, and brass andirons in its fire-place, over which hung old-time prints of historic scenes, cheaply colored and nearly a hundred years old. The other chambers were as bare as barracks. A low-ceiled hall, with two corner fire-places and a bench around the wall, was kept for dancing parties, which used especially to resort here in sleighing time, having gay times, and racing their horses, with tremendous jangling of bells, up and down the street; their sleighs were large, high-backed, green and yellow affairs, with yellow or red linings. The barns and sheds that stood north of this tavern, close to the road, were burned down a number of years ago. Here once stopped the gay stage-coaches that rattled over the Boston and Providence turnpikes, to give their horses a mouthful of water, and their passengers a chance to visit the bar within, if they chose.

President Monroe lodged at this tavern when on his tour in 1817. It was then kept by a Mr. Buckler. He was called upon by General Griswold and others of our first citizens, and was serenaded by the drum and fife corps of the artillery company. He probably occupied the "best chamber" during his stay. His passage through the country was a quiet one, without display of any kind.

Later in date was the tavern kept for many years by Mr. Henry Phelps. It stood on the site now occupied by the residence of Mr. Henry R. Hayden, on the corner of Mill street. The large elm overhung its roof in the rear. Just below the corner of Mill street stood the great roomy barns and sheds of the once prosperous hotel. Here stopped the stages while they ran, and here also were quartered the menageries with their strange animals, when they stopped in town to exhibit on Mill street, just below. Through its portals passed Gen. Lafayette upon his crutches on the occasion of his triumphal visit in 1824, and here the militia officers, gay with feathers and scarlet and tinsel, did most resort in the glorious old muster-days which gave them a shining prominence over all other men. And it was here they sold good French brandy for four cents a drink, and allowed the customer to help himself!

This hotel was kept by the Van Dorns, before Mr. Phelps took it in charge; and was owned before that by Richard Goodwin, and known as the old Goodwin tavern. The store and parts of the old rambling hostelry were moved down Mill street, and made into houses on the old training field. The main building was moved back and the frame used in the house now standing on its site.

In the meadow Mr. Daniel Pitkin kept a tavern, north of the ferry road, as has been said, and he probably had much to do with travelers. The stages passed here on their way across the ferry to the old Coffee House on State street in Hartford, where they put up. Pitkin's tavern was burned down accidentally in the day time. Later the Pitkins built a tavern on the Bridge Road near the site of the present lumber yard. This was also burned; and was rebuilt and again burned.

While Daniel Pitkin's tavern was in vogue on the ferry road, John Pantry Jones set up tavern-keeping on the line of the South Meadow Road, a little south of Mr. Chauncy Lester's house. The road at that time turned sharply to the east at this point, instead of taking its present course. Here Mr. Jones found business so good that he had to keep three flip-irons in the fire all the time. Apples were plenty, and cider-brandy was the favorite drink.

The hotel now kept by Mr. Luke Morse, was once kept by Mr. Joseph P. Jones, and was much patronized during the field days of the militia upon our meadows. Here General Pratt rode up to the door on the occasion of the grand review of 1843, when General Johnson of Tecumseh fame was here, and "something" was passed out to wet his potential lips.

"Cotton's tavern" and store, on the corner of the Tolland Turnpike and Burnside Avenue, was formerly owned by Euodias Bidwell, and probably by his ancestors before him. One "Biddell" is put down in an almanac of 1763, as keeper of a public house in East Hartford. It was bought by Mr. Henry Cotton in 1832. In the good old times before the days of the railroads this was quite a station on the road, and the jocund spirits of the neighborhood passed many a sociable evening here. On one occasion they bantered one of the sitters into selling his old greasy fur cap, which they immolated in the stove. The blaze it created set the chimney afire, and raised a considerable alarm.

Some facetious things were said at this tavern. "Well, well," said Lewis B——, one evening, as he came in; "G—— has really got to move his blacksmith's shop." "How so?" asked the chorus, while G—— himself looked up in mild surprise. "Oh, he strikes so hard he's jarring C——'s watermelons all off the vines."

There were other public houses, on the stage routes principally, in what is now the town of Manchester,—one at Buckland's corners, and one at Manchester Green, kept once by Capt. Hills, and afterwards by the Woodbridges. At the last, during the Revolution, is said to have disappeared a person of some note, who was traveling alone toward Boston at this time. His horse was found astray in the woods. Some children berrying afterwards found the missing man's body and told Mr. Corning, the spinning-wheel maker, who was in the woods for timber, and it was taken care of. His sword was found beneath an old stoop some years later. It was thought that he belonged in Philadelphia, and that he was murdered for his money. Indeed, one story has it that he was a paymaster of the army, and so was supposed to have a large sum of money on his person.

The restrictions in regard to the sale of liquors grew lax as time went on. In 1820, the selectmen were to license whoever they thought fit to sell them, provided they licensed no one who had, or would, sell to the town's poor. It was made their business, too, to inquire if any retailed liquors contrary to law.

In 1830 the town voted that no ardent spirits be furnished by the surveyors of highways—indicating that the road-making "bees" had sometimes taken a convivial tone.

In 1840, and again in 1841, the town voted that all persons might have liberty to sell wines and spirituous liquors during the ensuing year.

Nearly all the old time stores in town dealt in liquors. Among them was the "old red store" in Podunk, which stood just north of the "Island Road," north of Mr. Arthur Burnham's house. It was the bane of Podunk for many years, a haunt for drinking loafers, and a place for hen-shoots, and like amusements. About its fire were probably told some of the toughest fish and hunting stories that this locality has known. The building was moved down on to Prospect street and is now owned by Mr. Patrick McAloon; and through all the peaceful borders of Podunk no trace of its evil influence remains.

Pitkin's store (now Mr. G. W. Darlin's) in the meadow, and Goodwin's on Main street, with its low roofed cellar, were places of daily refreshment to the lounger and the passer-by, whose habits of imbibition were the result of general custom rather than of individual weakness, as it is regarded today.

In 1811 John Cotton was fined ten dollars for allowing liquor to be drunk on his premises. This was done in violation of some by-law of the town; but he showed that it had been done in his absence, and through fear of a stranger, and his fine was remitted by vote of the town. Mr. Cotton's store was the one now occupied by Mr. Luther Pratt, on Silver Lane. Mr. Cotton had but one leg, and he used to sit on his counter and serve his customers without getting down, when possible.

BURYING GROUNDS.

CHAPTER XI.

UNTIL the year 1712, or a little earlier, perhaps, our people buried their dead in Hartford, either in the old Center Burying Ground, in the rear of the Center Church, or in that other burial place on the north side of State street, near the State House, now completely obliterated. But the inconvenience of passing the Connecticut at difficult seasons of the year led them to ask for a burial place on this side the river.

April 8, 1709, the town voted "that Capt. Joseph Wadsworth, Capt. Cyprian Nichols, and Mr. Nathaniel Hooker be a committee to view a convenient place on the east side of the great river which may be suitable for a burying yard, for the people there, and, if necessary, purchase land therefor, and lay the same out at the town's charge."

In January, 1710 (old style, 1711 new style), one acre of ground was deeded to the town of Hartford by Mr. John Pantry. It was bounded on the east and south by land of John Pantry; on the west by the highway, and on the north by land belonging to John Goodwin; and was twenty rods in length and eight rods in width, and forms at present the northwest part of our Center Burying Ground.

The first burial in it is said to have been that of the body of Thomas Trill, an old soldier of the Narragansett War. The oldest stone is one in memory of Obadiah Wood, a fellow-soldier of Trill. His stone bears the following legend, in capitals:

"HERE | LIETH THE BO | DY OF OBADI | AH WOOD WHO | DIED APRIL THE | 11, 1712, IN THE | 64 YEAR OF | HIS AGE."

The ground set aside for sacred use soon became covered with wild growth, and in 1713 William Roberts was paid three shillings by the Ecclesiastical Society for cutting the bushes in the burial plot. He was also appointed with Joseph Meakins to "fort the burying place with a good five-rail fort, either to take the said burying place into John Goodwin's hill, or to fort it distinct, as they shall be advised."

In 1806 about an acre of new ground was purchased on the east side, of Joseph Goodwin, to enlarge the grounds. The price paid was at the rate of ten pounds per acre. Elisha Pitkin, Esq., and Dr. Samuel Flagg were appointed a burying ground committee. They were to fence the burial lot, and to rent it for pasturing sheep and calves only. This was an easy method of keeping down the bushes, briars, and weeds. They were also to move the stones in the old yard to make a road to the new purchase,—the use of a bier having made a road of any sort unnecessary before. These stones were moved only a few feet, north or south, to make room for the road between them, and this vote accounts for the apparent overlapping of some of the graves along this road. At this time the selectmen were directed to fence all the burying lots in this town, and to rent them for pasturing sheep and calves only.

In 1807 the town sold sixteen rods of ground on the south side of the Center Burying Ground, near Main street, in exchange for land at the rear on the same line. This probably was for the convenience of a road to the new addition on the south of the original plot. The ground was enlarged from time to time, both on the east and south sides, as was necessary, the land for the purpose being bought of the Goodwins.

The original south line of this burying ground ran along near the front of the tomb of the Pitkin family. For the site of this tomb a triangular piece was sold to Elisha Pitkin, Esq., by Joseph Goodwin, who set aside the land west of it for a burial place for himself and his family, and which is still retained by his descendants for that purpose.

The early burials in the Center yard were made without much attention to any orderly arrangement of families, and the seekers after a lost ancestry have sometimes a weary search before they get together those of their family name.

116   HISTORY OF EAST HARTFORD.

The slabs and tables and monuments in this yard bear hundreds of names, conspicuous in the history of our town, and to one at all familiar with our annals the study of them possesses a pleasant fascination. For him their quaint records raise pictures of times and customs and tastes serenely remote from the noisy commonplace of his own time, and as he meets name after name with which he became familiar in the records, and gets fresh information of the talents and the virtues of their possessors, he feels that he is indeed in goodly company, who yet speak to him in no uncertain tone. And not the least pleasant thing about these dear conscientious ancestors of ours is their fashion of mortuary inscription and device. Scrupulous in their tastes, their fancies flowered only heavenward, and then with a severe suppression which must have made the grave-stone cutter the most morbid man of his day. And we often wonder as we look at his flat-faced, bulbous-nosed cherubs, with their wings of escalloped stone, whether his inability to soar above his fettered art did not make him morosely skeptical of anything better in this life, or in that which is to come.

The epitaphs are freighted, also, with the somewhat somber cast of religious thought of their time. They are full of admonition and of doleful warning:

> "Death is a debt to nature due,
> Which I have paid, and so must you,"

is a very frequent one. And yet they express a wide range of feeling, and soar sometimes into the empyrean, as in this couplet:

> "The cloud's dispel⁴ the stormy danger's past,
> And I've attain⁴ the peaceful shores at last."

The following is one of the most curious in the yard:

"In memory of Mr. Phenehas son of Mr. Thomas and Mrs. Mary Burnham, who died TRYUMPHINGLY in hops of a goyful Resurrection in Dec. yᵉ 22, A. D. 1776, in the 23rd year of his Age."

Another on a young woman of thirty-three is peculiar:

> "Now she is dead and cannot stir,
> Her cheek is like the fading rose;
> Which of us next will follow her
> The Lord Almighty only knows."

But we have not space for more. A long list of names and of epitaphs from this yard is in the possession of the writer, who compiled it, and it furnishes odd and edifying reading for a leisure hour. Better than this, however, is a study of the old lichen-patched monuments themselves in the open air, beneath the same sky that was over the homely heroes they celebrate, when they visibly walked our streets or labored in our fields.

Buried in this yard, not far from the street, is the Hon. William Pitkin, for several years governor of the Colony, an office which he held until his death.

On the highest part of the hill is the soldiers' monument, in memory of those who died in the late Civil War.

SPENCER STREET YARD.

This yard (now in Manchester) was the second one laid out on this side of the river. Its oldest stone bears date of 1770. Here we find the names of Bidwell, Bunce, Cadwell, Elmer, Hills, Keeney, Kennedy, McKee, Marsh, Olcott, Spencer, and Symonds—most of them of people who had to do with the welfare of the "eastermost parish" in its early days.

SOUTH BURYING GROUND.

Of the two yards in Hockanum, the one on the meadow lane shows the earliest date—1776. The land for this yard is said to have been given for burial purposes by the Wadsworths, though no record of it has been found. The most prominent names found here are Arnold, Fox, Jones, Keeney, Porter, Wadsworth.

SOUTH MIDDLE BURYING GROUND.

On motion of Col. Jonathan Wells and others in 1777, the selectmen of Hartford were instructed to purchase a convenient place south of the Hockanum River, for a "decent burying ground," at the cost of the town. The earliest record of a burial here is in 1781. In this yard are buried many whose names fill important places in our records. Col. Jonathan Wells was a colonel in the Revolutionary War. There are also the names of Brewer, Ensign, Forbes, Hall, Hills, Kentfield, Lester, Little, Porter, Risley, Roberts, Smith, Treat, Warren, and Wells.

A new hearse-house in this yard was built in 1852. In 1875 the town appropriated $500 for the purchase of a new hearse. The old hearse was a low, mournful affair, with outside curtains and fringes of faded and weather-worn black, and ought to be preserved as a lugubrious relic of the past.

An effort was made in 1838 to procure the lay-out of a burying ground in Scotland (now Burnside); but, although continued to the next town meeting, nothing appears to have been done about it.

OTHER GRAVES.

In a few cases burials have been made in places outside the common burying grounds. This was oftenest done to prevent the spread of infectious diseases. There were, not long ago, several graves on the hillside east of the Ellington road, north of Gilman's brook. They were graves of persons who died with the small-pox, and were buried near their homes. A shattered grave-stone lies here on the sod, bearing the name of Capt. John Gilman, who died in 1761, aged 49. Of the burial of John Hurlburt near the small-pox hospital, on "Pock-House Hill," we have already spoken.

On the south bank, near Willow Brook, and many rods east from Main street, stands a leaning flag-stone with the inscription: "In memory of Serg't Heman Baker, Ju^r, of Tolland, he was captivated by ye British troops, Sept. 15th, 1776, son of Mr. Heman Baker & Lois his wife he died on his way home with ye small-pox Jan^r 21st, 1777, in ye 29th year of his age." He came up the river on a vessel, and was put ashore at Hockanum. He died shortly afterward, and was buried here.

FUNERAL CUSTOMS, ETC.

One hundred years ago, our people had no wheeled vehicles, excepting stout and clumsy carts, and hearses were not known. The bodies of the dead were carried to the grave on stout biers, borne upon men's shoulders. When the burial was from a distance—and bodies were often brought several miles,—many relays of bearers were needed, and the farmers assembled in such numbers as to far outnumber the mourners. And that none might faint by the way, there was usually provided a table of refreshments at the house of the dead. In the will of Ed: Vier of Wethersfield, brought into Court July 10, 1645, is this clause: "Item, my mynde is there shalbe 20s. bestowed vppon p^ruissions of wyne, bear, caks, and such like of what may be had for my buriall." Other funeral customs are shown in the will of Dr. Kimball, who gives to nine of his near relatives and friends, each a beaver hat, a pair of gloves, and a weed. To their wives, each a mourning hood and scarf, and to Mrs. Hannah Pitkin a mourning ring, etc.

The bier once in use in this town was a stout affair, made of timber from four to five inches square, and was in itself almost a load for four men. On this the plain, or newly-painted, coffin, with its narrow ends, was placed; with the initials of the dead on its lid in round-headed brass tacks, or in metallic letters—once to be had at Mr. Henry Phelps' store. Over the coffin was placed a heavy pall; and then the men lifted the bier to their shoulders, and the slow procession moved on, the funeral bell sometimes* tolling out the age of the deceased. The next Sabbath a funeral sermon was usually preached, the bereaved family occupying what was known as the mourner's pew

The following votes relate to the early equipments of this character. In 1723, Capt. Ozias Pitkin, by a vote of the Ecclesiastical Society, was chosen to pray the town of Hartford to procure a suitable black cloth for the solemnity of funerals in this society. The town at once added a sufficient sum to its rate to procure the same for them.

In 1756, seven shillings were voted to Jonathan Stanley for making a bier. This was the one described above, and it was kept in a little hovel, like a sheep-cote, near the highway in front of the burying-ground. For some years after light-wheeled vehicles came into use, the hand-bier was used, it

---

* There was no church bell in town until after 1835.

being thought a disrespect to the dead to trust their bodies to the jolting of a wagon. But innovation crept in; and the first horse-vehicle used was a frame on wheels, with mortices to receive the legs of the bier. A lighter bier was made at this time; and this was always taken off and carried to the door of the house to receive its burden. The front wheels of the gearing were small, so that the horse could be turned aside at right angles to the vehicle, to facilitate putting the bier in place. Over all was placed the black cloth as in former years. The driver sat on the slats of the bier, his feet resting on the whiffletree. The bier then in use, and the wheels of the carriage, which were used under the first hearse, are still preserved by Mr. G. S. Phelps.

Afterwards was purchased a hearse with a roof, and with heavily fringed black curtains on its sides. A house was built for it by Mr. Henry Phelps, in the Center Burying-ground, close by Main street. It was afterwards moved to its present site. The new hearse, which occupies it, was bought by contributors, and cost the town nothing.

The coffins in the early times were made to order, close at home, after the death of the person. In the will of Ed: Vier, mentioned above, is this " Item : My mynd is that John Carrington shall have 20s. for making my coffen." Mr. George Burnham, who lived on what is now Burnside avenue in our town, made many in his day, of that peculiar narrowed down shape to which the graves were also dug, a fashion which has happily gone out of use. A dreadful smell of fresh paint and varnish usually arose from these hastily constructed receptacles, a smell which came to be always associated with funerals.

SEXTONS, ETC.

The first sextons of the Center Burying Ground, of whom we know anything, were the Goodwins—Joseph and Hezekiah. Their familiar and helpful assistant was Uncle Hick Forbes, who slept in the loft of the old Polly Kendall house— a low gambrel-roofed house, half-hidden by lilac bushes, which stood just north of the site of the present residence of Mr. Albert C. Raymond, on the corner of Central avenue. The father of the writer used to say that, when a boy, he was often sent down for Uncle Hick when there was a grave to dig. He told the nature of his errand to "Aunt Polly," and she shouted up the scuttle-hole—"Uncle Hick! Uncle Hick! Mr. Goodwin wants ye." "Aye, aye!" he would respond, and slowly clamber down on the slats nailed to the studding. Uncle Hick dug graves until he was no longer able to get out of them when finished, without a ladder, which he always had at hand. It is a little curious that, while he was literally so near the grave for a long time, death should have exempted him so long; as if there had been a compact between the grim tyrant and the old fellow, which spared him in his feebleness, because of his faithfulness in serving.

After him "Old Ganzy" (Lewis Guernsey) dug graves. He was an interesting character who lived hereabout; and he was over ninety when he died. He had been a sea-faring man when young. Later he took care of the desperate or pestilential sick, and seemed to have an immunity from contagion and decay for many years. His knowledge of old fashioned weeds and herbs and their properties was something wonderful. The writer has come upon him in "the swamp," gathering his simples, with as much mystery as Roger Chillingworth in Hawthorne's Scarlet Letter. The old man lived to be almost a hundred years old.

Mr. Henry Phelps, who came here in 1821 to carry on the tavern which stood on the corner of Mill and Main streets, was chosen sexton of the Center yard in 1824. He was succeeded by his sons, Edward Phelps and George S. Phelps. The former held the office for a year or two only; the latter is the present incumbent. During the time this family has held the office there have been buried about 2,000 persons,—a number equal to two-thirds of the present population of our town,—and this in the Center Burying Ground alone. They have had several assistants in their work.

The present sexton of the Center Ground has had a varied experience. He began to drive to funerals when a boy, and when the wheeled-bier described above was in vogue. His first charge was of the body of Mr. Thomas Case, who had owned the "Calvin Hale place," on what is now Orchard street. The snow was deeply drifted, and the bearers who went beside the bier had great difficulty in keeping it from over-setting. Two of the bearers were Capt. John Pitkin, and Mr. George Reynolds,—the first a very short man, the latter tall.

Mr. Phelps once rode on this odd vehicle over the Hockanum Causeway when the water had already overflowed the road, and was beginning to touch the flooring of the bridge. While waiting at the house of mourning he noticed a large white flag thrust out of the chamber-window of the neighboring house ; and when the procession began to move, a gun was fired from the nearest cellar-window in that house, with a prodigious bang! This gratuitous celebration of the departure of the dead had been gotten up by the dead man's nephew, whom he had contemned in his will. Meantime the water had risen on the causeway, and the planks were nearly afloat in the bridge. The water was so deep that Mr. Phelps had to lift his feet from the whiffletree, and finally to climb upon the coffin to avoid a wetting.

ECCLESIASTICAL HISTORY.

CHAPTER XII.

OUR fathers came to this country in order to secure freedom to themselves in their religious beliefs and manner of worship. With them their religion was first and most important; based upon and secondary to it was the polity of the State. Much unjust contumely has been uttered against them, because when they sadly chose to isolate themselves from all their former comforts and life-long associations, simply that they might worship God in their own way, they also chose to purge out from among them many unruly spirits, vague and fanatical of belief and crazed with a sense of newly found freedom, whose practices were alien to the Puritan's notions of decency and order. At great cost they had left bitter intolerance and persecution behind them; their purpose was a single one,—above all essentially and rigidly exclusive in its nature, as is that of many church organizations in our land to-day, so far as every other church organization is concerned. When the good citizen began to prove himself more useful than the sound churchman, then the exclusiveness withdrew within the church doors, and there was freedom outside.

In the early confederation of the three towns of Hartford, Wethersfield, and Windsor, in 1638, the religious idea of government predominated. It was a " confederation . . . . to mayntayne and p^{r}searue the liberty and purity of the gospell of our Lord Jesus, wch we now p^{r}feese, as also the disciplyne of the churches wch according to the truth of the said gospell is now practised amongst vs; as also in our Ciuell Affaires to be guided "—by such laws as shall be made.

To some, of course, this exclusiveness was a genuine denial; but the colony was not inexorable. When, in 1664, William

Pitkin, one of our first settlers, joined with others in a prayer for some relief from the denial of their accustomed church [of England] privileges to themselves and their families, the General Assembly did "commend it to the ministers and churches in this Colony to consider whether it be not their duty to enterteine all such persons who are of an honest and godly conversation," and baptise their children, etc., and recommending their admission to half-covenant privileges, as they were called, by which they were allowed to participate in all the ordinances excepting that of the Lord's supper.

THE THIRD ECCLESIASTICAL SOCIETY OF HARTFORD.

To the history of the first ecclesiastical society formed on this side the Great River in Hartford much space belongs, because in its dual care of the spiritual and temporal well-being of its people it covers a wide period in our annals. Much of the material that has been found in its records has been used in other chapters of this volume,—in that on Schools, on Burying Grounds, on Roads and Bridges, etc. Its functions so nearly covered many of the details of the town's affairs, that for a time it seems to have been recognized in some matters as an equal power. Some of the business voted on at its meetings was also voted on in town meeting, and in 1798, after East Hartford became a town, the same vote is entered in the records of both the society and the town.

The inhabitants here first petitioned to have the "liberty of a minister" among them in May, 1694. In deference to this petition the General Assembly recommended that the two societies in Hartford (now the Center Church Society and the South Congregational Society), where our people attended, get together and consider the proposal. This was done, and in October of that year the societies again acted on the matter, as follows:

" Whereas . . . . . . sundry of both Societies being met together and the rest warned to meet, we have considered the motion of oʳ neighbors on the east side, and that in refference to their desire of setling a minister on the east side of the river, we doe declare we prize their good Company and cannot without their help well and comfortably carry on or mayntaine the ministry in two societies here, yet upon the earnestness of oᵣ neighbors to be distinct because of the trouble and danger they complayne they are exposed to by coming over to the pub: worship here, which difficulty they could not but foresee before they setled where they are and therefore is of less wayte to us, and upon these considerations we cannot be free to parte with our good neighbours";—still, if the Court saw cause they would submit; yet they wished that those good people of the east side who desired might continue with them; and that all land owned by west side people might pay its rate still to their ministry; and that all should continue to pay toward the support of the west side ministry until a minister was settled upon the east side.

The General Assembly accepted these conditions and granted liberty to procure and settle an orthodox minister on the east side of the Great River in Hartford.

In 1702, for the encouragement of the young society, all who lived on this side were ordered to pay rates toward the maintenance of the ministry here. Rate-makers were appointed, and the bounds of the society declared to include all of the town of Hartford upon this side of the Great River. Only the common lands were not to be taxed here, nor the lands belonging to residents of the west side.

This order found some reluctant to leave their old societies. Solomon Andrews, William and Thomas Warren, and Matthias Treat, of Hockanum, prayed the Court to be allowed to pay to the west side ministry, but their petition was not granted. The first two afterwards refused to pay their church rate, and the collectors levied on a brass kettle which belonged to the first, and on a horse which belonged to Warren. These the court (an "Inferior Court") ordered the collectors to return to their owners. The case, however, was appealed, with what result does not appear.

The first preserved record of a meeting of the society is of one held Dec. 29, 1699, when William Pitkin, Dea. Joseph

Olmsted, and Lieutenant Hills were appointed a committee "to see about the meeting house, and to do what they think needful in ordering the same, as they think best." To meet the expenses which would arise, a rate of three pence in the pound was laid on the property list of the society, one penny of it payable in corn, the rest in work, if any chose. A rate of three half-pennies in the pound was also voted, "to satisfy the Rev. John Rood for his pains in the ministry among us, and to defray charges about providing for him."

The next year sixty pounds were voted Mr. Rood for his salary; and a call was given him to settle here "in the work of the ministry." Meantime a house had been begun for him, and a rate of £200 laid to complete it. But he did not accept the call, and Mr. Samuel Woodbridge came here to preach. His first year's salary was £65, payable in wheat at 5s. a bushel, and in rye at 3s. a bushel,—all good and merchantable; afterward beef and pork were made acceptable as a part of the rate, money being scarce in those days.

REV. SAMUEL WOODBRIDGE.

Mr. Woodbridge was called in 1704, and ordained March 30, 1705, the society giving him £60 a year for his salary, and also promising him the minister's house, with two acres of land, and at least thirty or forty acres besides. The minister's house was still unfinished, and the next year £25 were voted to Mr. Woodbridge if he would complete it after the walls were filled up. Afterwards a deed of it was given him upon condition that he would stay here in the ministry during his life, or that it be not his fault if he removed sooner from the place. Its exact site we do not know. It stood on the west side of Main street, somewhere between Benjamin's Lane (Orchard street), and the old meeting-house. The deed was given by Daniel Bidwell, who owned the land, to Samuel Woodbridge, clerk; and was bounded south and west by Bidwell's land, north by John Case, and east by the highway. Much was done for Mr. Woodbridge, who had a strong hold on the regard of the people. In 1707, £4 were granted to such as had waited upon him, and Dea. Joseph Olmsted was given 50s. for the use of his son and horse to go to New York with him. In 1713, £9 in addition to his salary were voted him to procure firewood. Any person who chose could pay his proportion in wood delivered at the minister's door, at 3s. a load, each load to contain at least two-thirds of a cord. He was also given liberty to build a pew between the women's (widows') pew and the pulpit. In 1734 he preached the election sermon before the assembled ministers, legislators, and officers of the State, at the opening of the General Assembly at Hartford. In 1730 he visited Newport, and £2, 3s. were voted for a man to attend him on his way.

Mr. Woodbridge continued faithfully in service for many years, when he became sick and unable to work or to "supply the pulpit." The society obtained preachers,—Mr. Nathaniel Collins for the summer of 1736, and Rev. Mr. Samuel Newell afterwards. Mr. Newell's board was paid at Joseph Pitkin's until December, 1741.*

It was then proposed to procure a colleague for Mr. Woodbridge, he being still unable to preach, and declining to supply the pulpit. Calls were extended to several persons to "preach on probation," but without success, probably owing to the reluctance of all to come between Mr. Woodbridge and his people. There was occasional preaching only,—Mr. Newell being here a part of the time.

Finally the society declined to pay Mr. Woodbridge his salary,—he doing nothing about supplying the pulpit or providing that the ordinances be administered. Mr. Woodbridge carried the matter to the General Assembly, and that body ordered the society to pay him £150, old tenor, for his salary in 1743. This the society paid, crisply instructing Mr. John Pitkin to take his receipt therefor. After this his salary was paid him regularly, and he served the society as much as he was able. Probably no one regretted more than he that his necessities outlived his usefulness.

In 1745 Mr. Stephen Williams was called to preach on pro-

---

* Mr. Newell was afterwards settled as the first pastor of Bristol. He died there in 1789, aged 75, in the 42d year of his ministry.—*Barber, Hist. Coll.*

bation, and the following year he accepted, and steps were taken to settle him,—he being urged to take charge with all convenient speed,—when he drops from the record without a further word of mention. Probably he was the same Stephen Williams (son of Rev. Dr. Stephen Williams of Long Meadow) who was ordained at Woodstock, (Second Society,) Ct., in November, 1747.

Mr. Woodbridge "fell asleep" June 9, 1746, having, as his elaborately carved grave-stone says, been for forty years a minister of the Third Church of Christ in Hartford. His heirs were paid his salary for the last quarter year—£50 in old tenor bills. Little else than what these dry records show is now known concerning Mr. Woodbridge. He was a graduate of Harvard College, and without doubt fully qualified both by nature and education for his work here. And we have evidence that he was loved and respected by his people.*

---

* Mr. Woodbridge came of a long line of ministers. The following facts have been kindly furnished by Miss Mary K. Talcott, of Hartford.

Rev. Samuel Woodbridge was youngest son of Rev. Benjamin Woodbridge, and Mary, daughter of Rev. John Ward of Haverhill. His father probably received his education in England; he preached at Windsor, Ct., at Bristol, R. I., and at Medford, Mass. Rev. Benj. Woodbridge was second son of Rev. John Woodbridge, who was born at Stanton, Eng., in 1613, and came to New England with his uncle Rev. Thomas Parker, in 1634; married Mercy, daughter of Gov. Thos. Dudley, in 1639; was ordained minister at Andover, Mass., in 1645; and afterwards returned to England, where he was chaplain of the Parliamentary commissioners treating with King Charles at the Isle of Wight. Returning to New England in 1663, he became minister at Newburg, Mass., and died there in 1695. Rev. John Woodbridge was eldest son of Rev. John Woodbridge, Rector of Stanton, Wiltshire, Eng., who died in 1637, and whose wife was Sarah, daughter of Rev. Robert Parker, of Exeter, an eminent non-conformist author and divine.

Rev. Samuel Woodbridge was graduated at Harvard in 1701, and ordained in East Hartford, March 30, 1705. His first wife was Mabel, widow of Rev. John Hubbard of Jamaica, L. I., and daughter of Daniel Russell of Charlestown, Mass. Her mother was Mabel, (daughter of Samuel Wyllys, of Hartford,) who married for her third husband the Rev'd Timothy Woodbridge of Hartford, uncle of Rev. Samuel Woodbridge. Rev. Samuel Woodbridge's first wife died in New Haven, May 10, 1730, while on a visit to her son, Col. John Hubbard. His second wife was Mrs. Content, widow of Benj. Bull, Esq., of Newport, R. I.

Mr. Woodbridge was a Fellow of Yale College from 1732 to 1743.

THE FIRST MEETING HOUSE.

The meeting house in which Mr. Woodbridge preached was begun in 1699, on a small hill which once rose above the open ground near the junction of Main street and the South Meadow Road. It was not completed for several years. In 1707 a rate of £45 was voted for "seating and sealing the meeting house." Two-thirds of this rate might be paid in timber delivered at the water side of the meeting house. In 1713, the standing committee was instructed to seat the meeting house from time to time. This custom of assigning to the people seats that would accord with their social position, or the amount of tax they paid, was one which prevailed for many years. Galleries were built this year, and four green casements ordered for the south gallery windows.

This meeting house stood until 1735. We have no description of it, and only know it to have been a plain, barn-like building, without chimney or steeple, and probably innocent of paint, outside or in. Its frame was afterwards made into a corn-house on the premises on the corner of Main and Prospect streets, and some of its rough-hewn timbers are still preserved in the cellar of Mr. Arthur P. Moore.

THE SECOND MEETING HOUSE.

This was sixty-six by forty-six feet, and twenty-seven feet high "between joints;" and was built "on the same green" on which the first meeting house had stood. It was at first voted to build it of brick; this, however, was not done. A deed of the land was to be got of Daniel Dickerson, this matter having been long neglected; but we have been able to find no deed upon record. There were horse-sheds about the meeting house on the north, and on the east and southwest sides, and horse-blocks, upon which the ladies could alight from their pillions.

A committee was appointed to seat or "dignify the new meeting house," in 1742. "As a rule for direction in seat-

---

He died June 9, 1746; his widow died July 28, 1758. Their children were: Ward, Samuel, Elizabeth, Deodatus, Mabel, Capt. Russell, who was a prominent man in East Hartford, and Samuel.

ing the meeting house, it was voted, that to and in addition to each man's rate there be allowed at the rate of 20s. a year for their ages, as ratable estate, for each year from twenty-one to sixty years of age, and from sixty years upward there shall be allowed at the rate of four pounds for each year." Widows were to be seated at the discretion of the seaters. The deacons had seats directly in front of the pulpit.

Joseph Spencer was allowed to pay £12 toward the edifice and have equal privileges with the other inhabitants.

The meeting house was "colored" in 1754, and small seats were built about the walls and along the sides of the aisles for the children to sit on. This year four pews were built over the gallery stairs, conspicuously high,—two in each of the east corners of the meeting house (the pulpit was at the west end). These seats were for the colored people, slaves and servants of our good ancestors. A new pew at the right of the "broad alley" was set apart for the minister and his family. The front gallery, opposite the pulpit, and the lower half of the seats in the side gallery were for the singers to sit in.

Permission to subscribers to erect a steeple on the meeting house, at their own expense, was given in 1793; but it was never built. The structure did not possess even a chimney. A stove was not introduced until 1817; and then the pipe was thrust out of the window. The first Sunday after this stove was set up arose many complaints of headaches and warped back-combs, etc., when in truth there was no fire in it at all.

The following description of the old meeting house, written by Mr. Edward S. Goodwin, appeared in the *Elm Leaf*, in 1863:

"The old church was an unpretending edifice, two stories high, without steeple, cupola, or chimney. The pulpit was in the center of the west side—a high, antiquated concern,—but the most remarkable thing about it was the sounding board, a large sort of steeple over, and as large as the pulpit. This always excited the wonder of the young when they first went to church, for the good people of old used to take their children to meeting very young, and they were taught to venerate their Maker. They used to think that God was up in the sounding-board, for the minister, when he prayed, looked up there, and stretched up his hands toward it, as if waiting for the Lord to answer him.

"There were galleries on the north, east, and south sides, with two large pews on the southeast corner, and two on the northeast corner, with separate stairs leading to them. Those in the south corner were for males, and the others for females of a sable complexion.

"Below, the floor was divided into pews, or 'sheep-pens,' as some called them; they were about five or six feet square, with very high partitions between them, and a banister around the top. They were capable of holding six or eight persons.

"Directly in front, under the pulpit, was the deacons' seat.

. . . The people occupied the other pews according to their wealth, or rather the amount of taxes they paid to the society. There was annually a committee appointed to give the best seats to those who paid the most money." The age of the inhabitant was also an honorable factor in the position he obtained in the sanctuary, as has been shown.

A later writer (Rev. Theodore J. Holmes) says: "The galleries [excepting the singers seats'] were occupied by adults who had no place below, and by children, ... under the vigilant eye of the tythingman, ... and many a boy . . . . used to keep very still from a wholesome fear of the scuttle overhead among the bats, and the dark opening under the pulpit, where there might be imprisonment for misdemeanor.

"The singers, too, were, as now, in the gallery. . . . There was a single row of them in the front seats all around, —the tenor and counter or alto opposite the pulpit, the bass and treble on the north and south sides." Before the introduction of the viol and the flute and the worldly fiddle, "the only instrumental music," says the same writer, "came from the pitch-pipe in the hands of the leader, who [first pitched the key and then] marshaled his choir of seventy or eighty through all the old fugue meanderings of ancient harmony."

The early practice was for the leader to read a line of the psalm, which was taken up by the choir and sung. This finished, he read another line, and again the sacred tune took up its sonorous burden, and so on through the composition. It was not until the year 1772 that the society voted "that the singing in public on the Sabbath in the afternoon be without reading line by line." Several other votes about this time were for the purpose of "encouraging psalmody among us." Selah Norton, James Olmsted, and Jonathan Roberts, all staunch and prominent citizens, were appointed to be choristers to assist Captain Pitkin in setting the psalms. And there were later grants of money to procure some person "skilled in harmony," to teach the inhabitants. In 1795 Mr. Jonathan Benjamin sued the society for services in this line, a rather unharmonious proceeding.

The practice of "dignifying" the meeting-house prevailed until the year 1824, when the society had no longer a legal right to tax its inhabitants. The pews were then annually sold to pay the current expenses. Some quaintly humorous lines, written about a hundred years ago by Mr. Elisha Benton in regard to this now obsolete practice, may be fitly introduced here. They are from a copy found among Major Samuel Pitkin's papers, in the handwriting of Mr. Benton himself.

"ADVICE TO THE NEXT SEATERS.

"That each worthy member may rightly be placed,
The Seaters should have a fine fancy and taste,
Your fond proposition should also be strong,
Or else you'l be subject to act very wrong;
You ought to be furnished with very great knowledge,
And if you have not taken degrees at the College
You ought to be all of you masters of arts,
For you'l find work enough to employ all your parts,
The great art of pleasing you ought well to study,
But I don't mean by this you should please everybody;
If you can please yourselves and your favorite relations
'Twill answer exactly to our expectations.
As seaters 'tis certain you ought to be trimmers,
Even such as have made some advance in your primers,—
As mean folks should never be mixed with their betters,
You ought to distinguish and know the great letters,

Especially all the great capital P's,
And all the great round O's, and all the great G's,
The great H's also, and great W's,
Are all well entitled to elegant pews;
And the great crooked S's must be respected,
And the F's will fight you if they are neglected;
And the broad R's will rave and like Bedlam will roar,
If you leave them behind and not keep them before;
Your full blooded Heroes with Marshal Commission
Expect mighty reverence in every condition,—
They have keen sense of Honor, extremely high mettled,
If they think they are slighted you'l see how they're nettled,
They must be promoted at every new Seating
Though seldom you see them on Sunday at Meeting.
A person well dressed must attract your regard,
For them you may study no matter how hard,
However immoral, profane, or ill maner'd
There can be no doubt but they ought to be honor'd,—
Fine dress and rich Cloathing and fine handsome faces
Should always be sett in conspicuous places,
And men of fine learning whose Wives wear Silk Gowns
Should never be placed with Blockheads and Clowns.
What a fine show they make when these troops all appear
In the house when they're placed in the front of the rear,
While some in the center are ordered to rally
And form two Grand Colums to line the broad ally;
Those worthies first in such eminent station
Would beautify greatly our great Congregation,
But as for the rest, all the Vulgar, Oh, fy!
To please 't will never be worth while to try,
There's no place of honor to which you can fetch them
You may thrust them in any where just where you catch 'em.
But if you are bewildered in all your endeavors,
Dissolve and go home and plow with your heifers,
Those heifers which carry one end of the yoke
Will soon help get the pig out of the poke;
And as they're willing and apt to assist,
They'l scatter the fog and dispell all the mist;
By hearing their counsel no doubt they'l work wonders,
They'l rectify all your mistakes and your blunders,
For be your embarrassments ever so great,
They make all light, and crooked things straight;
They'l introduce order where you make confusion,
And bring things to a speedy and happy conclusion;—
Consult all the ladies you wish for to please
And the business may then be accomplished with ease."

"The author of the above annexed the following to his list on seating:

> "Five pounds and ten shillings my list is increased
> To what it was the last year,
> And wealth brings us credit, and credit preferment,
> So is a truth, evidently clear ;
> Should my riches augment to sufficient extent
> To answer my craving desire,
> Then how noble they'l treat me, and next time they seat me
> They'l put me full half a peg higher :
> Then I'll be so grand a pew I'll demand,
> And then I'll be known in my place,—
> One more precious tack—haw, gee, forth and back—
> Will fetch me up snug to Tom Case."

To any one familiar with the names of our older families the initials in the foregoing will need no explanation. Others may refer to the list of names already given in the chapter on Settlers and Inhabitants.

REV. DR. ELIPHALET WILLIAMS.

After the death of Mr. Woodbridge, the question came up in a meeting of the society whether Mr. Samuel Newell, who had for several years preached here, should be called to settle permanently. But the result proved that it was not the unanimous wish of the people that he should become their pastor. The next year (1748) Mr. Eliphalet Williams accepted a call to settle here. His salary was to be £65 a year and four contributions which were to be taken. Six years later the currency had reached so low a state of depreciation that the committee decided that it would require £867 in bills of the old tenor to pay his salary of £80. In 1755 a price for grain was agreed upon with him, that he might be paid in that commodity. His wood was at all times a part of his salary, and various persons were paid for cording it for him, that he might get good measure. At one time Mr. Benoni Hale and at another Mr. Jonathan Stanley performed this service for him, receiving 6d. per cord from the society.

In 1778 Mr. Williams was voted £90 salary, and £450 (old tenor) in consideration of the extraordinary price of provisions and the necessaries of life.

About the year 1799 Mr. Williams, having served his people long beyond the time usually allotted to such constant service as his, began to feel the weaknesses of old age. It became necessary to support another minister, and the society asked him to relinquish his claims upon them. He replied that this he could not do. He finally consented to retire on an annual salary of £110. This was in 1801. He died June 29, 1803, aged 77 years, and in the 56th year of his ministry. He was settled here about fifty-three years.

Many stories remain of Dr. Williams,—Parson Williams, or Priest Williams, as he was often called,—and there are still a few who remember him. He wore the old-time minister's dress, with black stockings and knee-breeches, a straight-buttoned waist coat, with the ends of his broad white band showing on his chest. A big white wig, so large that a child once called it a lamb, covered his head; on top of this he wore a large, stiff, broad-brimmed hat. He had a high sense of the dignity and sanctity of his office. Some thought him domineering, and David Crosby, in 1766, wrote him a long letter in which he stoutly arraigns the clergy in general, and Mr. Williams in particular, for trying to make themselves " lords over the heritage of God, and to make merchandize of the souls of men." Mr. Williams was certainly a sturdy theologian of the old school, who would not be likely to make concessions to any one. His was not a nature to be tolerant, and one of the phrases which he put into Governor Pitkin's epitaph pictures him most palpably to our conceptions as " Scattering away evil with his eye "—especially since we have been told that the children would crawl under the fences and hide when they saw him coming along the street. A man of that sort is never cordially loved, and no doubt he did call some of the wood which his parishioners were obliged to bring him, " crooked stuff," and, perhaps, with cause. It is said he told Benjamin Roberts that his load had in it the making of all the letters in the alphabet. Roberts promptly drove home and left none of his wood. A Mr. Warren came and began to unload. " I cannot have it put down there," said Dr. Williams. " I am going to leave *some* of it there," said Warren, and hurled it about so promiscuously that the good Doctor was fain to retreat into the house.

A man once mowing for Dr. Williams did not bend very low to his work. "My cow," said the Doctor, mildly, "loves the roots of the grass." "Just so," said the man, keeping right on with his mowing; "you see I am leaving them for her."

These trivial anecdotes, however, show only the surface humor of the man. His work here, the many honorable titles he bore, and his literary remains, show him to have been a man of large attainments for his day, and one of profound convictions, and a champion of them who hesitated at no inconvenience to himself to assert and maintain them. He clung to his dark views of what in the unlovely phraseology of that day was known as "infant damnation," until many of the mothers in Israel withdrew from his preaching and went to the Baptist meetings, which were then first held, and drew their husbands with them. Then he launched a dialogue pamphlet after them, entitled "Sophronistes: Persuading people to reverence the ordinances of God in the teachings of their own Pastors. Hartford: 1795." He did not remit his labors against the new sects even when his own son joined them, although he is said to have been less bitter against them from that time.

Of his home life we also know something. He had his favorite arm-chair by the fire-side, and after supper he would sit, while his daughter dutifully filled his long pipe for him from his smoking-box, which hung hard by the fire-place, and brought it to him with a coal in the little tongs. In his last days he smoked a good deal; but one day he put his pipe away, saying, "What right has a dying man to smoke?" and never took it again. His smoking kit, and pipes, and tongs are still preserved by the writer, who has many curious things from his household. Rev. Dr. E. P. Parker, of Hartford, has his old arm chair.

Like most ministers of his time, Dr. Williams thought he needed something warm to drink after his Sunday sermons, and one of his black women used to remain at home to have his flip iron hot when he arrived. Among his papers was found a recipe for making "shrub," a liquor composed of three quarts of grape juice and two-thirds as much "rumm," kindly copied for him by some friend, who pronounced it, when sweetened and diluted with about twelve quarts of water, an "agreeable liquor." Such were the customs and courtesies of this time.

Dr. Williams' study was a mere closet, not over five feet square, with a north window. It contained his chair and a small table, over which were shelves with his few books, all within reach. This was his sanctum, and his children, wanting him, came and rapped—once. If he did not answer, they went softly away. Sometimes he would open the door, without getting up, and pass out to them an apple, or a pear, or a piece of melon, and they would thank him reverently and go away.

His house, on the east side of Main street, near the site of the old meeting-house, and late the home of Mr. Edward W. Hayden, is a study in old-time architecture. It was built for him by Benjamin Roberts, and has a spacious hall, and low, easy stairway, with unpainted, hand-wrought banisters. There is much wainscoting and elaborate molding, even the "escallop shell" closets in the parlor being minutely molded and trimmed. The ceilings are low, and traversed by large beams; and there are endless cupboards and closets. The back rooms are finished in yellow pine and are unpainted. The house is gambrel-roofed, and over the chambers is an immense attic, until within a short time a perfect curiosity shop in old-time trumpery. A low, unceiled chamber, under the rafters, called the meal room, is the "black hole" where the negresses used to sleep,—a complete sweat-box in summer. The first paper hangings that were used in this town were really *hung* in the parlors of this house, having been tacked loosely to the walls. They are of a large brown velvet figure upon a green ground. This paper was sent from England expressly for Dr. Williams. Afterwards paper was pasted on the walls here, and the border, uncut, was put around under the windows in a broad strip, the use of it not being understood.

Dr. Williams' sermons cover a richly interesting period of our history, from 1748 to 1801. But they are so finely written, on such scanty sheets of paper, that most, beyond the scripture text, are utterly undecipherable, showing mere crooked pen-strokes across the page. He wrote in a time when paper was scarce and high in price.

Some of his printed sermons remain. One delivered on the Sabbath after "the late terrible earthquake," Nov. 23, 1755, by Eliphalet Williams, A.M., shows "The Duty of People under dark Providences or symptoms of approaching evils to prepare to meet their God." To which is appended an account of previous earthquakes in New England,—eleven in all,—of which this was the "fifth that has been general and very awakening,"—to wit: one in 1638, one in 1658, one January 26th and 28th, 1662-63, and one in 1727, and one in 1755. This sermon was printed by Timothy Green, New London, 1756. We have also a sermon (unprinted) of August, 1757, on the occasion of a public fast on the taking of Fort Henry. This was used again on some similar occasion in 1776. The text is, "Humble yourselves therefore," etc.

A thanksgiving sermon of March 6, 1760, on the taking of Quebec, was printed by Green of New London. Its theme is, "God's wonderful goodness in succeeding the arms of his people to be acknowledged and celebrated with rejoicing and praise."

Dr. Williams preached the election sermon before the General Assembly in May, 1769. His sermon on the death of Gov. William Pitkin, in October, 1769, delivered in our old meeting-house at the funeral, before many of the dignitaries of the State, was prepared in a marvelously short time, and indicates a capacity for work which few men have. It was on "The Ruler's duty and honor in serving his generation, and his dismission by death, and entering into peace. . . . . Acts, xiii, 36, ... by Eliphalet Williams, V. D. M. Hartford, Green & Watson, 1770." Dr. Williams also wrote

Governor Pitkin's epitaph, as he did many another notable one in our burying grounds. At the induction of Dr. Stiles to the presidency of Yale College, July 15, 1778, Dr. Williams, Senior and Presiding Fellow, made the opening prayer and delivered an oration in Latin. His Sophronistes pamphlet was published in 1795. Rev. David McClure of East (now South) Windsor, said of him in his funeral sermon: "He possessed quickness of apprehension, imagination, great sensibility, and zeal. He imbibed the principles of the Puritan fathers, and his diction was flowing, pathetic, impressive. He supported an unblemished reputation, and magnified his office." Niles & Pease's Gazetteer says of him that "he was distinguished as a man of science, a preacher, and divine."

Dr. Williams was a man of almost tireless industry, who let go no opportunity to impress the great concerns of life and of death upon his people. His talents, which belonged to another age than ours, we cannot rightly estimate. To his own generation "he was an able, orthodox, faithful, laborious, exemplary, and successful minister of Jesus Christ, patient under sharp bodily distress, resigned to the will of his Master, he committed himself to Him who judgeth righteously." (His tombstone.)

Dr. Williams came of a family famous for its ministers. He was born at Lebanon Feb. 21, 1727; graduated at Yale, 1743, and ordained, 1748. He was son of Rev. Solomon Williams, D.D., of Lebanon, and grandson of Rev. William Williams of Hatfield, whose ancestors came from England to Roxbury, Mass. He was a brother of William Williams, who signed the Declaration of Independence.

REV. ANDREW YATES.

Dr. Yates was a professor of Union College, Schenectady, and was ordained as colleague of the Rev. Dr. Williams in the ministry to the First Society in 1801, eighteen months before the death of Dr. Williams. A writer has said of him: "He was a man of wide learning, of strong sense, of simple, loving heart." He felt greatly interested in the children. In his day the catechism was taught in the common schools as well as arithmetic and geography; "and every year, in May, he gathered all the children of the different districts in the church, where, after hearing a review of the lessons for the year, he gave them each little tracts or books, some of which are preserved to this day." He was a friend and advocate of total abstinence in a time when it was the fashion among ministers to have liquors set out at their conferences. When the council met which was to dismiss him from his charge here that he might accept a professorship in Union College, he complied with this custom, and set out four bottles, saying, "Brethren, here is rum, gin, brandy, laudanum,—all poison, —help yourselves!" One veteran doctor, it is said, at once complied, saying, "Yes, yes. But I believe I will risk a little brandy."

Mr. Yates' wife died in 1806, and is buried here. He was dismissed from his charge in 1814, and went back to his post in Union College, followed by the affectionate regard of all his former people.

REV. JOY H. FAIRCHILD.

The pulpit was supplied by various persons until 1816, when Mr. Joy H. Fairchild was settled. His wife died in 1824, and is buried here. Mr. Fairchild was dismissed in 1827.

REV. ASA MEAD.

Mr. Mead was settled here in August, 1830. He died in October, 1831, while a memoir he had written on his little son was in press. From this we learn that "Mr. Mead was a nervous writer, an animating preacher, an active friend of every benevolent enterprise." He was graduated at Dartmouth College, and was also a student at Andover. Before settling in the ministry he was active in the temperance cause.

REV. DR. SAMUEL SPRING.

Dr. Spring was settled here in January, 1833, and was pastor of the First Society until December, 1860, when he resigned his charge on account of ill-health. His was a pleasant and faithful service of twenty-nine years. The sum of $400 was voted to him annually, in spite of his many protests, for many years after the close of his pastorate, and he remained among his people to the end of his days, honored and useful in spite of bodily infirmities.

Dr. Spring was sixth child of Rev. Samuel Spring, D.D., and Hannah Hopkins, daughter of Rev. Samuel Hopkins, D.D., of South Hadley. He was brother of Gardiner Spring, D.D., of New York. He was born at Newburyport, Mass., March 9, 1792. At seven he began the study of Latin; entered Exeter Academy at twelve, where he remained two years; then he went to Atkinson Academy, where for a year he had charge of the Academy in the absence of the principal. He was graduated from Yale in 1811. For a short time he took up the study of law, but soon went into mercantile life as clerk for a Mr. Tappan in his native place. In 1811 Mr. Tappan was burned out, and Mr. Spring assisted in saving many of his goods by plunging into the river and guiding them to a place of safety. In 1812 he ventured into the coasting trade with his brother Lewis, and became part owner of several vessels. Of one of these he was himself master, and was captured with his crew off Chesapeake Bay by Admiral Cockburn's squadron. After the war he went into trade in Boston in partnership with David Hale, who afterwards was editor of the *Journal of Commerce*.

Mr. Spring in 1816 married Lydia Maria Norton of Berwick, Maine. He entered the theological seminary at Andover to study for the ministry in 1819; and was graduated in 1821. He was settled in Abington, Mass., January 2, 1822, and continued there five years, greatly loved by his people. Afterwards he was pastor of the North Church in Hartford for six years, until 1833, when he came to East Hartford. After giving up his charge here he acted as chaplain of the Asylum for the Insane, in Hartford, six years. He had nine children, and died December 13, 1877, aged 85 years and 9 months. His funeral services were held in the meeting-house, Rev. Dr. Burton of Hartford delivering the principal address.

Dr. Spring was a person of high culture, and of fine tenderness of feeling; he had a literary as well as a moral conscience, and his sermons are models of perspicuity and orderly arrangement, and of faultless phraseology. He was universally loved and respected, not only at home, but among his brother clergymen, in all the wide circle in which he was known. Dr. Burton said of him : " In all matters of doctrine he was conservative and quiet—a gentleman of the old school in two senses of that expression ; for while he held on by the old and safe ways, he did it with a geniality and suavity reminding one of the careful and gracious manners of long ago. . . . . As a preacher [he] was calm-minded, instructive, Scriptural, putting his thoughts forth in the clearness of Addisonian diction, never rising to thunders of eloquence, and never sinking to thinness, ... a model preacher whom to have heard is a pleasant and abiding remembrance. . . . . If all clergymen could lead the worship of a congregation like him, some of the strong arguments for the use of a liturgy in the common worship of God would be brought to naught." . . . . "Around such a man all sorts of confidence slowly gathers. On his true and tried character all men gradually rest. . . . . The lines of his influence stretch off into the unfathomable dimness of the everlasting."

Dr. Spring preached for three years in the old meetinghouse, and during the rest of his pastorate in the one at present occupied by the society.

REV. THEODORE J. HOLMES was settled here in 1861. In 1863 he received leave of absence, and enlisted in the army as chaplain of the First Regiment Connecticut Cavalry. During his absence Rev. Mr. Walker preached. Mr. Holmes returned from his regiment in 1865. He resigned his charge in 1872, and accepted a call from a society in Brooklyn, N. Y. Mr. Holmes was very much liked by his people, and the results of his labors in Sunday-school matters and among the young people were marked and abiding.

MR. FRANK H. BUFFUM was settled in 1873. He was dismissed in 1876.

REV. RICHARD MEREDITH, the present pastor, was installed

in April, 1878. Prior to his installation the pulpit was mainly occupied by Rev. T. T. Munger.

The salaries paid by this society to its ministers have gradually risen from the £60 paid to the Rev. John Rood in 1700, to $2,000 paid to Rev. Mr. Holmes in 1871, in addition to the $400 voted to Rev. Dr. Spring the same year.

To several matters relating to this society which have been passed by in our sketch of its ministers, we will now recur.

As has been said, the society included in its limits all the present towns of East Hartford and Manchester until November, 1748. Then the society voted to release the inhabitants of the Five Miles (now Manchester) from such proportion of their minister's rate as would procure preaching for them three months in the year. This probably referred to the winter season. The people there were set off as the Parish of Orford in 1773.

The name of the old society was changed to the First Society after 1784, when East Hartford was made a town.

An institution of the by-gone times was a Sunday ferry over the Hockanum River and swamp, near the meeting-house. Boats were run on lecture days and on Sundays, when needed. The first appropriation for it was made in 1731, when £3 a year was voted for five years, and Joseph Dickerson, Joseph Pitkin, and Jonathan Hills were appointed to manage the affair. This ferry was kept up many years, and the up-town people were wont to say, when the water was high, "Well, Hockanum will turn out to-day so as to get a sail."

The old society has occupied three meeting-houses since its formation. The first and second stood near the junction of Main street and the South Meadow Road, and have been described. The third (dedicated in 1836) is still standing, although it barely escaped destruction by fire in 1876. Since then its interior has been altered, repainted, and re-seated. Its conference room was built and its organ purchased (partly by contributions) in 1866. The tower-clock and a new bell costing $1,200 were given to the Society by Mr. Albert C. Raymond, in 1878. Suitable dedicatory services were held in the church November 8, and the poem and addresses published in pamphlet form.

When the second meeting-house, which so long stood conspicuously on its hill near the river swamp, was broken up, its material was scattered about town, and still exists in various shapes. The house owned and occupied by Mr. George S. Phelps is made almost wholly from it; and has one of the large semi-circular door stones at its side door. The little balusters from the pew doors made convenient toddy-sticks, and have been kept as relics by some of our people.

About the old meeting-house was formerly a sort of town center. In it were held the meetings of the town, and of the society,—the latter sometimes obliged to adjourn, on account of the cold, to the house of Mr. Jonathan Pratt, who lived on the west side of Main street, just north of the little brook or hollow. Near here was the minister's house,—the General Pitkin house, across the street from Mr. E. W. Hayden's late residence, being used for that purpose after Dr. Williams died. A school-house stood near the meeting-house in 1748. Elisha Pitkin, a great trader, had a store (still standing) near his house, supplying a good part of the town with stores and notions, about the time of the Revolution. A mill was in operation under the hill upon which the hatters' shop lately stood, in which grain and plaster were ground, and carding was done. Besides all this the locality was very nearly the geographical center of the society, and people naturally resorted hither upon their many occasions.

The first attempt to warm the meeting-house was made in 1817 or 1818, when a single box stove was put in on the north side of the meeting-house. The pipe was run out of the window. Prior to this time the ladies used to carry little square foot-stoves to meeting with them, in which a pan of coals furnished the heating power. The effect of a hundred or more of these contrivances in one room was to make the air smoky and blue to a choking degree. After the morning sermon, the people flocked to 'Squire Pitkin's kitchen, with its huge fire-place, and to Mr. George Roberts' house (late Ozias Roberts' house), and elsewhere in the neighborhood, to thaw out and gossip until time for the afternoon service. Then they filled their little stoves from the hearth, and went back to the meeting house, to shiver another hour. The boys sometimes during the noon hour stole away from the presence of their parents and from the surveillance of the tything man, and went under the hill and wrestled and jumped and got entangled in clannish fights—Podunk against Hockanum, or Pirate Hill against Bear Swamp. One of our staidest citizens still tells of vanquishing the bully of an alien neighborhood there on a Sunday in his youth. Indeed, we find that the good boy of the past is as occasional a phenomenon as the good boy of to-day.

In the days when there were no wheeled vehicles, save the stoutest carts, the men came to meeting on horseback, bringing their wives, and perhaps their youngest child, behind them on a pillion. The rest of the family followed afoot, coming across lots, the nearest way, often barefooted in warm weather, until near the meeting house—men and women too —then putting on their shoes which they had brought in their hands.

A plant which was supposed to have been long extinct came up on the site of the old meeting house, after it was removed and its ancient site bared to the sun and rain. The little hill has since been razed by the roadmakers to a level with the street.

OTHER SOCIETIES.

The sway of the First Society was undisturbed until about the year 1795, when the Baptists began to hold meetings here at some of the houses, and by means of circuit preachers to draw off the people. Meetings were held at the house of 'Squire Elisha Pitkin, which for its hospitality to the old society and to the new orders was called the ministers' hotel,—at Benjamin Roberts' (now Hezekiah Roberts'), and at other places. At this time residents in the old society began to present certificates showing that they supported the gospel with the Baptists, or with the Methodists, and obtained exemption from the old church rates. Among these was

Isaac Lester, a Baptist (1795), and Nehemiah Smith, a Methodist (1798).

Perhaps the hard theology of Dr. Williams may have hastened these withdrawals; but they were, of course, inevitable, as was the growth of the sects which prompted them. At any rate the good Doctor was much troubled about the secessions from his flock, and launched his pamphlet against them with a sincere hope of winning them back again.

A gazetteer, published in 1819, says there were four societies in East Hartford (including Manchester)—two Congregational, one Baptist, and one Methodist society. The only settled ministers were Congregationalists. The Baptists held meetings for a time in the old school-house in Scotland, where a Mr. Nelson came occasionally to preach.

SPENCER STREET MEETING HOUSE.

The Methodist Society first had its meeting-house on Spencer street, now in the town of Manchester, a half-mile east from Spencer Hill. It stood nearly opposite the head of Keeney street. The land for its site was given by Thomas Spencer, who deeded it to the trustees in Feb., 1800. The meeting-house was built with a steep, pointed roof, the gable end toward the street, and it had a cupola upon it. It is no longer standing. People came from a distance,—some from Main street,—to attend the meetings here, the women riding on pillions.

Thomas Spencer was a somewhat coarse, noisy person, who preached at times, and prayed always with a loud unction. Of his illiterate fervor some amusing stories are told. It is said he once prayed that the "Lion of the tribe of Judah" might be slain. Once, at a camp meeting, finding no opportunity to exhort, he mounted a stump in the outskirts of the camp and cried, "Fire! fire! fire!" until a wondering crowd had gathered. When asked where the fire was, he answered, "Why, my soul is all on fire," and began preaching vehemently to them. Once, at table, he said he felt as sure of heaven as he did of eating a piece of meat he held on his fork. That moment it fell under the table, and a dog snapped it out of sight in a twinkling. These stories indicate positive traits of a character which probably was vigorously useful in its day.

HOCKANUM METHODIST EPISCOPAL SOCIETY.

In the roll of names of members of this church some are put down as having made a profession of faith as early as 1798. Its earlier meetings were held at the houses of widow Simeon Smith, and of Mr. John Porter, at a time when it relied on circuit preachers for its ministrations. The site of its present meeting house was deeded in May, 1827. The people became a separate charge in 1846.

BURNSIDE METHODIST EPISCOPAL SOCIETY.

The first meeting-house of the church society in Scotland stood on the street just east of the residence of the late William Hanmer. It was a plain brown house, built sometime before 1834, without cupola or steeple. It was moved back, and is now used on the Hanmer place for a horse barn. The site of the present meeting-house in Burnside was given to the society by Mr. George Goodwin. This church has now a fine organ, and a live and growing membership.

ST. JOHN'S PARISH.

In May, 1854, Thomas H. Harding, George Hills, Agis Easton, Moses Chandler, and others, associated themselves in a society under the name of Grace Church,—a Protestant Episcopal Society. They fitted up a little chapel south of Mr. Easton's house, in Scotland, now Burnside, using for the purpose the frame of the old ancestral Easton house. This chapel is now a tenement house. Meetings were afterwards held on Main street, in Elm Hall. The society was reorganized, and was named St. John's Parish. The substantial stone church of this parish on Main street was erected through the instrumentality of Mr. John J. McCook, its present pastor. It was begun in 1867.

ST. MARY'S CHURCH.

This church has the spiritual care of all the Roman Catholics in East Hartford and in adjacent parts of South Windsor. It first began raising money for a church edifice in April, 1873. It held its first service in Elm Hall in July of that year, and was made a separate parish at that time. Its church edifice was completed in 1877, and first occupied in November. Rev. Patrick Goodwin was its first pastor, taking charge in August, 1873. He died in 1876, much beloved by his people. Rev. John A. Mulcahy succeeded him. The present pastor is Rev. John T. McMahon.

HOCKANUM ECCLESIASTICAL SOCIETY.

This society was formed in 1876. Among its members are many once connected with the old First Society. Its meetings were for a time held in the hall of the Second South school-house. Its pleasant and commodious church edifice was begun in 1876, and was dedicated and the society duly formed in September, 1877. Its pastor is the Rev. William P. Clancey.

PARISH OF ORFORD.

CHAPTER XIII.

The present town of Manchester was originally called the Five Miles, that being the length, east and west, of the new territory purchased by the town of Hartford of Joshua Sachem, in 1672. Much information concerning its earlier history has been incorporated in another chapter (Early History, 1670–1774). This tract continued to be known as the Five Miles until 1772, when it was set off from the Third Society of Hartford, and named the Parish of Orford. This name the territory bore until the year 1823, when the town of Manchester was incorporated.

The lands in this tract lay in common for many years, subject only to such occasional grants as the General Court might make, or to such orders as the proprietors in common might vote. Meetings of the proprietors were held in the court house in Hartford, many of them being residents of the west side of the river. More votes were passed at these meetings than were acted upon, and they are to the investigator somewhat confusing in their nature. So early as 1682 it was decided to divide the last grant of land between the inhabitants. But in 1728 we again find a vote ordering a division of the whole tract. Later votes still indicate that even then nothing was done about a real division.

In 1729, 200 acres were ordered laid out for the first minister who should settle there, to be laid out in one, two, or three parcels, as should be deemed best. The place where the copper mines were supposed to be was to remain undivided, "to lye for the general benefit of the proprietors." A committee was appointed to make "a model or scheme," showing in what manner the whole could best be divided. The following vote was also passed,—a formal taking possession of real estate being then necessary under the English law:

"Voted, that two of said committee forthwith go and enter upon said propriety and take possession thereof by Turf and Twigg, fence and enclose a piece of the same, break up and sow grain thereon within the enclosure, and that they do said service in right of all the proprietors, and take witness of their doings in writing under the witnesses hands."

Other votes in regard to the lay-out of tracts for division were passed, as well as votes ordering highways, and a sale of a part to pay the charges of laying out the rest of the land; and James Church was chosen to draw the allotments for each proprietor. But still nothing appears to have been accomplished, save the making of expense, and in 1730 a tax of £49 4s. was laid on the proprietors.

The following year (1731) a record was made of the grant made pursuant to the allowance of the committee of Dec. 30, 1677, to the heirs of Thomas Burnham and of William Williams, of "equivalent lands" allowed them by said committee, "what Windsor line had cut off their lots,"—a tract of 300 acres, bounded west by the line of the upland lots (three mile lots), and the five mile lots, and running easterly by Windsor line 300 rods, and in breadth north and south 160 rods, bounded north by Windsor line, and east and south by the undivided lands.

By this grant William Williams encroached somewhat upon the land of Solomon Gilman; and the committee gave Gilman fifty acres in compensation, beginning south of Williams's land upon Jamstone plain, west of the cart path; thence south one half mile to Mill River (now Hockanum River), &c., leaving twelve rods for a highway across said piece of land, east and west, upon said plain.

The first general division of a part of the Five Miles, lying "next to Bolton, from Windsor to Glastonbury," was made in 1731.* The surveyors began east and went west on the

---

*There was a difference among our own townsmen about the proprietorship of the "five miles." A paper exists signed by Samuel Makens and twenty-nine others, binding themselves to hinder (by attorneys and committees) sundry of their neighbors, who call themselves proprietors of the said five miles, in laying out or possessing the whole or any part thereof,

line between Glastonbury and Hartford 240 rods to the thirty-rod highway (said highway extending north to Windsor bounds, and being the west end of the eastermost tier of lots), and butting east on Bolton bounds." They began at Glastonbury bounds and laid out the lots, beginning at No. 1, as they were drawn by vote of the proprietors. The width of the several lots is given in chains and links—as Thomas Thornton, 4 chains, 60 links, and so on. As few—perhaps none—of the grantees settled on their land, it has not been thought worth while to give the whole list, which may be found in Hartford Land Records, volume 2.

This same year "the line run by surveyor Kimberly between the Five Miles and the three-mile upland lots" was declared to be the permanent dividing line between the two sections; and it was then voted that three miles one hundred rods at the east side of said Five Miles be laid out, including highways, and excepting the copper mines, to the proprietors. The remainder, excepting Court grants and the grant to Burnham and Williams, to remain in common. For the protection of small trees and green timber in these common lands, votes were passed, as well as other votes allowing the cutting of elm, beech, maple, ash, black birch, and piperidge, above eighteen inches in diameter.

Encroachments were made upon these lands from time to time. In 1719 some Windsor men had set up a saw mill here without a shadow of right. And, in 1753, a committee was again appointed to oust trespassers who had taken possession of land here.

This year (1753) it was voted to lay out and draw by lot the whole of the common and undivided land, " to each pro-

---

by demolishing any monuments, fences, &c., which they shall erect there. The paper is apparently dated March 24, 1731. It is signed by Samuell Makons, Daniel Dicinson, Richard Burnham, Richard Gilman, Richard Olmsted, Thomas Spencer juer, Jonathan Cole, Sam[ll] Easton, John Bidwell inner, Joseph Bidwell, Joseph Simonds, Jonathan Pratt, William Worren, John Hassaltine, Daniel Williams, Dan[ll] Bidwell, Disbrowe Spencer, John Makons, Benjamin Cheney, Timothy Williams, Obadiah Wood, Jacob Williams, Gabrell Williams, Gabriel Williams, Juner, Will[m] Williams, iunr, Timothy Easton, William Forbes, Joseph Robarts, Samuel Smith, Thomas Trill.

prietor his equal proportion according to the payments of the purchase of said lands," as entered in the records. Col. John Whiting and Mr. Thomas Hosmer were to draw the lots in the names and behalf of the original proprietors. Other votes occur, one passed the next year appointing Capt. Samuel Wells, Capt. Stephen Hosmer, and Messrs. Josiah Olcott and John Haynes Lord, a committee to view the land and "draw up a scheme or model" of how it might best be divided, according to the vote. We find no record of the lay-out of this last division, although it was ordered recorded the same year (1754).

There has been found, however, a copy of the survey or "scheme" made by order of this committee by William Wells, surveyor. It is in the possession of Aaron G. Olmsted, Esq., of this town. The tract laid out bounds south on "Glassenbury" 574 rods, and on Windsor bounds 410 rods. The east line runs straight from Glastonbury to Windsor 4½ miles, and is north 1° east. The west line is straight also. The special grants already set off are: To Burnham & Williams 300 acres in the northwest corner; the Gilman lot lying south of this and about 60 rods from the west bounds, and running south about 60 rods wide to the river, 57 acres; the Col° Pitkin lot, lying about 100 rods south and west of Gilman's, and just east of the present powder mills, and bulging into the new lay-out in an irregular curved line, 50 acres; the Olcott's and Simons' lots, an irregular square near the center of the whole lay-out, 357 acres and 100 rods; Mr. Olmsted's lot lies about 60 rods south of this and contains 201 acres; Mr. Wyllys' lot, 92 acres, Porter's 168 acres, and Capt. Jonathan Hills' 80 acres, are laid out in the southwest corner of the tract and are of the same length, east and west, as Burnham's and Williams' —320 rods.

Prior to this time some had settled within the Five Miles, and, under the fostering Court grants, several industries had sprung up along its streams. The people had become numerous enough in 1745 to have their school money improved among them, and in 1748 they were allowed their part of the minister's rate to procure preaching at home during three months of the year. They petitioned to be made a separate

PARISH OF ORFORD.

society in 1763, and afterwards; but because of a lack of unanimity among themselves, their petition was not granted until June 5, 1773, when they were set off as the Parish of Orford. A site for their meeting-house was decided upon in 1774, and is still occupied by the Center Meeting-House, in Manchester.

There was some opposition to the formation of the new society on the part of the old. This arose principally from the fact that the petitioners asked to have the west line of their society fixed five and one-half miles from Bolton line, thus coming over the old line of ditches between the Five Miles and the three mile lots, one-half a mile. But notwithstanding this, the line was here established, and although it was afterwards contested, it was never restored to the old line of ditches. The present line of the town of Manchester is about 80 rods (one-quarter of a mile) west of the east end of the three mile lots, which, at the south side of the town, end at Keeney street, so called. No record has been found of this line, but it is marked by suitable landmarks, we have been told.

In 1784 the town appointed a tax collector in the new parish, and its assessment list was separately made out. In 1792, Dr. George Griswold was allowed to set up a hospital to practice inoculation here.

In 1812 the Parish of Orford unsuccessfully aspired for town privileges of its own; but the town of East Hartford refused to unite with it in its petition, and voted to oppose it in the General Assembly, unless the line were made at the end of the three mile lots.

The town of East Hartford held its annual town meeting in the meeting-house in Orford, in 1813, and from that time it was held here alternately with the First Society, until the year 1823, when the town of Manchester was incorporated, with bounds identical with those of the Parish of Orford. The new town held its first meeting June 16, 1823. The accounts of the old town and its poor were divided, and Manchester assumed its proportionate share of them.

Further facts in regard to this section will be found in the chapter on Industries, and elsewhere.

INDUSTRIES.

CHAPTER XIV.

THE excellent water privileges furnished by the Saw Mill (now Hockanum) River, and its tributaries in our town, and in the present town of Manchester, were early utilized by the settlers. In 1639 William Goodwin and John Crow bought 776 acres of land on the east side of the great river, bounded west by the "boggy meadow," and continuing east to the east end of Hartford bounds (three miles), for the purpose of establishing a saw mill upon the site of the present mills in Burnside. The present village of Burnside was formerly known as Scotland, said to have been so named by some of the Forbes family who came from Scotland, Great Britain. The site of the mills long owned by the Pitkins was also known as Pitkin's Falls. Our town at first was nearly covered by forests of white and yellow pine, and the work of converting them into lumber for the uses of the young settlement was of prime necessity. In 1654 Mr. Goodwin bought other adjacent lands of John Talcott, with all privileges and rights. The same year the General Court gave him liberty to take timber from the "waste lands" to keep his mill on Saw Mill River running. Goodwin's mill stood on the site of the present lower mill in Burnside. John Crow, who married William Goodwin's daughter, became owner of a one-third interest in this mill and a corn mill which had been added to it. This interest he sold in 1686. Afterwards the Pitkins acquired possession of it, and used a part of the power for a fulling mill. Goodwin & Co. bought a controlling interest in this mill in 1826, adding at a later date buildings for making paper. The title passed to Hanmer & Forbes in 1863, and is now held by the Hanmer & Forbes Company, which has greatly improved the

INDUSTRIES.

buildings and manufactures paper only; and the old gristmill is one of the institutions of the past.

John Allyn, secretary of the Colony, had a mill somewhere on the Hockanum prior to 1671, and was granted 100 acres about it, with the privilege of taking timber from the commons, "for his encouragement in the improvement of a saw mill he hath built for the public benefit." This was laid out to him, "a neck of land abutting on Saw Mill River, commonly called Hockanum River, toward the south, and toward the east," containing 80 acres; and twenty acres on "Saw Mill River on the south and on a brook running in Spar Mill Swamp toward the west." This is the site of the present powder mills in Burnside. The swamp lying directly north of them is to-day known by its owners as Spar Swamp.

In March, 1673, there was laid out to Corporal John Gilbert two hundred acres of land, "on the east side of the great river, about two miles eastwardly from Mr. Crowe's saw-mill, upon a brook called Hop Brook." Hop Brook is the South Manchester branch of the Hockanum. Probably the first value of the land was for the timber which stood upon it, and the opportunity to convert the timber into lumber.

Another saw-mill was built just below the present bridge in Burnside, on the site now occupied by the East Hartford Manufacturing Company, prior to 1669, by John Bidwell and Joseph Bull, and they were granted two hundred acres in the next commons, "with liberty to take timber out of the commons for the improvement of their mill as their need shall require." This land, with forty acres granted to Thomas Harris,—240 acres in all,—was laid out to them in May, 1671, on what is now known as Chestnut Hill, east of Burnside. John Bidwell had a tan-yard on an island in what is now Bushnell Park in Hartford, in the early days. An interest in the mills in Burnside remained in the Bidwell family for some time. A story is told of the conscientiousness of one of the family. Worn out with overwork in a busy season, he fell asleep in his clattering saw-mill and slept twenty-four hours, unconscious of the lapse of time. Awaking, he saw the sun going down the west. He stopped his mill, and started out. At the grist mill he stopped and shouldered his grist (the mill was never locked then) and plodded homeward. Arriving there he was questioned in regard to his long absence, and he was horrified to find that his mill had been making idle noise all the Lord's day, and that he had borne a secular burden in holy time. He straightway sat down with his Bible and passed the next twenty-four hours as piously as he thought he ought to have kept the preceding day.

A fulling mill, for fulling homespun goods, was in operation next below the Burnside bridge, prior to 1690. During that year it was burned and rebuilt. A white oak tree which was one of the landmarks on the eastern boundary of its site is standing to-day, just north of the bridge. This mill was owned by William Pitkin (2d), who had in connection with it a large clothier's trade, conducted by his sons, William (afterward Governor) and Joseph (afterward Colonel) Pitkin. This mill site was occupied by Gen. Shubael Griswold and Amariah Miller in 1784, for a paper mill and a fulling mill. A saw-mill stood below this mill and above the grist mill. Hudson & Goodwin bought this site in 1811, together with the adjacent saw-mill. It passed to the Hudsons in 1821, their deed naming two paper mills and a saw mill. Boswell, Keeney & Co. bought it in 1851, using the works entirely for the manufacture of paper. They owned it until 1864, when Hanmer & Forbes became the purchasers, selling in 1865 to the East Hartford Manufacturing Company, who manufacture fine writing paper.

The upper mill site in Burnside, just east of the bridge, was bought by William Pitkin in 1690, and leased to Thomas and Daniel Bidwell, Thomas Spencer, and John Meakin, who built a saw-mill there. This mill was burned in 1713, and the Pitkins erected a saw and corn mill on its site. Hudson & Goodwin built a paper mill here in 1789. An oil mill stood at the north end of the dam in 1807. Other improvements were made, and George Goodwin purchased two paper mills on this site in 1815. They were bought by Hanmer & Forbes in 1863, who sold the south mill to F. R. Walker in 1864, who still manufactures paper there with enlarged facilities.

Perhaps worthy of mention among the early industries of our town are the copper mines, in what was then the Five Miles, although they were never profitably productive. The land about them was reserved to the proprietors in common in 1728. A shaft was sunk into the hillside, but the work was afterwards abandoned. They are situated just below Case's mills in South Manchester.

The second use which we know was made of the water privilege at the present powder mills was in 1747, when Col. Joseph Pitkin set up iron slitting there, he having been given the sole privilege of that industry by the General Court for fourteen years. But the British Parliament, with an eye to the promotion of trade in English manufactures in his majesty's dominions, prohibited this industry, with others, in 1750. This mill site is still called "The Forge" by some of our older people. It was long owned by the Pitkins, who in 1775 began the manufacture of gunpowder, for which purpose the power has been more or less used ever since, the Pitkins having been succeeded in that industry by Messrs. Hanmer & Forbes (1846), and they by the Hazard Powder Company (1860).

In 1784 William Pitkin, having suffered losses in the manufacture of powder for the public use, asked for the privilege of using his mill in the manufacture of snuff. The sole privilege of making snuff in the State was granted him for fourteen years, exempt from taxation. The town also leased ten acres of highway on the Hockanum River to William, George, and Elisha Pitkin, Jr., for a snuff mill site this same year. This was in the Parish of Orford.

Iron working was carried on again at The Forge about the year 1782, anchors, mill screws, nail rods, etc., being made there. The guns of our old artillery company were cast there in 1797,—the gift of Elisha Pitkin, Esq., to the company. In 1812 powder was furnished to the State from the mills, and several bills for the same are still preserved.

During the Revolution powder was also manufactured just

east of the Burnside bridge, and the mill exploded and killed a man. Many similar explosions, attended with death of workmen, have happened at the Forge mills.

The first paper mills in town were set up in Orford Parish in 1775. They were owned by Watson and Ledyard. Three years later these mills were burned, it was supposed by design, and the widows of their founders asked the State for a loan, showing their loss to have been £5,000. They also stated that their mills had supplied the press of Hartford with 8,000 sheets weekly, and had made a great part of the writing paper used in this State, beside large quantities for the Continental Army and its officers. Permission was given them to hold a lottery to raise the sum of £1,500, and managers, good and substantial men, were appointed.

In 1783, the Pitkins again started out in a new field of industry; William Pitkin, Elisha Pitkin, and Samuel Bishop being granted the sole privilege of making glass in the State for twenty-five years. In October, 1789, they came forward with a petition asking to be allowed to set up a lottery to raise the sum of £400 to cover heavy losses incurred by the employment of an unskillful superintendent of their works,— one Robert Hughes, of Boston. Their prayer was granted, and Jonathan Stanley (town clerk) and Elisha Pitkin and Shubael Griswold (selectmen) were appointed managers, "to pay all the prizes which shall be drawn in said lottery to the persons holding such fortunate tickets," the residue to go to the petitioners. The picturesque stone walls of the old glass factory are still standing in Manchester, south of the Green, and near the house of Mr. J. R. Pitkin.

SILK CULTURE.

The culture of silk in this section was begun about the year 1783, and was at first encouraged by premiums given by the General Assembly,—10s. a year for three years for every 100 mulberry plants, and 3d. an ounce for raw silk. This Multicaulis business, as it was called, after the Morus Multicaulis trees, was at its height thirty or forty years ago. It is said to have received its greatest impulse from the endeavors of Samuel

Whitmarsh, of Northampton, who had been abroad studying silk culture, and who planted trees and built cocooneries with large promise of success. The subject was much discussed in the public prints, and thousands went into the business. The young trees, on the leaves of which the worms were fed, commanded extravagant prices, and a few, who sold out their nurseries just before the public became convinced that silk culture could not succeed in our climate, made fortunes. Many met with serious losses, rooting up their trees and throwing them away at last. The white mulberry trees, still growing in neglected hedges and about our fields, are the offspring of this culture.

Our townsmen went very generally into the business. The trees were propagated by means of twigs buried in trenches, each bud sending up a new plant. Some raised trees only; others bought and sold the eggs of the moths, and fed the caterpillars in "cocooneries" built for that purpose. Dr. Pardon Brownell had one of these cocooneries, and Mr. Thomas Burnham,—a sort of hot-house structure, with shelves, on which the caterpillars were daily supplied with fresh leaves from the mulberry trees. Other breeding-houses were built or fitted up; but the worms died in large numbers, and were swept out and buried. Some, however, produced cocoons, and the writer remembers seeing a large bin of them in Dr. Brownell's barn. The cocoons, when completed, were gently baked to kill the chrysalides inside, and then the silk was reeled off on a common hand-reel and wheel, and sent to the mill. Sewing-silk was made from home-raised stock in the mills in Lisbon and in Mansfield in this State; also in South Manchester, where the present extensive silk manufactures were begun at this time by the Cheney Brothers, who at first wrought in native silk alone.

When this industry was at its best there was a little eight-page monthly magazine, "The Silk Culturist and Farmers' Manual," published in Hartford, in which the different processes are discussed with great interest and minuteness. The "Silk Growers' Guide," another publication of a similar nature, says (1835) that for seventy years silk has been raised in Connecticut, and that it has become a regular and profitable employment, although but primitive machinery is used—the common reel and spinning-wheel—and the worms fed anywhere without fires. The financial troubles that culminated in 1837 knocked the bottom out of this roseate belief, and to-day there is probably not a silk-worm in town.

Butler & Hudson built a paper-mill in Orford in 1784, probably on the site of Keeney & Wood's present mill.

The first cotton-mill set up in Connecticut was built on the site of Hilliard's mill in Buckland in 1794. It was owned by Samuel Pitkin & Co., and made velvet, corduroys, and fustian. (Barber, Hist. Coll.)

Some of the smaller streams in our town were employed in various industries. There was a saw-mill set up at an early date on the site of Hills' mill, on Pewter Pot Brook, in Hockanum. This afterwards (1802) became a grist-mill, and is still used for that purpose. Higher up on the same brook, just north of Brewer Lane, stood an old oil mill, for making linseed oil from flax seed, in 1802. A part of the dam may still be seen. An oil mill also existed in Burnside about this time.

Opposite the site of the lower mill in Burnside once stood a nail-cutting mill, carried on by Timothy Bidwell and Joseph Hale in 1808 and later. Its site was used afterwards for a saw-mill, which was carried away by the disastrous freshet of Oct., 1869.

A gazetteer of 1819 gives the following as comprising the industries of our town at that time: seven paper-mills constantly running, with a double set of workmen,—several with two engines; eight or ten powder-mills; two cotton and one woolen factory; "two glass works, where vast quantities of bottles are made and sent into various parts of the country for sale"; a hat factory, with water power and patent processes, making abundant low-priced hats for the southern (slave) markets; also tanneries, clothiers' works, hatteries, four carding machines, six or eight grist-mills, several saw-mills, "and various other mechanical establishments and

INDUSTRIES. 161

employments." This description of course included the present towns of East Hartford and Manchester.

The old hat factory mentioned above stood near the north end of the Hockanum causeway, just across the road east from the old meeting-house site. Its water-power was derived from a dam across the Hockanum, 40 or 50 rods east of it, with a race-way conducting the water to the hillside in a nearly east and west line. An older mill, used for grinding grain and plaster, and for carding wool for the hand-looms of our ancestors, stood at the foot of the "hatters' shop hill" in the olden times. It was built by Elisha Pitkin, Esq., and was not a very profitable investment. The "head of water" was small, and much back-water from the floods made its use uncertain at some seasons of the year.

Another of the hatteries, now a dwelling, stands on the west side of Main street, next south of the Hockanum Bridge. Hats were made for thirty or forty years in a shop which stood in the dooryard of Mr. Martin Stanley, now the Wm. H. Olmsted place.

A saw and grist-mill once stood on the brook near the Daniel Winslow place, in the South Middle District, and was run by Benjamin Roberts of Hockanum. There was also a saw and grist-mill lower down on this stream, near the house of Mr. Allen Wadsworth. It was on this site that Mr. George Curtis began the manufacture of plated goods about 1840, afterwards removing to Naubuc.

Willow Brook was once used for manufacturing purposes. It industriously turned a nail mill about eighty years ago. There was a tannery here beside it, owned by Mr. Perez Comstock. The vats, now filled up, still exist under the small house next south of the brook, on Main street. The tannery was a rough building, with shutters arranged for drying the hides. There was also a tannery (Hallet's) in the rear of the premises now owned by Dr. S. L. Childs.

One of the largest tanneries ever conducted in town was one established may years ago by Asahel Olmsted, father of Giles and George Olmsted, in the hollow north of the late Geo. Olmsted (later A. P. Pitkin) place, on Prospect street.

It was run afterwards by Selah Webster, Esq., who died in 1831.

Ashbel Warren and Isaac Lester carried on a tannery back of Mr. Austin Warren's house on Silver Lane, and had their vats near the hillside. They also made shoes, and traveled South winters and sold them. This was about 1820. There were a number of shoe shops on Silver Lane not many years ago.

Seventy-five years ago or more several clothier's shops stood about Main street; one by the Stanleys, north of Mr. Norman Webster's; and one by Col. George Pitkin, north of the Root house; and one in Burnside near the lower mill. The fulling for these shops was done at the power mills in Burnside.

"Poudrette," a patent fertilizer, was made twenty-five years ago in buildings on the meadow hill north of the Ashbel Olmsted place, by the Liebig Manufacturing Company. "Poudrette lane" leads to the site from Main street.

The house now owned by Dr. L. W. McIntosh was long a tool shop, carried on by a Mr. Brooks. He labored on a "perpetual motion machine" for years,—and his invention, I was ingenuously told, operated successfully—"at least for a time."

Much tin ware was once made by the Foxes, in the shop on the west road below Pewter Pot Brook, in Hockanum.

Bricks have been made in various places in town. Among the earliest places is the locality of Pock-House Hill in the river swamp, known also as "clay pit." Later they have been numerously made in Burnside, and on the Connecticut at Colt's Ferry.

At this last locality was once a ship yard and a store. Some of our people remember launchings here, and the boys used to find pennies on the site of the old store.

During the late war of the Rebellion a steam "shoddy" mill was built on Main street, just north of the railway station. Its business was the picking to pieces of old rags, which were then sold to manufacturers to work into new goods. It was first built of wood, but was burned, and afterwards rebuilt of stone; this, however, was burned out by fire,

INDUSTRIES.

and was not rebuilt. It was owned by Andrew Farnham and others. Messrs. Stedman & Bancroft's lumber yard now covers its site.

Mill street, in the center of the town, was named from the steam grist and saw mills which were carried on here in connection with the sale of coal. They stood a little way from Main street a few years ago, and are now dwelling houses. The original firm was Hurd & Perkins, who bought out Jared A. Ayres' coal yard.

The spoon shop on Main street, south of the railroad, was established by J. H. and W. L. Pitkin.

The making of syrup from sorghum was carried on by Dea. Edward Hayden a few years in a small mill, in what was then an old "sand pit," now a part of Central avenue. It was not attended with profitable success.

Other small industries have been carried on in town, but have become obsolete and forgotten in the changes of the passing years.

SCHOOLS.

CHAPTER XV.

THE town of Hartford made early provision for the education of its children. The first mention of a public school occurs in the record in 1643, when Mr. William Andrews was appointed "to teach the children in the school" for one year. He was to have for his pains £16.

In 1650 the General Court made it obligatory upon towns having fifty householders to "appoint one within their town to teach all such children as shall resort to him, to write and read, whose wages shall be paid either by the parents or masters of such children, or by the inhabitants in general by way of supply." Towns of one hundred families were to "set up a grammar school, the masters thereof being able to instruct youths so far as they may be fitted for the University." The reasons given were as follows:

"It being one chiefe project of that old deluder, Sathan, to keepe men from the knowledge of the Scriptures, as in former times keeping them in an unknowne tongue, so in these latter times by perswading them from the use of Tongues, so that at least the true sence and meaning of the originall might bee clouded with false glosses of saint-seeming deceivers; and that Learning may not bee buried in the Grave of our Forefathers, in Church and Common Wealth, the Lord assisting our indeavors," etc.

In March, 1660, the town gave Mr. William Pitkin liberty to teach school in Hartford, and in November of that year empowered the townsmen (selectmen) to hire John Church's house for his use. A year later he was granted £8 from the town rate to teach the ensuing year, and each scholar was either to send a load of wood "within a month after Michimas" (Michaelmas, Sept. 29), or pay 3s. to procure wood. In 1662 he was paid £5 for keeping school from October to April.

There were no schools on this side of the Great River prior to 1708, although travel to Hartford in the winter season was often impossible. That year the Ecclesiastical Society petitioned the General Court to allow them to improve their own part of the school rate among themselves for a writing and reading school. In 1710, Rev. Samuel Woodbridge, Mr. Samuel Wells, and Mr. William Pitkin (2d) were appointed to hire a school master, and to take especial care that the money so obtained be improved. A school-house was ordered "built and sott up in ye most convenient place between ye meeting house and ye house of David Forbes." There is no evidence that this house was built, or that there was any school taught here until eight years later. But it is hardly probable that after such decisive action no further steps should be taken. We think the school-house was built somewhere on Main street, between the Hockanum causeway and Central avenue.

Two schools were established in 1718; one north of the Hockanum on Main street, 16 by 18 feet, "besides the chimney space." This house was set by the committee "who have viewed the road, in the country road or highway a few rods southwards of the east end of the lane that leads from Joseph Olmsted's into the other highway, not exceeding six rods." Its site was in the middle of the highway, near the present Second North school building, the custom for many years being to set the school-houses in the highway on public land, or just through the fence on somebody's lot, with entrances directly upon the road, which was the only playground. A permanent goose-pond stood in the highway near this school-house.*

The school-house south of the Hockanum was to be 16 by

---

* Regarding this pond a story is told. "Uncle Thad." Olmsted once discovered wild ducks in it, and crawled out behind the fence with his old flint-lock musket, but the "pesky thing" failed to go off. His wife crept out after him with a brand from the fire-place, and touched off the gun, killing some of the ducks.

16 feet " beside the chimney space "—a huge fire-place, forming one end of the building, into which great logs were rolled by the boys. Its site is not known, though probably it stood south of Willow Brook.

A separate teacher was not hired for each of these schools, but Capt. Pitkin and Lieut. Olcott were to provide a master, and have the time divided, " according to the inhabitants from an east and west line from the bridge on Hockanum River." This practice of having but one teacher, who spent his time in the different schools according to their share of the rate, prevailed for many years.

In 1721 the sum of £9 12s. 4d. was voted to the schools. The next year a master was to be hired for five months, and a dame for the other six months of the school year.

In 1723 all male children, more than seven and not fourteen years of age, were to pay their equal part of schooling from year to year, whether they went to school or not; and the females from seven to eleven years were to pay their part. The parents and masters of male children were to furnish the wood in equal parts, or pay a fine of 4s. a load for neglect.

In 1727 the society voted to relieve the children of one-half the expense of the schools; in 1729 the society assumed it all.

The inhabitants living two miles east of the country road (Main street) were allowed their ratable part of the school money in 1735, to be improved, by direction of the committee, among themselves for a school. This was the first school in Scotland (now Burnside), and it meant only that the common school teacher should spend a proportionate part of his time in that neighborhood.

A school was kept in Hockanum in 1738, a proportionate part of the eleven months, between the house of John Hill on the north, and that of Samuel Wells on the south.

In 1741 the Colony sold " seven townships " in Litchfield County, and divided the money among the societies for the use of schools. Our society received bonds and cash equivalent to £172 in silver. This money was let out at interest, and was known afterwards as the School Society Fund. It continued a snug help to our schools until the year 1863, when, by the failure of its treasurer, it vanished for ever from sight.

A school was allowed in the Five Miles in 1745, with the one sole teacher, and under the direction of the same committee the rest of the town had.

In 1748 a new school-house was ordered in or near the middle of the society, on the "point of land near the meeting-house somewhere near the bridge or hollow near Mr. Pratt's northwardly and the causeway southwardly." Mr. Pratt lived across the hollow north from the house of Mr. W. A. Wright. The schools on Main street were this year divided into three parts, "as near as may be, and kept according to the former vote."

Richard Gilman and others living north of Gilman's Brook were granted their proportion of the school money for a school in 1750.

Four schools were ordered on Main street in 1751, the society voting to allow school-houses to be built as follows: Near the house of Abraham Hills, north side the brook. This was made a wooden building, and stood just north of Pewter Pot Brook, in Hockanum, on the west road (Main street). It was succeeded by a brick building, which was burned out a few years ago,—when the site of the school-house was changed to near the Methodist meeting-house.

The next school-house was to be near the house of Silas Easton, we think near Silver Lane, on Main street. To accommodate the inhabitants from Hockanum River to Stephen Olmsted's, one was to be set near the line between Russell Woodbridge's (now Wells' tavern) and John Hurlburt's (the house now occupied by Mr. James Bancroft).

The fourth school-house on Main street was to be set south of John Gilman's house and north of Gilman's Brook, in Podunk, on what is now known as the "old road." A Gilman lived on the site now occupied by the house of Mr. N. L. Anderson about this time, and possibly the present "Pirate Hill" site was then taken.

A school-house was to be placed " in the center " between the houses of John Bidwell and Timothy Spencer on the country road (in Burnside, perhaps on the site of the old Scotland school-house, nearly opposite Mr. Mahlon Forbes'); and one to accommodate the Olcotts, the Simons, and those that lived near them (on Hop Brook in Manchester),— " always provided that the houses be built without cost to the Society."

A school was also to be kept on Jamstone Plain (west of Buckland's Corners); one near Ezekiel Webster's; one " in the center between Sergt. Samuel Gaines' and Alexander Keeney's (now Hillstown?); and one near Doctor Clarke's. The schools in the Five Miles were to be kept only at the discretion of the committee.

" And it was further voted, that each of the six places where the school-houses are allowed to be built shall each have their part of the public money for the support of schools according to the lists of the respective districts, on condition that they add so much money as will keep the school three times as long as the public money " . . . . would have kept them.

The " north division for schooling " on Main street was given one-half of the old school-house which stood north of the Hockanum River, and near the meeting-house; and the division next north the other half of it. The old school-house south of the Hockanum was also divided between the two divisions there. The last two divisions afterwards became the South (now Hockanum) and the Second South Districts. The school-house in the latter stood for many years in the highway, near the present residence of Mr. George A. Williams. It stood near the west side of the street, with only a pathway between it and the fence. It became much dilapidated,—" you could throw your hat through it anywhere," the boys having ripped off the boarding to kindle the fire. It was superseded by the present building on the east side of Main street.

In 1766 was passed a state law ordering the division of the societies into districts to draw the public money; and from about this time specific appropriations for schools were no longer made by our society,—the districts managing their own affairs, although the society still appointed the committees.

A new district was formed in the southeast corner of the town in 1768, extending from "Glastonbury line to the north side of Mr. Ritter's lot, west so far as to take in Mr. Samuel Roberts, and east to the end of the lots." Its territory is now occupied by the South East and the South Middle Districts. Its school-house stood west of the brook on the north side of the Hillstown road. It was burned down during a state of ill-feeling, which just preceded the division of the district.

The fifth district (now Burnside) was extended east on the country road (Spencer street) in 1779, to the end of the three miles, so as to take Silas Spencer into the district.

This year also the two districts north of the Hockanum were made into three, as follows: From the river to Bidwell's Lane (Burnside avenue,) and Benjamin's Lane (Orchard street,) so called, "from the east to the west bounds of the present district to be one district; from said lanes to the north side of Timothy Cowles' lot, running easterly in said line until it comes to the Highway that leads from Gilman's to Samuel Bidwell's, thence by said highway to the east bounds, to be one district; and all north of said line to East Windsor bounds to be one district."

Of these divisions that first described was the first lay-out of our present Center District. Its school-house was built near the south end of the plot in front of the Center Burying Ground. It was a wooden structure, and had a large fire-place occupying one end, and a loft overhead, to which the boys used to climb to evade their tasks, or to escape punishment. The desks were planks, fastened aslope around the walls, with benches also of rude planks upon which the children sat with their backs toward the center of the room. Pending the displacement of this house it was assailed one night and part of its chimney torn down. It was succeeded, a little north of the same site, in 1819, by a two-story brick building, with a chimney at each end and a belfry in the middle of the roof. The upper hall was sometimes used for lectures and meetings, and for artillery sword exercise; afterwards a school was kept in it. This building was known as the "bell schoolhouse," because of the sonorous bell in its cupola. It was razed in 1858, and the present Center School building erected opposite the head of the Bridge Road.

The second division north of the Hockanum became afterwards the present Second North District. Its school-house was built in the center of the highway, in front of the present school building, where had formerly stood the first schoolhouse known to have been built north of the Hockanum. South of it was the "goose-pond." This building was afterwards (about 1812) moved away and became the present "Cowles house," next south of Mr. William Stanley's homestead. The arched ceiling in the second story still remains: it once crowned a hall in which social dances, etc., were held. A brick building succeeded it, which in turn was replaced by the present west building in 1856. The east building was added in 1878. A primary school was once taught in this district in a little house which stood in what is now Mr. Henry Bryant's garden. It was moved back upon the hill and became the home of Mr. Levi Bemont. It is now a part of the tobacco house of Mr. Norman Webster.

The north division of the three districts formed at this time is our present North District. Its early school-house was built on "Pirate Hill," very near the site of the present school building.

The Meadow District was formed in 1795 by setting off all of the Center District west of the meadow hill, excepting what lay south of the South Meadow Road. This exceptional part was afterwards taken from the Center District and divided between the Meadow District and the Second South District.

THE SCHOOL SOCIETY.

School societies were formed in the towns in our State in 1796, in accordance with an act of the General Assembly, creating them for the purpose of receiving the income from our present State School Fund. This fund arose from the sale of certain lands lying west of and bounded east by the State of Pennsylvania, one hundred and twenty miles in length from east to west, and about seventy miles wide. This land was included in the original charter of Connecticut, which gave the grantees all the land within certain lines "from the said Narrogancett Bay on the east, to the South Sea (Pacific Ocean) on the west part." The original sum arising from the sale of this land was $1,200,000. The State School Fund now amounts to over two millions. On the question, What shall be done with this fund? our town voted with the majority, that it should go wholly to the support of common schools, instead of partly to the schools and partly to the ministry.

The school societies were really no new body of men—they were simply the old ecclesiastical societies meeting in the new capacity of school societies, keeping their records from this time separately. They yearly appointed a committee of eight or nine persons for all the districts until 1839, when the districts were made corporations, with power to elect their own officers. The societies chose the visiting committee, and a committee to receive the town's share of the income from the School Fund; they also had power to form districts, which could tax their inhabitants for the maintenance of schools. After 1839 the school societies still had charge of the boundaries of the districts, of the public money, and held the appointing power in regard to the visiting committee. In 1856 they were dissolved throughout the State, and the towns assumed their duties.

Long Hill District was first formed in 1819, being set off from the east end of the North District. In 1830 all within its bounds, "south of the south side of the middle turnpike," was set off to the Mill District. In 1837 it was made a "union district" with District No. 6 in East Windsor (now South Windsor).

In 1830 a change was made in the lines of the North District,—the alteration placing Col. Solomon Olmsted's homestead (now Mr. W. H. Boyle's) in the Second North District.

Col. Olmsted was to pay $2.40 to the North District annually for five years.

The first school-house in the Scotland or Mill District (now Burnside) stood nearly opposite the dwelling house of Mr. Mahlon Forbes, south of a small pond. It is now a dwelling house. This district was divided into the North Mill and the South Mill Districts in 1841, the Hockanum River being the dividing line. In 1873 these two districts were united again for the purpose of better grading the schools,—a higher department being set up in the office of the mill northeast of the bridge. The name of this district was changed to Burnside in 1878. A post-office of that name had been established here in 1865.

The name of the South District was changed to Hockanum District in 1878.

In 1857 the South Middle District was formed from the western part of the South-East District, and new school houses were built in both these districts.

We have now traced the origin of all our present school-districts, and for their definite boundaries refer to a volume of historical notes gathered by Mr. Walter A. Riley and now in the town clerk's office. The names and numbers of our ten districts are: 1. North. 2. Second North. 3. Center. 4. Second South. 5. Hockanum (once South). 6. South Middle. 7. South-East. 8. Burnside (once Mill). 9. Meadow. 10. Long Hill.

Our schools under the present law are supported by the town by a system of appropriations, under the supervision of a joint board consisting of the selectmen and the school visitors. For this purpose the town receives from the State the sum of $1.50 for every child enumerated between the ages of four and sixteen years; this amount being annually appropriated by the legislature for that purpose. It receives also from the School Fund $1.00 for every child so enumerated. The origin of the School Fund has been given.

Besides these helps there is an annual income of about $350 from the Town Deposit Fund. This fund came from a distribution, by act of Congress in 1836, of surplus money in the United States Treasury to the different States, according to their congressional representation. It is to be held as a deposit, subject to recall at any time. It was to be paid to the towns in four equal installments, in January, April, July, and October, 1837. The last was never paid, owing to the financial revulsion of that year. What was received was deposited with the towns according to their population. The conditions imposed by the State are: 1st. That it must be held as a trust fund. 2d. That all income arising from it must be given to the support of schools. 3d. That the towns must make good any loss or deficiency in the original amount. 4th. That the same must be fully repaid to the State Treasurer when called for.

The amount our town received from this fund was $5,745.48. The town is at present using a large part of this fund, having given its note to the treasurer of the fund for the amount used. From these sources the town receives enough to pay more than one-fourth of the expenses of its schools. The annual appropriations for the last two years have been $7,000 (1877), and $6,500 (1878).

THE ACADEMY.

Aside from the public schools, special efforts have been made at different times in behalf of education in our town. Most prominent among these was the institution of the English and Classical School Association, which erected the brick building known as the Academy, on the Wells tavern property, and for a time maintained an excellent school. It was a joint stock investment, divided into 170 shares of $10 each. The names of the associated members, with the rules for the management, will be found in the town records, vol. 17, page 574. The trustees were Col. Solomon Olmsted, Dr. Pardon Brownell, and Mr. Erastus Woodruff. The school was established in 1833, under Mr. Theodore L. Wright, and soon obtained a wide patronage, many attending from out of town, and finding temporary homes here. In 1836 Mr. Edgar Perkins was principal. The school afterwards fell into less efficient management and was finally closed. The property was bought by Jonathan T. Wells in 1858, and merged into the Wells estate.

Our Ex-Governor, Richard D. Hubbard, was a pupil at this academy, and his name appears in the catalogue of 1833, and also, in several places, in the "exhibition" programme of 1835.

Rev. Increase N. Tarbox, D.D., distinguished also as a poet, was also a pupil of this institution, as were many of the present residents of our town.

A select school was kept by Mr. Salmon Phelps, a veteran teacher, and sometime town clerk, in the house opposite the First Congregational Church; and afterward in the Academy building with a good attendance and satisfactory results.

Other private schools have been taught; one for primary scholars being at present maintained by Mrs. Harrison on Burnside avenue.

ROADS, BRIDGES, AND FERRIES.

CHAPTER XVI.

THE primitive road was a mere bridle path through the forest, with marks blazed upon the trees to guide the traveler. These paths led from one settlement to another, or reached out into the wilderness to the clearing of some venturesome pioneer, or stretched, a thin trail through the woods, to far Mohegan (Norwich), or to the plantation at Pequot, now New London. Often they led to some isolated mill site, on Saw Mill River perchance, or upon Hop Brook, one of its tributaries. The early settlers on this side the Great River set their houses in the most eligible places, on slight eminences to overlook the country for the Indians, or near localities favorable to pasturage and cultivation. The early roads had reference only to these, and, in many cases, are now wholly obliterated. The settlers had no vehicles save heavy carts, wains, or tumbrils, and pairs of wheels upon which they loaded one end of their timbers, leaving the other end to drag upon the ground behind them. These vehicles were drawn by oxen by devious ways through the woods, pounding over stumps, and splashing through the bridgeless streams with far-resounding jolt and shout and clatter. Later there were roads laid out with regard to through travel, and men built their houses beside them for convenience as well as for safety and sociability.

One of the earliest roads used in town was one which ran north from the landing place on the Great River to Windsor. The Island road in Podunk was a branch of this road, and was laid to his dwelling by Thomas Burnham, who lived on the north side of the present home lot of Mr. John A. Burnham.

A road must also have been made very early to the mill

sites in Burnside, where much timber was sawed for use in building on the west side of the Great River. Other early roads were used, of which no record exists. Some of them were afterwards laid out as town roads with no hint of their earlier use; indeed, short cuts through the wilderness probably indicated the most feasible courses for many of the roads which were afterwards laid out. It will be well to bear this in mind while reading the following pages, which have to do only with dates that are upon the records.

FIRST ROAD THROUGH THE UPLAND LOTS.

The first record of a highway laid out in our borders is of a road along the meadow hill, a part of which is still a public way, and is now called Prospect street. It was ordered laid out at a meeting of the proprietors of the three-mile lots in 1640. "The proprietors that were present at the laying out of these lotts did mutually consent that there should be a highway of four rods wide through all these lotts, which shall be layed out by Mr. John Crowe and Mr. Wm. Pitkin, as near the swamp and boggy meadow as conveniently may be." This road once ran along the meadow hill from Windsor to Glastonbury, crossing the Hockanum near the mouth of "the Gulf," and following the hill again down through Dowd's Grove, southward, until it came out, just north of Pewter Pot Brook, into the present highway, near the site of the old Hockanum school-house. Some of the earliest houses in town were built along this road, in places where no road at present exists.

The same year (1640) a committee was appointed to order the highway in the meadow from the river to the upland,—now the "North Meadow Road,"—in regard to which later action will appear.

EARLY BRIDGES.

The first bridges were ordered built in Hockanum by the General Assembly in 1663:

"This Court orders Tho: Edwards and the rest of the inhabitants at Hockanum, all above sixteen yeares old, to

ROADS, BRIDGES, AND FERRIES. 177

take some speedy oppertunity to make two Bridges, the one over the Brook at the place called Sadler Ordnary, the other at Frog Brook, where may be most sutable; in each Bridge to lay three Trees, so hewed that they may be sufficient for horses to passe safe over. Thomas Edwards is to oversee the work, and is empowered to call the rest of the p^{r}sons forth to performe the work, according to the Courts expectation herein; and the Court allowes ten shillings towards the work, out of the Publiq' Treasury; it is to be finished before May Court. They are to mark out the way from ye common way to the Bridge at Frog Brook."

Thomas Edwards was a resident of Naubuc, but the bridges were probably for the accommodation of travel toward Hartford. Sadler kept a public house, as will be seen in the chapter on that topic. Frog Brook is the stream which crosses Main street near the house of Mr. Joseph H. Porter.

MAIN STREET.

Our present Main street was ordered laid out in 1670, by the General Assembly:

"The Court orders that the selectmen in the respective plantations on the River shall lay out a highway six rod wide upon the upland on the east side of the great River, that men may pass to their lotts there as occasion shall require; and they may order the fence to be sett up in the place where they shall order the highway to be sett out. And this Court grants the severall plantations that their bownds shall extend to the eastward twenty rod farther then their three miles formerly granted, in consideration thereof."

Whether the proprietors took the twenty rods granted them is not known. Mr. Agis Easton, county surveyor, thought the lots did not indicate it. By a vote of the town of Hartford in 1679, these roads were to be known as country roads, or King's highway. The course of this highway through our town is as follows: Beginning on the main traveled road (better known as the New London turnpike), below the house of Mr. Ira W. Porter, near Glastonbury line, and running northwesterly around by the house of Mr. Joseph H. Porter, it continues northerly to the house of Mr. Osmyn Roberts; thence it turns westerly until it crosses Pewter Pot Brook. From that point its course is northerly, past the town farm and the South Middle Burying Ground,—north of which it runs side by side with the New London Turnpike for more than a fourth of a mile, when both roads unite and form our principal street. After crossing the Hockanum causeway the turnpike turns west toward Hartford; the old highway continues northerly until it reaches the house of Mr. R. A. Olmsted, where it forms the right fork over the brook, and, afterwards, the left fork to South Windsor bounds.

The town instructed the selectmen to straighten Main street, from East Windsor line to the bridge road, in 1826. No records show that anything was done.

HIGHWAY NEAR WILLOW BROOK.

In 1678 a highway was to be settled "from the country road upon the upland on the east side of the great river through Widow Andrews her land to the great river," there being opposition by some of the town. This was near Willow Brook, and in 1679 the committee reported that they had "determined a highway for common use to be and remain fower rods in bredgth from the mouth of the Hoccanum river to run by the great river southerly uppon the highland until it pass cleere of the south side of a ditch that was formerly William Houghtens, and from thence to run easterly over a bridge that was made by Edward Andrews, and from thence to run on the north side of the Widow Andrews ortyard and then to be six rods wide and beare southerly to the east until it meete with John Dix his fence, and to continue the same bredgth on the north side of said Dix his lott to the end of Hartford bounds east, for publicke use."

Edwards Andrews was one of the first settlers here, and lived on the meadow hill just north of Willow Brook. It is thought that this road entered Main street just north of Mr. Ralph Ensign's house, but its other courses are uncertain. It did not become a permanent road. In 1728 the selectmen were instructed to care for it from the mouth of the Hocka-

ROADS, BRIDGES, AND FERRIES. 179

num " up to the upland and so to the north side of Dick's lot to the end of Hartford bounds, and endeavor what may be proper to be done that the said highway may be accommodated for passage."

In 1743 it was superseded by another road, as will be seen under the title of "Brewer Lane."

NORTH MEADOW ROAD.

A road was to be laid out by the committee of 1678 from Main street to the river, " somewhere between Mr. Crow's and Mr. Pitkin his house." John Crow lived on the Ozias Roberts place, and an old road runs down into the meadow near it; but William Pitkin lived near the present railroad, and probably the road laid out by the committee was that known as the North Meadow Road. The committee appointed a highway two rods wide from the north end of "Mr. Jonathan Gilbert's* Island and that land north that lyeth between the great river and the highland east up to the mere-stones of the lotts to be for a landing-place, and from thence where the carts have already made a passage down the bank to run easterly to the swamp that is next the upland on the north side of a ditch that is near the sayd swamp on the south side of Mr. Olcott's land, which highway is ordered to be two rods in bredgth, and through the swamp to be fower rods wide to the upland, to run upon a white oak tree uppon the side of the hill which is markt by us, and on the side of that hill to turn north towards William Buckland's lott, and from thence a highway fower rods wide is appoynted to run between Mr. Aaron Cooke his lott and sayd William Buckland's lott east

---

* Jonathan Gilbert was a merchant, and dealt in wines and liquors and other commodities. He owned a warehouse on the west side of the river, and was a prominent citizen. He bought the island named after him in 1660, of Thomas Bird. It contained fourteen acres, and was bounded east by Dutch Island and the meadow lots; south against the Little River's mouth, and west by Connecticut River. This island was in later years called "Pomp's Island," because Pomp Equality, a negro, harbored his sloop in a cove below it. Pomp also owned land upon it. Though then in part or wholly an island, it is no longer so, except in time of high water. A gradual filling up of the meadows has left the ancient merestones three feet or more below the present surface of the ground.

to the country road [Main street], and we judg it convenient that the highway run to the end of Hartford bounds the same bredgth."

"Also we have ordered a common landing place upon Mr. Jonathan Gilberd's island on the east side of the Great River, where now it is, to be fower rods wide uppon the banck next the river, and to be two rods wide upon the banck or highland belonging to Mr. John Pantry, and from thence to turn north two rods wide to run untill itt meetes with the common highway north upon the highland by the meerestones of those lots as bounds with meere-stones."

Land for this road was afterwards sold to the town by John Easton, in 1696, who deeded two rods in width from the river to the land of Samuel Olcott. It was agreed, however, that said two rods in width "should only extend to the highway upon the bank leading from Potuncke to Hartford landing-place on the banck of the meadow next to the low land leading to the river." Easton also deeded "20 feet in breadth of land from said highway on the bank of the river, some few rods northerly from the above mentioned place where the two rods cometh into the highway to belong to said town for a highway, which hath been the town's for many years," and bounds by the river west, by highway east, by Easton on the south and north.

Samuel Olcott also deeded a strip across his land for this road, two rods in width, bounded north and south by his own land; eastward by "the bridge causeway or highway newly repaired or built at the charge of the town of Hartford," west by land of John Easton, "forever as a country rhoade or highway for traveling, driving, or any other improvement whatever."

That this road was ever carried beyond Main street there is now no evidence. It came in a nearly straight line from the landing place north of the present bridge, where for many years the ferry was kept. Sometimes at low water the stream was forded near here, and hay and grain from our meadows carted across.

HOCKANUM BRIDGE.

The first bridge across the Hockanum River in this town was built at Burnside, where the teaming about the mills made it necessary. Lower down the stream was probably passed by fording, when it was possible so to do. William Pitkin, Capt. Nichols, and John Marsh were appointed in 1700, " to view a convenient place for a bridge, and order the building of a bridge at the town charge." In 1724 passed the following vote: " Whereas the town hath been at great cost from time to time to erect and support a bridge on the east side of the Great River in Hartford on the road leading to Hockanum, and yet the inhabitants on that side do not sufficiently make the landway at the ends of said bridge, sufficient for persons to pass without a vessell to pass the water, even when there might be good passing on the bridge if the ends were sufficiently causewayed: It is therefore ordered that the town will not for the future pay anything towards building or repairing said bridge until the inhabitants of the east side make the land at each end of said bridge." This work was done by the society in 1731, when the surveyors of highways were asked to call out the persons obliged to work on the highways two days in the year, and " employ them to work in the swamp . . . . near the meeting-house, to raise a causeway across the swamp." The causeway has since been raised to a higher level at different times. The trees were placed along it by vote of the town in 1837. A new bridge was built over the river in 1828, in place of the old one, which had fallen. The present bridge was built in 1854, and has been subsequently altered and repaired.

NORTH PROSPECT STREET.

The road from Richard Burnham's to Joseph Olmsted, Jr.'s, as then fenced, was accepted as a town highway in 1717. This is the present road from Main street, near the house of Mr. Putnam, to the meadow hill, near the house of the late Mr. Ashbel Olmsted. This road was widened one-half a rod from Jared Hurlburt's to the Meadow Hill in 1858.

BURNSIDE AVENUE.

In 1722 the selectmen were ordered to lay out a highway from the end of a street leading by the house of John Bidwell, "to run northerly on the western side of a swamp, about a rod within the improved land of Daniel Bidwell, Jr., extending on that course the said breadth of four rods from the said two lots of Bidwell and Case [Case then owned Mr. C. C. Moody's place], and then eastward," etc. They reported in 1725 that they had done the same "from ye east end of ye lane which runs by John Bidwell's north across ye lotts belonging to ye heirs of Daniel Bidwell, dec^d, four rods wide, butting west on ye fence now standing near bear swamp:* Then runns round on ye brow of ye hill four rods wide in Benjamin Cheeney's land so far on ye heighth of ye hill as to make ye highway convenient, till it comes to ye lott of Daniel Bidwell dec^d, before mentioned. Then turns east on ye north side of said lott four rods wide till it comes to ye next turn of ye hill. Then turns to ye top of ye hill on John Bidwell's land so as ye way may be convenient: To be and remain for a highway forever, till it comes to ye north line of ye abovementioned lott of ye heirs of Danl Bidwell; then continue east on ye north side" said lot four rods wide, to the west end of Daniel Bidwell's field "near ye mills." Then south, four rods wide, across said lot and lot of Lieut. John Meakins and Ensign Samuel Meakins; from thence continue four rods wide on the lots of heirs of William Pitkin to the Fulling Mills.

Attached to this report is a quitclaim deed of the land taken, signed by Daniel Bigelow (the road was once called Bigelow Lane, and Bidwell's Lane), Benjamin Cheeney, Daniel Bidwell, William Bidwell, John Meakin, Samuel Meakin, John Bidwell, William Pitkin, Joseph Pitkin.

---

* This "bear swamp" is said to have derived its name from the fact that a Mr. Corning, a spinning-wheel maker, who lived in Scotland, killed a bear here. The people made a barbecue of the beast, and made Corning the mock hero of the feast, crowning him in a ludicrous fashion, and drinking many toasts in token of his exploit.

SOUTH ROAD TO BOLTON.

The above road was continued from the Fulling Mills (in Burnside) to Bolton line. The proprietors along it signed a paper signifying that if the said continuation of the highway from the "great street" toward Bolton be made but four rods wide, instead of six, they would "take up full satisfied with the security the said committee do give us for the payments of our respective sums annexed to each of our names [to wit]:

John Pitkin and Joseph Pitkin acquit the town from paying anything.

James Forbes, £3.

Benjamin Roberts, gives his as the jury returned.

Daniel Bidwell, gives cross his land as the jury returned.

Thomas Spencer, for what it takes off the side of his lot (he gives what it takes cross his lot), £5 16s.

William Corbett, gives cross his lot.

Joseph Pitkin, for what it takes on the side of his lot, £6 15s."

SILVER LANE.

In 1728 the selectmen were directed to view a place for a road south of the Hockanum River. Two years later their return concerning a road from Benjamin Hills was accepted, and the sum of £76 7d. was voted to pay for the land. In 1731 the deed of the land was given for a roadway three rods wide. There were nine grantors, among whom was divided the £76 7d., according to their respective proportions. The road abuts west on the country road (Main street), and began at Benjamin Hills' land, he selling 83 rods in length and 3 rods in width,—"reserving to myself a few foots round my well." Next came John Hazelton's land, he selling 36 rods in length and 1½ rods in width,—"reserving 8 foots south of my house;" then Samuel Hills, who sold 105 rods in length and 3 in width, as also 1½ rods wide and 106 in length, to run the same course; then John Abbey, 62 rods long and 1½ rods wide; then John Kilbourn, 22 rods long and 1½ wide, abutting south on Samuel Hills' rod and a half; then Samuel Smith, 25 rods, 22 of which were 1½ rods wide, abutting south on Samuel Hills' 1½ rods, and 3 rods on Joseph Roberts' 1½ rods. Then, turning due south 14 rods, and 4 rods in width; then east 3° north, on John Cadwell's land, 76 rods and 4 rods in width; then on Thomas Kilbourn's land, the same course, one mile and 140 rods (4 rods wide), abutting east on the country road that leads [from the Fulling Mills] to Bolton. The deed is signed by Benjamin Hills, John Hazeltine, Samuel Hills, John Abbey, John Kilborn, Samuel Smith, Joseph Roberts, John Cadwell, Thomas Kilborn.

This road was afterwards changed at the "Sand blow," to pass around the hollow there, and also at the angle near the head of the mill road, so called. When this was done we do not know,—perhaps by the committee appointed by the General Assembly, in 1798, who altered the road from Orford meeting-house to the Hartford Ferry, for the " convenience of publick travil."

ROAD EAST, NEAR GILMAN'S BROOK.

This road was viewed by the selectmen in 1728, and surveyed in 1734. The deed was not given until 1744; it is signed by John Goodwin, John Goodwin, Jr., and Caleb Goodwin, in consideration of £15 formerly paid to William Goodwin by the treasurer of Hartford. The survey is as follows ·

"I began at said Country Road, and thence ran parallel to the dividing line between Hartford and Glassenbury, 1 mile 75 rods east, taking 2 rods out of Decon Goodwin's lot, and 1 rod out of heirs of William Goodwin: Then South squarewise across said Goodwin's lot 27 rods 13 links: Then East between John Goodwin and Timothy Cowles's lots 27 rods near a swamp, taking 2 rods out of Goodwin's land and 1 rod out of Cowles's lot: Then South across Timothy Cowles's lot 22½ rods: Then East between Cowles's lot and Capt. Roger Pitkin's land 27 rods, taking 2 rods out of Pitkin's and 1 rod out of Cowles's land: Then south 91½ rods and 3 links across Roger Pitkin's, Capt. Ozias Pitkin's and Susanna Bunce's lots, and lot of heirs of Nathaniel Pitkin, deceased: Then east between lots of Nathaniel Pitkin and Capt. William Pitkin to the end of the three mile lots, taking 1½ rods out of William

Pitkin's land, and 1½ rods out of Nathaniel Pitkin's land; Said highway to be three rods wide in all parts."

Other deeds and surveys carry this road by various courses to the bounds of the town of Bolton.

The easterly part of this road was to be viewed and made more convenient by exchange or otherwise in 1735. Beyond the point where an intersecting road turns south toward Burnside, it is now a mere track through the woods, emerging on the Long Hill road, just north of the railroad crossing. For many rods east of this place it has been obliterated by the railroad, the road-bed of which lies along its course. Farther on it is represented by the Tolland Turnpike.

ROAD EAST ALONG WINDSOR LINE.

Joseph Talcott and Daniel Goodwin were appointed in 1743 to view and enquire about a piece of land about two rods wide next to Windsor bounds, said to be left vacant, and see whether it were best used for a highway. In 1744 the town voted to obtain it for that purpose, provided it could be had without cost. In January, 1744-5, it was deeded by thirteen persons, who give as a reason, "especially for the necessity to reach their lands, and also for conveniency of having a town highway." It was laid out one rod and fifteen links in breadth from Windsor line, and bounded north by that line, and west by the country road (Main street),—" which way is now opened on the north side of the dwelling house of John Burnham the younger, and is bounded the whole length east ward on the south side by the land of said John Burnham, Jabez Burnham, and Jonah Williams; and from the country road eastward until it comes to the land of Jonah Williams being near a mile and a half." It was to be one rod and fifteen links in breadth from the west line, " and after it comes on the land of Jonah Williams until it meets a road in the bounds of Windsor coming to the dividing line, the said way is to be two rods in breadth."

The deed is signed in the following order :—by John Burnham, Sr., John Burnham, Jr., and by Charles, Jonathan, Jabez, Caleb, David, and Timothy Burnham, Jonah Williams,

John Wood, John Anderson, Samuel Burnham, Joseph Burnham.

BREWER LANE.

A place for a highway eastward to the commons, between Hockanum River and Glastonbury, was viewed by Joseph Talcott and Daniel Goodwin in 1743. The following year representations were made to the town in meeting assembled of a highway supposed to have been formerly left, or set out, near the proposed new road, and a committee was appointed to examine the records for the same. It was "said to be on the east side of the great river leading from Tim: Williams eastward through the three mile lots." (See "Highway near Willow Brook.") This, if found, was to be sold, or exchanged "for land that may be more accommodable for the use of a highway." Where this was first laid out we do not know; but in 1751 the General Assembly made void the doings of a jury appointed by the County Court, and directed the court to appoint another jury for a new lay-out. They were "to begin at the said road [now the west road leading from Hartford to Glastonbury] and to lay-out a highway from thence eastward, to be on the south side of said Samuel Wells's lot, of suitable width until it fall in with the said highway on said lot laid out by the former jury, and assess the damages," etc. The Wells family owned land from this road north to the north side of the house lot of Mr. Addison Pitkin, and extending, I am told, to the three-miles end.

THE "NEW ROAD" IN PODUNK.

William Wolcott of Windsor, and others, petitioned for a highway westward from the common road, from near the house of William Cowles northward to Windsor bounds, and so into the country road against the house of Thomas Elmer, in 1752. This was opposed by the town of Hartford, and again in 1762, when it was again prayed that it might be laid out "between the meadow fence and the old road."

In 1769 Col. John Pitkin and Elisha Pitkin were appointed to confer with East Windsor and endeavor to get alterations in the new highway "west of the old road," to have it come in above where the jury had laid it, so as to open east on the old road at the place where most likely to communicate with a new road proposed eastward to Pitkin's Mills, but without success. We think the place of "the road proposed eastward" was taken by the road branching from the road east from Richard Gilman's, and leading now to Burnside, and known as the Mill Road, but find no record of it.

ROAD TO PRATT'S FERRY.

The west road from near Pewter Pot Brook toward Naubuc was projected in 1763. The town of Hartford appointed a committee to attend the County Court in regard to a road from Glastonbury to the country road near the house of Samuel Roberts, and, if it is found necessary, to get it at as small expense as possible. But it does not appear to have been opened so late as 1784, when the town agent was instructed to apply to the court "to have the road opened which leadeth from this town to Pratt's Ferry in Glassenbury."

OTHER ROADS.

When the South Meadow Road, west from the old meeting-house, was laid out, we do not know. Probably very early. £12 were granted to build a bridge upon it in 1795.

The New London Turnpike (chartered in 1795) afterwards passed over it. This turnpike follows the main road south until near the house of Mr. George Brewer; then it runs along the east side of the old country road to the new meeting-house site, where it forms the east fork, and from thence is the direct road to Glastonbury.

A petition was sent to the County Court in 1805 to straighten the old ferry road from the old meeting-house to the ferry, it being represented as "very circuitous." The old road turned north just west of Pantry's Pond drain, and afterwards west, coming out just north of the house of Mr. Janeway Brewer. From thence it cut across the corner in front of Mr. Chauncey Lester's house to the ferry road. The new lay-out was probably very nearly that of the present South Meadow Road, running directly to the river, where two ferries were carried on in 1805.

Assessments were made for a road from T. Wadsworth's to T. Keeney's in 1798. Of this, and of other roads subsequently laid out, the records give us only hints, if they are not altogether silent about them. We think this road is the one running west from near Mr. H. U. Holmes's store in Hockanum.

Assessments were made the following year for a road from Ashbel Hills to Hosea Keeney's. This was for the road easterly from the South Middle school-house, although it had probably been for years a traveled road.

In 1802 the road in Podunk west from Tim: Burnham's to the "new road" was made public. This road was laid out at the time of the first settlements by Thomas Burnham, and is the cross-road on which Mr. Julius Burnham lives.

The Hartford and Tolland Turnpike was chartered in 1801. It is the road coming from the ferry landing direct to the present post-office in the Bigelow Hall building, and passing thence over Main street to Burnside avenue, of which it forms the left fork, running straight to Buckland's Corners.

The Middle, or Boston Turnpike, through Burnside and by the powder mills, was chartered in 1797.

The town opposed the opening of turnpike roads, and by its efforts succeeded in preventing any toll-gates within its borders. The turnpikes have all been abandoned to the towns, and are now town roads.

Assessments were made for the Ellington road, so called, in 1806.

The road in Podunk next south of the school-house was made a town road in 1825, when it was voted that the road from Jacob Williams' house up the hill to the old road be a town road. This road, followed west, descended the meadow hill and went straight to Gilman's Landing on the Connecticut, where vessels unloaded molasses and other commodities for the "old red store," which stood just north of Mr. Arthur Burnham's.

In 1826 the town of East Windsor petitioned for a public road down through our meadows to Hartford, but it was not granted.

A road was to be laid out from the mills in Burnside to

near the house of Nehemiah Smith, on Silver Lane, in 1834; but in 1839 a similar vote appears for the lay-out of a road from near Timothy Risley's (near Mr. E. C. Brewer's), and running east to near the house of Elijah Forbes. This road was straightened and made three rods wide in 1872-4.

From 1836 to 1846 steps were taken to lay out a highway on the meadow hill from the Bridge Road to the house of Timothy Buckland, and it was finally opened. The first road on the upland north and south through our town had once run along this hill.

The road from Hillstown to Eagleville was laid out in 1844-5.

The road in the Meadow on which the school-house stands was laid out in 1852.

This year also the road in front of the Arnold place (Mr. Chauncey Lester's) in the Meadow was considered,—whether to lay out a new road or to alter the old one. Of the road from this place north to the lumber-yard no record has been found. It is an old-time road, once the only way from the North Meadow Road to the lower ferry landing.

The road in front of the west row of houses in the South Meadow was laid out by the selectmen, but never became a public road—Mrs. Arnold refusing to give her land.

A road was to be laid out from Mr. George May's to Eri Eldridge's east line in 1853, if it could be done without expense to the town. This was on the line of the present "Tobacco avenue," where an ancient right-of-way existed. It was laid out two rods wide from Main street east, and then north to Silver Lane, in 1863.

From the east Glastonbury road to Manchester line a highway was laid out on "the Neck," in 1867. It runs easterly between the two brooks next north from the eastern terminus of Brewer Lane.

The Mill Road, from Burnside north, was extended toward the house of Mr. Thomas Burnham in 1872, coming out on the Ellington Road south of the brook. It is three rods wide.

William street, in Burnside, from the Middle Turnpike

to the Tolland Turnpike, became a town road in 1873. The land for it was given by Mr. William Hanmer.

In regard to some of our roads no record has been found; among these are the Long Hill Road; East Main street, or the East Glastonbury Road, which south of Brewer Lane was laid out by the Porters, 4 rods wide, in 1775. Orchard street, once called Benjamin's Lane, and later Woodruff's Lane. Several private streets have recently been laid out, and building lots sold. Most prominent of these are Central avenue, laid out by Edward W. Hayden, and running east from near the First Congregational Church; Prospect street, along the railroad, by Jas. H. Ranney; and Woodbridge avenue, a little north of the latter, by Alfred Woodbridge.

There are several votes on record (1800 and later), by which the town authorizes its selectmen to maintain ferries over the overflowed roads in time of freshets, and to find good and sufficient ferrymen, and to fix the fares that may be charged. In 1818, an ice blockade at the bridge over the Great River damaged the roads seriously, and gouged out what is known as the "Gulf" in the pastures near the meadow hill. Bridges were also carried away at this time by freshets in the eastern part of the town, now Manchester. An account of the ancient ferry across the Connecticut River will be found in a separate chapter.

METHODS OF REPAIRING ROADS.

The methods of repairing the roads in town have been various. The system of district taxation,—most citizens working out their highway taxes,—prevailed for many years. Under this system neighborhood road-making "bees" were held; and sometimes bounties were given to the districts having the best roads, which were probably spent for the common refreshment of the laborers who won them.

In 1841 the roads were divided into sections and let out to the lowest bidders. At present all the roads are under the supervision of the selectmen.

SEWERS.

A sewer was laid from the railway station on Main street to and through Orchard street, to the meadow hill, in 1875. Branch sewers drain the adjacent streets. In digging for this sewer on Main street, near the head of Orchard street, a skeleton was exhumed from about two feet below the surface. Probably it was not that of an Indian. Its mystery has never been explained.

A sewer was also laid in Burnside, down the Main street there, to the river below the mills. Other smaller sewers were put in at this time; one near Mr. Charles M. Bidwell's on Burnside avenue, and one near Mr. George E. Pratt's, on Silver Lane; and others.

BY-LAWS *de* HIGHWAYS AND SIDEWALKS.

Sundry by-laws for the protection of public ways have from time to time been passed by the town. One in 1842 provides a fine of one dollar a load for the removal of earth from the highways.

For the protection of sidewalks against the travel of vehicles and beasts, a fine of $3 was fixed in 1838. In 1859 this fine was made two dollars.

In 1872, for willful damages to fences, gates, etc., a penalty of $25 was provided.

In 1842 it was made a penal offence for any person to bathe in any stream within one-fourth of a mile from any road or dwelling.

Plank walks were built on the Hockanum Causeway, and over Elm Brook on Burnside avenue in 1876, for the first time.

THE STREET ELMS.

CHAPTER XVII.

In regard to the first planting of the noble elm trees which are still allowed, in places, to beautify our streets, no exact information has been obtained. Mr. George J. Olmsted, writing in the *Elm Leaf* in 1863, inclines to the tradition that the good work was begun by a Mr. Warren, who is said to have put out the trees in front of Dr. Williams' house, on Main street, and that others followed his example in other parts of the street. One pretty well authenticated account has it that a general gathering was held for the purpose, and Mr. Timothy Deming says that Mr. Thomas Case told him that the young men did the work, and the old men furnished the "fixins." When asked what the "fixins" were, he replied, "rum and sugar." Tradition further says that this gathering was held,—probably by a mere coincidence,—on the day of the battle of Lexington. Individual enterprise, however, did some of the work. The trees in front of the house of the writer were set out by his great-grandfather, Joseph Goodwin, Sr., (about 1773) when he built the old house which until recently stood on this site. Those in front of the house of Mr. S. O. Goodwin were set out by his grandfather, Joseph Goodwin, 2d, when he fixed over the old house which once stood there for his home.

At first there was opposition to the tree-planting. Some some said the forest was only just subdued, and why again obstruct the highways with trees? But most of our people to-day bless the enterprise and taste which gave President Monroe occasion to say, when on his tour in 1817 he lodged in our town, that our elm trees were the finest he had ever seen.

The story that our elms were set out by English prisoners of war, or at the suggestion of the French when here, we regard as untenable. It arose from the fact that in South Windsor work of this kind is said to have been done by the Hessian prisoners there, during the Revolution. We can not ascertain that there were any prisoners quartered in our town.

Other ancient trees are still standing in town. The large oak in front of Mr. W. H. Olmsted's house is said to be an aboriginal forest tree, and certainly has the appearance of being 300 years old. An old oak near the Burnside Bridge, a boundary tree in 1690, has been mentioned elsewhere.

HARTFORD FERRY AND BRIDGE.

CHAPTER XVIII.

THE ferry over the Connecticut River was first leased to Thomas Cadwell in 1681; he was to "keepe the ferry for seven years," with sufficient boats to carry over horses and men, and a "connoe for single persons." The fares were regulated by vote of the town:

"Fare for horse and man 6d. if not of this town.
Fare for a man . . . . 2d. if not of this town.
Fare for a man . . . . 1d. in silver if of this town, or 2d. in other pay.
Fare for horse and man 3d. in silver if of this town, or 6d. in other pay.
And for those of this town whom he carrys over after the daylight is shutt in, they shall pay sixpence a horse and man in money, or 8d. in other pay." For a single person 2d. or 3d.

After this lease expired the ferry was leased to Cadwell's widow for seven years more. In 1737 the fares were regulated by the General Assembly.

The town of Hartford applied to the Assembly in 1728 for a charter for the ferry; and in 1737 the petition was renewed for the settlement or grant of the ferry to the town of Hartford.

The money arising from the rent of the ferry was divided among the schools to procure firewood in 1748; and in 1756 it was applied to the repair of the bridge over the Little River in Hartford.

When East Hartford became a town in 1783, it was given one-half of the ferry privilege. The new town at first leased its privilege, selling the same at vendue for many years.

Two ferries are mentioned in 1805,—the upper and lower. So nearly as we can find, one of these crossed to State street in Hartford, the other to Ferry street. In 1808 the Hartford Bridge Company was incorporated, overshadowing the ancient rights of the people in regard to the transportation of passengers across the Connecticut River, although its charter was not at first thought to be strongly inimical to those rights. Its bridge would provide a way across the river at seasons unfavorable to navigation, and the charter provided that "nothing in said act shall now or hereafter injure said [ferry] franchise." But the troubles which arose would make a long chapter. We give simply an outline of what followed.

In 1812 the Bridge Company attempted to buy the ferry franchise from the town, but were unsuccessful. In 1813 they petitioned the General Assembly to suppress the ferry. A compromise was talked of, and the town voted to relinquish the ferry if its inhabitants might pass over the bridge at the ferry rates of toll. This vote was, however, rescinded. In 1818 a new act was passed, suppressing the ferry, and making no compensation whatever to the town. This was done on condition that the Bridge Company should repair their bridge and raise their causeway three feet, and the piers of their bridge four feet, and place the draw at the west side of the river. These changes were necessary because the bridge had been badly damaged by the ice and its draw swept away. The bridge here referred to was the second one that had been built by the company. The first was an uncovered structure, hanging low over the river, with the travel on the crown of the arches. It was soon swept away.

This arbitrary action of the General Assembly resulted in the erection of the present bridge, and in gaining for the company a troublesome opponent in the town of East Hartford, which did not withhold its appeals to the General Assembly until that body consented in 1836 to reëstablish the ferry by a repeal of a part of the act of 1818. The clause compelling the Bridge Company to keep three boats was also repealed, and the towns of Hartford and East Hartford were ordered to keep one-half of the Bridge Road in repair from Main street to the Tolland Turnpike, with one-half of the "dry bridge." This obligation was repealed the next year.

In 1838 the Company, by its attorney, addressed a letter to the town, asking for an amicable and mutually advantageous settlement, stating that they thought the bridge adequate to the wants of all. The town laid this letter on the table, and immediately voted to continue the ferry. A suggestion to unite with the town of Hartford in buying all or a majority of the stock of the company was not adopted, and in 1839 the town was defending the ferry again before the Legislature, but without the aid of Hartford, which had no share in the reëstablished ferry of 1836.

This year (1839) the ferry having proved remunerative, the town ordered that the surplus fund be loaned at interest.

In 1841 the Legislature took action unfavorable to the town, and the ferry franchise was lost again. The town voted to sell its scow and skiff, and to let the horse-boat and the horses. The tolls of the Bridge Company were changed to the rates followed by the company until 1879.

The town, though again worsted, was not beaten. It appointed a committee to investigate the works of the Bridge Company, and to question whether their causeway was half bridging as the law demanded, and to prevent their operations if they could.

A fresh appeal for a restoration of the ferry was made in 1842, which appeal was granted; and the following year the ferry was reëstablished and run by the town.

The Bridge Company, determined to have the matter permanently settled, then carried it to the courts; the town was sued and beaten, but, assisted by many contributions from Hartford people, it appealed its case to the Supreme Court of the United States. The higher tribunal sustained the decision of the State courts. The gist of this decision is, that the new grant of the ferry to the town in 1842, by the General Assembly, was in violation of that body's contract with the Bridge Company in 1818, which suppressed the ferry. It decided that—whatever ancient privilege Hartford may have had in the ferry—East Hartford (which alone was party to the suit) had no other title than that acquired by its act of incorporation in 1783, which was subject to the pleasure of the General Assembly.

The town, seeing no further hope for its cause, except by some dereliction on the part of the Bridge Company, abandoned the field, and passed an indignant resolve to hold this " aggressive monopoly to a rigid compliance with its charter."

The town had to pay the Bridge Company $12,363.36 damages awarded by the courts.

In 1857 the Legislature ordered the Bridge Company to raise its causeway, and to add 250 feet to its bridging.

In 1869 it passed an act authorizing certain towns to purchase the bridge and causeway. The towns might associate themselves for that purpose; and the mayor and common council of Hartford, and the selectmen of the other towns, were to be a board of management; and the towns might obligate themselves for $150,000, with the right to appeal to the Superior Court to fix the price of the property, if the parties could not agree. But nothing has yet come of this.

In 1878 the free bridge question was again agitated, but with small result. The petition was continued to the next session of the General Assembly, and the towns authorized to report what action they would take in regard to the matter.

MILITARY AFFAIRS.

CHAPTER XIX.

1653-1865.

THE General Court passed the following vote in 1653:
"The inhabitants of the East side of the greate River are exempted from training with the Towns on the West side, this present time, & are to meete on the East side as Will: Hill shall appoint & traine their together, and so to continnue on theire training dayes untill the Courte take furder order: & Will: Hill is to returne the names of those that doe not meete according to appointment, as notis shall be given them."

From the date of this order until about the year 1850 our town had its annual "training days,"—days resplendent with commissioned tinsel, and yet often mortifying to official dignity with their slovenly presentment of a citizen soldiery in ragged homespun clothes, and with the most ridiculous substitutes for arms. Indeed, our old militia came to be known as the "rag toes," a name said to have been suggested by the appearance of our East Hartford company, a member of which, from Long Hill, came on parade barefooted and with a bandage around his toe. There was a time when training two days in each year, with a field muster in the fall, was obligatory; but each man came in the garb he chose, and shouldered a corn-stalk, an umbrella, or a musket, as pleased him best. Many quaint parades of this sort have passed through our streets, or tramped unsteadily about the convenient fields near by, to the rude inspiration of a drum and fife, and much to the delight of the assembled populace.

The principal training grounds were either upon the meadows in the fall, or upon Upper Quag Plains, or upon the once open field on the south side of Mill street—the latter conveniently near the old tavern that stood on the corner. The charges of the bar of this tavern were bravely met by every "trainer" who meant to thoroughly do his duty to the usages of the time. To drink three times before ten o'clock was a common thing on such days, and before night the training was very "general" in its character. Sometimes the companies took pains to uniform and equip themselves, and their appearance on muster days was tidy and creditable.

A gazetteer of 1819 says there were four infantry companies and one artillery company in East Hartford (and what is now Manchester) prior to the re-organization of 1816, and that afterwards there were two companies of infantry and one of artillery. We have been able to trace the organization of only one company of infantry, and that of the artillery company. The past-commanders of what was in 1824 the 4th Company, 1st Regiment Connecticut Infantry, as copied from a list found among the papers of Gen. S. L. Pitkin, and completed, so far as possible, by the writer, are as follows:

Hon. Ozias Pitkin.
Gov' William Pitkin.
Col. Joseph Pitkin, 1738.
Col. John Pitkin.
Hon. William Pitkin.
Russell Woodbridge, 1772.
Jonathan Roberts, 1786.
  (Capt. of Hockanum Co).
Col. Ashbel Stanley.
Joseph Carver, 1793.
Levi Goodwin.
Martin Pitkin, 1800.
John Pitkin, Jr., 1802-4.
Timothy Forbes?
Amos Pasko, 1805.
John Spencer, Jr., 1806-9.
Martin Stanley, 1810-13.
Joseph Goodwin, 1814-16.
Moses Ensign, Jr.
  (Formerly Capt. H'kanum Co).

Col. George Pitkin.
Elisha Pitkin, 1776.
Zebulon Bidwell.
  (Killed near Saratoga, 1777).
Stephen Roberts.
John Pitkin, Jr., 1786.
Joseph P. Jones, 1817-19.
Eli Olmsted, 1820-3.
Samuel L. Pitkin, 1823-5.
Samuel Williams, 1825-8.
Elisha Risley, 1828-9.
Charles Forbes, 1830-1.
George Barber, 1832-3.
Thomas C. Franklin, 1834-5.
Samuel Brewer, Jr., 1836-8.
Ashbel Brewer, 1839-41.
Sylvester Wiley, 1842.
S. A. Brewer, 1843-5.
Ira Anderson, 1846-7.
James Spencer, 1848.

This company was at first attached to the 19th Regiment, and remained a part of that regiment until the re-organization of 1816, when it was attached to the 1st Regiment. In 1830 it was returned as the 3d Company of the 25th Regiment, and so continued until 1848, when it appears as the 1st Regiment "riflemen."

A company was kept up in Manchester from 1848 to 1855. In 1862 there were no regiments organized in the State; a few scattered companies only retained their organization.

Some of the officers of our East Hartford company were promoted to higher stations, and a number of regimental officers were chosen from our town. This is indicated by the titles appended to some of the names in the foregoing list.

Jonathan Wells, of Hockanum, an officer of the Revolution, was lieutenant-colonel of the 19th Conn. Regt. in 1786; and Dr. Timothy Hall, also of Hockanum, was surgeon of that regiment.[†]

Shubael Griswold was lieutenant-colonel of the same regiment in 1800, and for several years thereafter. He was afterwards a general, as his grave-stone indicates.

Samuel Leonard Pitkin was lieutenant-colonel of the 25th Regiment in 1829, and colonel of the same from 1830 to 1835. He was appointed brigadier-general (1st Brigade) in 1835, and held that office for two years. He then became major-general of the 1st Division (1st and 2d Brigades) in 1837, and continued in office until 1839, when he became adjutant-general, an office to which he was re-appointed in 1840.

Elihu Geer, of our town, was colonel of the 1st Regiment, 1850–2. He afterwards held the office of brigadier-general from 1853 to '62.

Mr. Thomas Dowd was paymaster of the 1st Regiment in 1854.

Mr. Heman A. Tyler has held various offices in the present 1st Regiment, and in 1878 held the office of colonel in that regiment.

With the adoption of the commutation system the old picturesque training days passed away for ever, and only the quaint traditions of their absurdities remain. Some of the votes on record concerning the old militia organizations are curious. For instance, in 1701 the town of Hartford voted

MILITARY AFFAIRS. 201

that 40s. in the hands of the selectmen resulting from the sale of a town bull be expended for colors for the east side company. A standard held by our company was destroyed in 1822; it was one that had been entrusted to it by a member, and a certificate signed by the officers, and found among Gen. Pitkin's papers, was issued to set at rest certain malicious rumors regarding it, whatever they may have been.

THE ARTILLERY COMPANY.

An institution of the past was the old artillery company, for about twenty years attached to the 19th Regiment, and known as the Matross Company. It was organized by Elisha Pitkin, Esq., in 1797. Mr. Pitkin had the two cannons,—a four-pound and a six-pound brass piece,—cast at his mills at the Forge, Seth Clark making the molds, and the machinery to bore them out. They were mounted on carriages, and made a very formidable appearance on parade. The uniform of the members of this company consisted of a leathern cap, with a white feather and gilt cord and buttons; blue coat and pantaloons, with gilt cord and buttons, and a yellow sword-belt. The guns were stored for a long time in the old Merrow barn, which stood on the lot just south of Mr. Samuel G. Phelps' house. Afterwards they were stored in Scotland at Ebenezer Kimball's. One of them was split and torn from its trunnions while firing an election salute in Hillstown. Afterwards some enterprising person sold them both to a peddler for old brass, and the company obtained the use of a State piece—a six-pounder—giving bonds for its safe return.

This company was known as a matross company until 1812, when it was called the artillery company, being at this time attached to the 19th Regiment, infantry. In 1817 it was made the 3d Company in the 2d Regiment of light artillery. In 1825 it was called the 1st Company; it ceased to exist in 1853. Its commanders were:

George Pitkin, Jr., 1797–8.
Maj. Samuel Pitkin, 1800–2.
John Sage, 1803.
John Kennedy, 1805–11.
Nathan Pitkin, 1812.
Amherst Reynolds, 1813–15.
Col. Giles Olmsted, 1816.
William Jones, 1817.
Col. Aaron F. Olmsted, 1819.

William Porter, 1820.
Col. Solomon Olmsted, 1821–5.
Edward P. Harrington, 1826.
Col. Charles H. Olmsted, 1826–31.
Col. N. W. Spencer, 1838.
William C. Cowles, 1839–41.
Horace Shipman, 1842–3.
Ebenezer P. Kimball, 1844–7.
Martin O. Hills, 1848–53.

Some of these captains and lieutenants were promoted to higher offices, as their regimental titles indicate. Col. Giles Olmsted was major in 1818, and Joy H. Fairchild chaplain. Solomon Olmsted was major in 1826, and colonel in 1829–30. Andrew K. Goodwin was paymaster in 1837.

Of the absurdities and dissipations of the old field days of the militia much has been written, and, grotesquely as such scenes are usually painted, they are hardly exaggerated. Yet in its later days decency and order were evolved out of the crude system, and tales are told of grand field days, like that in our meadows in 1843, when General Pratt reviewed the militia of the State in the presence of Gen. "Tecumseh" Johnson, of Indian-fighting fame. That day a row of tents stretched far away up the bank of the Connecticut, and thousands of people assembled to hear the inspiriting music, and to watch the evolutions of the troops. General Johnson was the guest of the day, and the Hartford Light Guard waited upon him at his tent, as his body guard. Jones' tavern (now Morse's Hotel) was then the great rendezvous of the officers and their aids, and to its portal, now and then, would dash up some gilded son of honor, toss his rein to a bystander, and hasten in to communicate with his associate officers, or for some other purpose as mysterious to the boys outside. Gen. Pratt himself, it is said, deigned to reign up here and moisten his throat,—dry with the utterance of magnificent commands. Ah, we may well sigh for the departed splendor of those days!

THE WAR OF 1812.

Our part in the Revolution has been treated in another chapter. The war of 1812, so far as we know, called very few of our citizens beyond the borders of our State, excepting such as went upon adventurous cruises upon the seas. There was a draft of eight or nine persons from our town in 1813, to serve against the enemy, and the whole of our artillery company was called into service to assist in manning the fortifications at New London and on the east side of the Thames. The names of the infantry recruits we have been unable to ascertain. A pay-roll of the artillery company, preserved in the comptroller's office, shows the following names:

Pay-roll of Capt. Amherst Reynolds' company, showing the amount they received from the State in addition to the United States pay:—

Amherst Reynolds, captain.
Giles Olmsted, 1st lieut.
Sergeants:
Daniel Easton,
Solomon Spencer,
Timothy Buckland.
Corporals:
Augustus Stoughton,
Moses Ensign, Jr.
Musicians:
Timothy Deming (fifer),
Sylvester Treat,
Sala J. Rathbun (fifer),
Jemison Cady.
Matross:
Edward Warren,
Anson Cowles,
John Brewer,

Matross:
Nehemiah Abbey, Jr.,
James Warren,
Leonard Fox,
David Keney, Jr.,
Ephraim Warfield,
Marvin Evans,
Reuben Stedman,
William Baker,
Orrin Evins,
John O. Slater,
Leonard Hills,
Erastus Rathbun,
David Brainard,
Ebenezer G. Marble,
Stephen Gleason,
Harvey Risley,
Lewis Smith.

The commencement of this pay-roll was Aug. 3, 1813, and it ended Sept. 16, 1813,—covering a period of one month and fifteen days. It shows only the amount of compensation given by the State above what was paid by the United States government. The captain and first lieutenant got nothing; the sergeants and corporals one dollar per month, each receiving $1.50. Musicians and privates received two dollars per month, each man receiving $3.00. The total amount paid to the men was $75.79, some having served only a part of the time.

Mr. Timothy Deming, one of the last survivors of this company, pleasantly remembered his visit to the sea-shore, and said they had no arduous service, although some shots were exchanged with the British men-of-war which came in sight. They were on the Groton side of the Thames. Among other incidents of their service we have been told how a visitor at the fort was knocked down by a passing ball. He afterwards unearthed the missile, and was given a bottle of wine for it by the officers, who sent it immediately back to the enemy. Some of the men fired their muskets *at* the enemy, wishing at least to have something to tell the people at home.

"Our old friend," Horace Risley, was in the army on the northern border, but nothing of his experience could be elicited. It is said he left the army rather irregularly, and went among the Indians of his own accord. When approached on this topic he was darkly reticent, long after any need of concealment remained, it having become a habit with him.

Upon the ocean, some of our citizens assisted the common cause by embarking in privateering enterprises. Two generations ago, and earlier, there were many seafaring men among our people—the West India trade then coming directly to Hartford. Many horses and mules, etc., were shipped hence,— Col. George Pitkin making a business of buying.

Of the exploits of these during the War of 1812, we have been able to gather little information. Mr. Ozias Roberts, afterwards captain of merchantmen, went privateering under Capt. Josiah Griswold of Wethersfield, in the privateer "Blockade." This vessel was fitted out on the Connecticut River, and was owned by Thomas Belden and others. It carried six guns. After cruising for some time with little success, it was captured by a brig of war and taken to the Bermudas, and the crew were confined on a prison ship. Mr. Roberts and Dr. Wm. Cooley, of Manchester, surgeon, managed to escape, and were secreted by a negro until they found opportunity to return home.

Dr. Samuel Spring was in early life a merchant, and during the War of 1812 was in command of one of his own vessels, and was captured off the entrance of Chesapeake Bay, by the frigate Laurustinus. His pilot, crew, and cargo were taken off, and his vessel burned. On board the frigate Mr. Spring, by his cheerful, gentlemanly ways, soon won the favor of his captors, and was allowed to eat at their table, where his own provisions were generously served. The frigate pursued a French letter-of-marque out to sea, but did not overtake it. Returning, they bore down upon a vessel which Mr. Spring recognized as from Newburyport, Capt. John Caldwell master. He pleaded that his old townsman be allowed to go on his way unharmed, and for some reason was successful. His own freedom was also given him, and he sailed with Caldwell to Charleston, S. C. Thence he returned home, and ventured on another voyage. He reached Charleston, when an embargo was declared, and he returned home by stages.

The effect of the draft of 1813 was to wonderfully recruit the home militia—the governor, Hon. John Cotton Smith, having announced that none of the State troops were liable to the draft. We are told that nearly every man in our town became an active militia-man. There was an unusual muster and parade that fall near the old meeting-house. The parade was conducted on the green just east of it. Later, there were refreshments served in the meeting-house, and "something else," that was not kept in sight. Some drank till they were tipsy, and then threw cheese all about in the sacred place, and several good citizens, it is said, slept awhile, hidden away in the singers' seats. These afterwards stoutly laid the trouble to the cheese they had eaten.

WAR OF THE REBELLION.

In treating of events so recent as those of the war of 1861, it has been thought best to confine our record to the vote books of the town. Of the names and deeds of our citizens who took part in the struggle to preserve our nation, various records exist, among which is the printed catalogue of Connecticut Volunteers, and the "Soldiers Record," 1861 to 1865, in the town clerk's office. From these a list of our volunteers has been taken and appended to this chapter.

The first meeting of the town to provide for the equipment of volunteers, and for the support of their families, was held April 29, 1861. A spirit of eager patriotism is evident in the votes passed at this meeting; but under different requirements of the general government it became necessary to rescind most of them in regard to bounties, etc.

In July, 1862, a bounty of $100 was voted to three years' men, and, later, the same was extended to nine months' men, with $25 additional. Provision was made for the families of volunteers, and, in September, the selectmen were able to declare the quota full without resort to a draft.

In April, 1863, the town voted to issue bonds, not to exceed $15,000, to cover its indebtedness and its liabilities; and $15,000 was appropriated the following August to enable a committee to relieve the drafted men according to their circumstances,—no one to receive over $300. The taxes of volunteers and of drafted men were abated while they continued in the service.

The call of the President for 500,000 additional men was considered in July, 1864. A bounty of $200 was voted to every man who had or should enlist personally or by substitute so as to count on the quota under this call. In September $300 additional bounty was voted to volunteers, or to persons furnishing substitutes, provided no man should receive within $200 of what he actually paid.

This year the town voted to issue bonds to the further amount of $35,000. Also to pay the mother or guardian of each child of every soldier who died in the service the sum of fifty dollars for one year. January 9, 1865, a substitute was to be furnished for every man who paid the selectmen $200.

The number of men who enlisted, or for whom substitutes were procured, with the amount of bounties and commutation money paid, are given below. They are taken from the "war book" kept by the selectmen, and are reasonably accurate— some omissions in the record being supplied by a computation of averages.

Under the first bounty of $10, with $10 a month pay from the town, there enlisted ten men, to whom was paid $545

Under call of July 5, 1862, for 400,000 men, there enlisted 139 men, who received about $100 each (some amounts not carried out), ... 13,900

Under call of Aug. 4, 1863, for 800,000 men for nine months' service, there enlisted 59 men, to whom was paid about $125 each, ... 5,800

Paid commutation money on draft of Aug., 1863, 24 men, partly paid by the men and partly by the town, in varying proportions, ... 7,200

Under draft of July, 1864, by vote of Sept. 21st, each man paid $200, the town paid for each $300 —for 59 men, ... 27,555

Under vote of January 9, 1865, 9 men had furnished substitutes and received from $150 to $200 from the town, ... 1,585

Under the same vote there were 11 men who received about $200 each from the town, and who paid $200 each, beside, for substitutes . . . 4,450

Making a total of 311 men on all calls, and a total expenditure of money by individuals and by the town for recruits, ... 61,035

Seventy families of soldiers drew . . 9,698

Making a total expenditure, by individuals and by the town, of $70,733

War debt bonds were issued by the town to the amount of $41,750

Of which there remains unpaid in 1878, . . 9,000

The "Soldiers' Record" in the town clerk's office gives the number of men who enlisted from this town voluntarily as 210 ; and gives only 51 men as drafted or furnishing substitutes, a total of 261 men in all. The names of the substitutes of many who paid commutation money are not entered in this record, and the names of reënlisted men are entered but once, which may account for the discrepancy.

A fine monument was erected in the Center Burying

Ground in 1868 (mainly by the aid of voluntary subscriptions) to the memory of those soldiers who died in the war, and annual memorial services are held at its base on "decoration" or "memorial day," the town giving one hundred dollars each year to assist the surviving comrades in procuring music, and in meeting the expenses of the occasion. On that day, while the band plays a dirge at the monument, the veterans file slowly away along the avenues of the burying ground, laying flowers upon the graves of all their old associates in arms who have gone to rest. Usually there is an address delivered afterward, and a short march upon the street, followed by a table of refreshments at Elm Hall.

LIST OF VOLUNTEERS FROM EAST HARTFORD, 1861-1865,

With Name of Connecticut Regiments to which they were attached (see Catalogue Conn. Volunteers). Those marked with (*) are on the Soldiers' Monument.

Aldenhofen, Joseph, 5th,
*Allen, John F., 10th,
   Died at Morris Isl., S. C., Oct., '63,
Amidon, Chas. D., Corp. 21st,
Arnold, John F., 8th Missouri,
Bailey, Josiah B., 1st Art.,
Burnham, Spencer H., 7th,
   Wounded May 14, 1864,
Bond, Joseph L., 7th,
Bidwell, Julius, 1st Cav.,
Bidwell, William E., 16th,
Bidwell, Henry E., 12th,
Bantly, Anton, 6th,
Bantly, Francis, 6th,
   Died at Andersonville Aug., '64.
Brewer, John M., 16th,
Brewer, William H., 21st,
Brewer, Ralph C., 21st,
*Brewer, George E., 21st,
   Died at Andersonville June, '64,
*Brewer, Jason F., 21st,
   Wounded Pet'sb'g, died Sept., '66,
*Button, Leroy M., 21st,
   Killed at Petersb'g July 30, '64,

Button, Leander W., 25th,
Button, Jerome K., 25th,
*Button, William, 25th,
   Died April, '63, of wounds rec'd at Irish Bend.
Brogator, Antonio V., 10th,
Barnum, Phineas, 11th,
   Wounded May 16, 1864,
Best, Valentine, musician, 11th,
Bennett, Edwin, 11th,
   Wounded May 16, 1864,
Bissell, Harrison H., 21st,
Bryant, William B., Corp., 21st,
Barnard, Daniel B., 25th,
Bliss, Walter J., 25th,
Brown, Jacob C. (col'd), 29th,
Cowles, William J., 1st Art.,
Cowles, Henry S., Corp., 1st Art.,
*Cowles, J. Francis, Corp., 21st,
   Died Aug., '64, of wounds rec'd at Cold Harbor,
Champlin, Henry A., 7th,
Corbett, Daniel, 10th,
Carlin, John, 12th,

Cleary, John, 16th,
  Wounded Sept. 2, 1862,
Currin, Michael, 20th,
Craw, Charles, 21st,
Carter, A. Russell, 21st,
Cleveland, John E., 21st,
Case, Andrew A., Corp., 21st,
Casey, Chester, 25th,
*Carroll, John F., Sergt., 24th,
  Killed at Port Hudson, May, '63,
Chalker, Daniel B., 25th,
Cotton, Leander, Corp., 21st,
Cadwell, George, 11th,
Dailey, Bartholomew, 11th,
Deming, Henry O., 13th,
Douglas, William W., 21st,
Erving, Waldo, 6th,
Elmer, Elizur B., 13th,
Edwards, William, 13th,
Eagan, Thomas, 24th,
Easton, Arago, Corp., 11th,
Flynn, Andrew,
Fitch, Charles J., 1st Cav.,
*Forbes, Andrew J., 10th,
  Killed Aug. 16, '64, at Sharpsb'g,
Forbes, Charles, 21st,
Forbes, Monroe, 21st,
Forbes, George H., 25th,
Forbes, John W., N. J. Reg't,
*Flint, Alvin, 21st,
  Died in service, 1863,
*Flint, Alvin, Jr., 11th,
  Killed at Antietam, Md., Sep., '62,
*Flint, George B., 21st,
  Died at Falmouth, Va., Jan., '63,
Frome, Otto, 21st,
Ferner, William, 22d,
Francis, George (col'd), 29th,
*Francis, Samuel W. (col'd), 30th,
  Died in hospital,
Griswold, John D., 1st Art.,
Grassell, George A., 21st,
Garrison, Isaac, 21st,
Griswold, George T., 21st,

Goodwin, George H., Sergt., 25th,
  Afterwards Quarter-Master 29th,
Graham, Francis A., 25th,
Holmes, Theo. J., Chap., 1st Cav.,
Hills, Richard M., 1st Cav.,
Hills, Ferdinand, 25th,
Hills, Chester M., 25th,
Hills, John B., 25th,
Hughs, Lewis G., Corp., 1st Art.,
Harding, Thomas H., 1st Art.,
Haley, John, 1st Art.,
Haling, William H., 25th,
Handel, Christian, 6th,
Hollister, William G., 7th,
Hollister, Morgan, 21st,
Harris, Henry W., 8th,
House, Marshall D., 16th,
House, Elisha E., 25th,
Hawkins, Daniel S., 21st,
Hayden, Edward W., N. Y. 61st,
Harman, Adamson J., 25th,
Jones, Thomas, 1st Cav.,
Jackson, Calvin, 7th,
  Captured June 2, 1864,
Jordan, Joseph, Capt., 21st,
Judson, Albert A., 21st,
James, Thomas, 10th,
Kenney, Patrick, 1st Cav.,
Kramar, Frederick, 1st Art.,
Kramar, Ferdinand, 25th,
Kimball, Samuel M., 21st,
Kimball, Clarence, 21st,
Kostenbader, John, 22d,
Lyman, William C., 1st Cav.,
Lathrop, Frederick O., 6th,
*Lucas, Clinton G., 7th,
  Killed Oct.7, '64, near Deep Bot'm,
Long, Julius F., 13th,
Luce, Henry B., Corp., 21st,
Luce, Otis F., 21st,
Lord, Walter T., 25th,
Lathrop, Charles W., 25th,
Lewis, David, 25th,
Lewis, William J. (col'd), 29th,

210 HISTORY OF EAST HARTFORD.

Loomis, Joel A.,
McWilliams, Henry, 1st Cav.,
McCormick, John, 2d,
McGrath, Henry, 11th,
McLelland, Matthew, 11th,
McLelland, William J., 21st,
McLelland, Robert, 21st,
McMann, Miles, 24th,
Moore, Thomas, 1st Cav.,
Moore, Arthur P., 25th,
Moran, Michael, 25th,
Moldaner, Valentine, 27th,
Mattler, Abram, 12th,
   Died Aug. 26, 1862, in La.,
Mandeville, Frederick G., 16th,
*Munsell, William S., 21st,
   Killed near Drury's Bl'ff May, '64,
Miller, Titus (col'd), 29th,
Norton, James, 15th,
Newberry, Samuel, 21st,
Olmsted, Arthur G., Sergt., 21st,
Olmsted, Horace B., Lieut., 25th,
*Olmsted, Edgar C., 13th,
   Died Feb. 2, 1865,
*Olmsted, Evelyn H., 21st,
   Died Dec., 1862,
Olmsted, Elihu, 21st,
Olmsted, Conrad S., 3d U.S. Reg'lars,
Pfeiffer, Ortmar, 6th,
   Wounded July 18, 1863,
*Pratt, Samuel A., 7th,
   Died Oct., '62, at Hilton Head,
Pratt, Dodridge, 12th,
Parker, John B., 11th,
Parsons, Norman D., 21st,
Peaslee, Loverin, 12th,
Porter, A. Leroy, 20th,
Porter, Nelson L., 21st,
Proctor, Jared, 21st,
Pearl, Jared, Jr., 21st,
Persons, Henry S., 25th,
Quimby, Daniel W., 21st,
Roberts, Richard W., 1st,
   Afterwards Capt. 25th,
*Roberts, Edmund M. B., 1st Bat'y,
   Died June 24, 1862, at Beaufort,

Roberts, Hamlet F., Lieut., 21st,
Roberts, Joseph, 21st,
Riley, William E., Capt., 1st Cav.,
Riley, Edmund D., 1st Art.,
Rockwell, Lester A., 1st Cav.,
   Captured March, 1865,
Reynolds, Peter, 1st Cav.,
Risley, Sanford L., 1st Art.,
Risley, Julius A., 21st,
Risley, Eugene, 25th,
Risley, Charles O., 25th,
Robinson, John, 5th,
Reid, Robert K., 7th,
   Wounded.
Reid, William, 7th,
   Wounded May 4, '64.
Rowell, George D., Corp., 21st,
Ruoff, George, 22d,
Rock, John, 24th,
Ryan, Charles H., 2d Art.,
   Wounded Sept. 19, '64.
Saunders, Thomas, 1st Cav.,
Skinner, Hervey D., 1st Bat'y,
Symonds, Charles A., 1st Art.,
Symonds, Sylvester, 25th,
Symington, John, 1st Art.,
Stowell, George, 1st Art.,
Schoemehl, Carl, 1st Art.,
Smith, Jason, 25th,
Smith, Richard, 25th,
Scarborough, John W., 5th,
   Supposed killed May, '64.
Stewart, James E., 7th,
Stewart, Robert, 10th,
Stewart, David (col'd), 29th,
Sloan, Adrian P., 7th,
Shields, Peter, 10th,
   Killed in action Aug. 14, '64.
Speirs, Robert, 16th,
   Wounded.
Spafford, George L., 21st,
Shepard, Jason J., 21st,
Stearns, Oliver E., 21st,
   Died at Mansfield, Conn., Sept.'64.
Schmidt, Ferdinand, 22d,
Schoonhann, Casper, 22d,

Sweeney, Christopher, 24th,
Strickland, William W., 25th,
Snow, Samuel A., 21st,
* Thomas, George D., 10th, [ston.
   Died Dec. 7, '62, of w'nds at King-
Tremer, Joseph, 10th,
Taylor, Charles G., 11th,
Tripp, Samuel N., 12th,
Turner, Jacob A., Sergt., 25th,
Talcott, Daniel L. (mus'n), 25th,
* Vibert, Geo. N., Harris Light Cav.,
   Died Nov. '62.
Vibert, Edward, 1st Cav.,
Vibert, Oscar B., 7th,
Vaughn, George L., 21st,
Wadsworth, William, 11th,
Wolfer, Simeon, 6th,
Wakefield, Elhanan, 21st,
Wilcox, Benjamin F., Corp., 25th,
Wright, Henry, 21st,
* Wright, Francis H., 16th,
   Died at Falmouth, Jan. '63.
* Warren, Marshall E., 25th Mass.,
   Died at Chesap'ke Hosp., Oct. '64.
* Woehrle, Charles A., 7th, ['64.
   Died at Ft. Trumbull, Conn., Feb.

The following are names of drafted men and of substitutes furnished by drafted men:

Brown, Edward, 5th,
Brown, Henry, 12th,
Bowen, Charles A., 5th,
Burke, Charles, 8th,
Burke, Michael, 15th,
Carpenter, Daniel G., 13th,
Clark, Benjamin, 12th,
   Died at Hilton Head July, '65.
Dignan, John T., 1st Art.,
Dallye, Ernest, 13th,
Donnelly, James, 13th,
Erving, James, 1st Art.,
Elmer, George, 13th,
Faraden, Frank, 7th,
   Wounded Oct. 13, '64.
Freeman, George (col'd), 29th,
Gordon, James, 1st Art.,
Gaynor, Thomas S., 13th,
Howard, Charles H., 10th, ['65.
   Died at Point of Rocks, Va., Jan.
Howard, Charles, 1st Art.,
Hanley, John, 1st Art.,
Harris, George, 6th,
Harris, James, 12th,
Harper, Henry, 13th,
Hanly, John, 20th,
Hutton, Andrew, 13th,
Jones, Charles, 20th,
Jones, Henry F., 5th,
Jones, Thomas, 1st Art.,
Johnson, Charles, 1st Art.,
Keleher, John, 13th,
King, William, 20th,
Larave, Peter, 7th,
Lenthard, Carl F., 8th,
   Killed May, '64, at Petersburg.
Manyote, Francis, 5th,
Martinneu, Gilbert, 7th,
Myer, Emil, 12th,
McGregor, Peter, 13th,
Newton, Horace, 13th,
O'Brien, John, 12th,
Pombriand, Paul, 7th,
Reese, John, 1st Art.,
Russell, Robert E., 12th,
Sullivan, Owen, 12th,
Sullivan, Patrick, 13th,
Sullivan, John, 13th,
Singer, Martin, 12th,
Stino, William, 13th,
Smith, John, 20th,
Spruce, Charles (col'd), 29th,
Shanly, William,
Smith, Franklin, 1st Art.,
Tracy, James, 6th,
Tarrac, Camile, 10th,
Whitney, Joseph D., 13th,
Willis, James A., 13th,
And probably others.

OLD HOUSES.

CHAPTER XX.

FROM the first inception of the purpose to study the history of our town we have had in view a chapter which should describe the early homes of our ancestors; but in its preparation we have met with many difficulties, the records being no certain guides, and have reached no complete knowledge at last. We give nevertheless what fragmentary information we have gathered, hoping some time to supplement it with further facts.

The earliest houses built by the first settlers were small, and usually covered with a thatch of bark, reeds, or straw. The combustible nature of their material made fires frequent. One of the early votes of the town of Hartford required each house to have a "ladder or tree," to reach within two feet of the roof. "Chimney-lookers" or viewers, were regularly appointed, and strict orders were passed that chimneys should be frequently burned out. Many years later (1784) we find smokes (spelled "smoaks"), afterwards called fire-places, subject to taxation. They were classed as first, second, third, and fourth rate smokes.

Typical old-fashioned houses were built later, low upon the ground, with two large rooms and an immense central chimney between them; a low sloping roof at the rear, called a lean-to, usually covered the kitchen and pantry and bed-room. These houses stood length-wise to the street, with a shallow front yard, or sometimes none at all. Usually the cellar was dug under the north rooms only. A long well-sweep showed over the roof at the rear of the house. Often a gambrel roof shut steeply down over the front of the house, through which protruded dormer windows, like great blinking frog's eyes.

The vast chimney afforded fire-places in all the lower rooms and often in each of the chambers. Occasionally these were set at an angle in the corner of the room with pleasant effect. Below they were furnished with cranes and pot-hooks and extension hangers to hold the immense kettles for trying lard, or melting tallow for candles, or for culinary operations; and there were ovens and ash-holes in the lower part of the chimney, and frequently a blackened smoke-closet, for curing meat, in the chambers or the attic. Mysterious cupboards and caverns have been found in them also, when taken down, which no one could explain. In front of the chimney was usually a small hall-way with a stair-case ascending sharply by three cramped angles to the landing directly overhead. The outer door of the house was oftenest a double one, sometimes in upright sections, sometimes divided horizontally, that the upper half might be opened to admit the light and air. When the sections were upright they were often pierced near the top by queer little eye-like holes for lighting the hall. The handle and knocker of the door were of elaborate pattern; and generally a wooden cornice or pattern of scroll work surmounted the portal, with something of quaint ginger-bread or honey-combed ornamentation under the heavy eaves. Larger houses were built two stories high beside the great gambrel roof, which covered a capacious garret, as in Dr. Williams' house, elsewhere described.

The rooms of the houses were ceiled across the chimney front with wide panels of yellow pine, not always painted. The corner posts and ceiling-beams were cased and sometimes heavily molded. The frames of these old houses were prodigiously strong, and covered with oak planking, upon the outside of which the clapboards were nailed, and the lath and plastering were placed directly upon them within. The walls were often not more than three inches thick.

Of the earliest houses in town, we have already mentioned that of William Pitkin (1661), which stood on the meadow-bank near the railroad. This was fortified against the Indians. His son, William, built about twenty-five rods from Main street, a little southwest of the house of the late Capt. John Pitkin.

William Hills, one tradition has it, settled about eighty rods south of Mr. Overton's, on Tobacco avenue, before 1653. Another says his house stood a little way north of the old Hockanum school site. The latter seems most probable, though he may have occupied both.

Thomas Burnham lived just across the street from Mr. Julius Burnham's present residence, settling here about 1659. His house is described elsewhere. The house occupied by Mr. Samuel P. Burnham is the oldest Burnham house now standing. Here lived Joshua Burnham, cashier of the U. S. Bank, at Hartford. The old house on the hill, opposite Mr. N. L. Anderson's, was once occupied by Cornelius Burnham, perhaps as early as 1759. Phineas Burnham lived in the old house which gave place to Mr. Z. Arthur Burnham's residence (once Mr. W. Alexander's).

Edwards Andrews lived on "Pigeon Hill," just east of Dowd's Grove, near Willow Brook, before 1679. This property afterwards went, by marriage, to the Williams family, and their descendants have lived in this neighborhood ever since.

The Treats also acquired land near here, by marriage, and lived near the meadow hill in Dowd's Grove. Traces of their house cellars still remain.

Matthias Treat lived later in the little old house that lately went to ruin on Tobacco avenue, near Main street. It was a quaint cabin, about half its space being filled by a great clay-built chimney.

South of Colt's Ferry landing are sites of old houses,—the "Perkins place," Daniel Brewer's, and others of later date.

John Crow built early, near the Ozias Roberts homestead, and an old well, long disused, and covered by a stone, exists there, with currant bushes growing north of the barn. Crow owned much land, his lot extending north to the neighborhood of "Smith's Lane," and south across the Hockanum, and eastward to the three mile's end. Crow Hill, in the river swamp, north of Mr. Frank Roberts' house, was named after him. His house site is still called by some of the older people the Eddy lot—why, we do not know.

William Roberts lived on the meadow hill, at the foot of Smith's Lane, about 1668, and his cellar hollow may still be seen there. His son, Benjamin, lived on the Hezekiah Roberts place. He brought up his family in the rear L of that house, which is very old and has a vast chimney. He afterwards built his main house, with a cellar having unusually solid walls, and a staircase down which hogsheads of rum could be, and probably were, rolled, for some of our citizens were West India traders in those days. His son, George, built the house on the Ozias Roberts place for his home.

Dr. Eliphalet Williams' house was built by Benjamin Roberts about 1750. It is described elsewhere (see page 137).

Deacon Joseph Olmsted, our first deacon, lived on the meadow hill, in an old house on the site now occupied by the house of the late Mr. Ashbel Olmsted. He was the first of the Olmsteds who settled in town. Here at a later day lived Elihu Olmsted, who died in 1844.

William Olmsted, a surveyor and public man, lived east of Elihu Olmsted, on Main street, in the house later occupied by Persius Olmsted, and now by Mr. Arthur P. Moore. He died in 1822.

The Capt. Aaron Olmsted house, lately burned, stood on the corner of Main street and the Bridge Road, and dated back about a century. It had a long L in the rear, and, when first built, a gambrel roof, but this was changed to a gable roof, adding a third story to the house. It was long the home of the Olmsteds. The first piano ever brought into town was burned in this house.

Epaphras Olmsted, an old cavalry man of the Revolution, lived on the present site of the First Congregational Church. He died in 1836. Jonathan Olmsted lived on this site before him.

Gideon Olmsted, a privateer of the Revolution, lived in an old house where now stands the residence of Mr. R. A. Chapman.

The house once occupied by Capt. Joseph Goodwin, and now standing on the lane east of the post-office, is one of the oldest remaining in town. It once stood south of Mr. A. A.

Waterhouse's, and was occupied by Caleb Goodwin, who was a hypochondriacal bachelor, and died in 1769. It was moved to the site of the present house of Mr. S. O. Goodwin about the year 1800, and repaired. Afterwards it was moved to its present site. Joseph Goodwin, Sr., lived in the old brown house, which, in 1876, gave place to the house of the writer. Goodwin's store on Main street, for many years our post-office, dates from the time of the Revolution or thereabout. Its rear door came from the old Caleb Goodwin house. Its front door was formerly very capacious, and divided horizontally into two sections, and fastened with a stout wooden bar.

Governor Pitkin lived in a house on the site now occupied by Mr. L. D. Richardson, on Main street. He died in 1769. The house was unpainted and brown, and had a long "lean-to" roof in the rear; its chimney was wholly of hewed stone.

Col. Joseph Pitkin lived in the house now occupied by Mr. W. H. Olmsted. It was later owned by Capt. Martin Stanley, and later by Mr. Walter Pitkin. An oak tree in front of it is thought to be a survivor of the primeval forest. On the south side of this place Capt. Stanley built a hat shop, where he made hats for thirty or forty years. This hat shop was moved away and made a house on the mill road, by Mr. Frank Tryon. In the house next north of Mr. William H. Olmsted's lived Mr. David Pitkin.

Ashbel Pitkin lived in the house now fitted up by Mr. Wm. Sargent (late J. C. Bull place).

In the house now owned by Mr. Loren C. Terry once lived Timothy Pitkin, and after him, for a time, Elisha Pitkin, Esq. This house was shingled on the day of the battle of Bunker Hill, and was not re-shingled until a few years ago. Elisha Pitkin built the house on the corner of the South Meadow Road, and here Dr. Edward Pitkin lived after him. The house now occupied by Mr. Henry Bryant, the artist, was once owned by Mr. George Pitkin. The house next north was Mr. Charles Pitkin's, the humorist; and before him was his father's, Mr. Nathan Pitkin. There was once a clothier's shop north of this house. On the hill just back of this site once stood the house of Epaphras Pitkin, the cellar being still traceable. A wag rapped Mr. Pitkin up one night to tell him that, as he was passing, it struck him what a favorable chance he had to drain his cellar, and then hurried away—as he had need! Roger Pitkin, 2d, lived just south of the present railroad, on the corner of Orchard and Prospect streets. This was known as the Joshua Pitkin place. Ezekiel Pitkin, son of Roger, 2d, built a house on the site that was later occupied by his son, Dennison P., for his home.

Col. George Pitkin lived in the Jas. Root house, now Comstock's. A clothier's shop stood north of the house. Col. William Pitkin (4th) lived on the site now occupied by Mr. Wm. G. Comstock. His house is still standing, having been moved down on "Poudrette Lane," on the J. C. Bull place.

The house next south of the silversmith's shop, on Main street, was once occupied by Col. John Pitkin, who was a lieutenant-colonel in the expedition against Crown Point in 1755. Afterwards Capt. John Pitkin lived there.

Maj. Samuel Pitkin lived on the site of the house of Mr. John B. Smith. He had a rich garden, filled with choice fruits and flowers. He died in 1839. His son, Gen. Samuel L. Pitkin, lived in the house nearly opposite Mr. E. W. Hayden's. Later this was used for a parsonage. Mr. Osmyn Pitkin lived (1800) in the house next north of Mr. R. A. Chapman's. Others of the Pitkins settled in Manchester.

Deacon Timothy Cowles, the first of the name here, lived on the site now occupied by Mr. L. Carney, before 1700. Here, after him, lived Dea. William Cowles, until 1771.

Levi Goodwin once owned a tavern at the north end of Main street, standing between the roads, where Mr. Ralph A. Olmsted's house now stands. He afterwards built the house now owned by Mr. Aaron G. Olmsted, and lived there before 1800.

His son Buckland Goodwin built the house opposite Mr. Aaron G. Olmsted's. It was owned later by Col. Solomon Olmsted; then by Mr. Albert C. Raymond; and at present by Mr. William H. Boyle.

George Gilman lived (before 1800) north of the brook, in

the house now owned by Mr. John Whalen (once E. W. Hayden's).

In the house next north once lived Jacob Williams. He died in 1828.

Joshua Williams lived behind the two trees on Mr. Ackley's lot, above Mr. Patrick Burnham's.

Deacon Israel Williams lived on the old road, on the place lately owned by Mr. Ralzaman Gilman.

Mr. Jonah Williams lived in the house now owned by Mr. Elijah Ackley. He died in 1846.

Serg't Elias Gilman (1751 and earlier) lived in the fork of the Ellington and Mill roads in Podunk.

Gilmans also lived on the site now owned and occupied by Mr. N. L. Anderson for his house.

On the south side of the site of Mr. William M. Stanley's homestead once lived Mr. Ashbel Cowles, Sr. On the north side, Mr. Reuben Cowles.

Anson Cowles lived in the second house north of Mr. William H. Olmsted's.

The old Cowles house, south of Mr. W. M. Stanley's, was once the school-house of the Second North District and stood in the highway, near the site of the present school building.

On what is now known as the Stillman Putnam place once lived Theodore Stanley, a prominent man in his day. Here, before him, lived Lieut. William Stanley, the first of the name who settled in our town. He was great-grandfather of our present selectman, William M. Stanley, Esq.

Across the way, on the Norman Webster place, lived Col. Ashbel and Elisha Stanley. They had a clothier's shop north of the house, and were engaged in that business. This shop was afterwards moved to the north side of the Charles Pitkin house, and the business carried on by James Stanley and Nathan Pitkin until 1817.

John Hurlburt lived in the house now occupied by Mr. James Bancroft, next north of the railway station, prior to 1778.

Timothy Olmsted, a man of much musical talent, lived in a house which stood on the west side of Main street just south of the railroad. He composed many pieces and went about the State as a teacher. He was fifer in the Boston relief company of 1775, and chorister in the church. He afterwards moved to Hartland and went "music mad."

Gen. Shubael Griswold lived at the corner of Orchard and Main streets in the house now occupied by Mr. John L. Olmsted. He had a store on the corner. This site was occupied in 1776 by Benjamin's tavern. West of it, on "Benjamin's Lane," stood a weaver's shop owned also by the Benjamins. Prior to his location here, Gen. Griswold kept store in a house near where Mr. R. A. Chapman's now stands, and lived in the house now Mr. Norman Webster's.

The old Wells tavern on Main street dates back many years. It was formerly owned by the Woodbridges, and in 1817 was kept by a Mr. Buckler. It was a busy place in the old stage-coach days, with their through travel, and the scene of many sleigh-rides and dances.

"Uncle Russ," an odd character described in the *Elm Leaf* of July 18, 1863, once lived in a poor hut, half underground, where the academy building now stands. He was the last of his family, and clung thus literally to the soil of his ancestors until removed to the poor-house.

(Another odd character, known as Captain Jack, lived for some months in a hut built into the swamp hillside, north of Mr. Nathaniel Warren's, on Silver Lane. He was often inebriated, and usually morose when so; still he sought companionship in his sprees, during which his hermitage furnished a safe retreat from the public eye.)

Dr. Samuel Flagg (1770) lived in the house now occupied by Mr. Samuel G. Phelps. The small house next south was the Doctor's office, and was once attached to the house.

The vacant lot next south of the above, now owned by Mr. E. O. Goodwin, was once known as the Merrow place, and was occupied by the houses now standing on the "sand-pit" lot, east of the burying-ground. One of these buildings was an old yellow store, with heavy down-dropping window shutters. The Merrows also owned a house behind the large maple trees south of Mr. Joseph Merriman's residence. On a slight eminence, now also in Mr. Merriman's grounds, and near the front of his mansion, stood an old house amid old-fashioned shrubbery,—once the home of the prominent Meakins family.

Next south of Mr. Merriman's door yard, on the site once owned by Mr. Joseph Clark, stood the Metcalf house, formerly occupied by Capt. Amherst Reynolds, of the artillery company, in 1813. Earlier this site was occupied by the Olmsteds. A little wagon-shop which stood on this place was moved to Prospect street, and became a currier's shop; afterwards it was several times moved,—was a shoe shop south of Mr. Waterhouse's, was a part of Phelps' store on the corner of Main and Mill streets; and is now the back part of Mr. John Stewart's house.

Thomas Spencer built a house near the site of the present post-office before 1761. Afterwards Lemuel White—"'Squire White"—lived here. The latter was a prominent magistrate, and had an office east of his house, where the store and hall now stand. Next south of this was the Phelps tavern described elsewhere.

Col. Giles Olmsted lived in an old house on the site of that lately owned by Mr. L. T. Pitkin, nearly opposite the Center church. It was a story-and-a-half house, with a low-browed gambrel roof, and had a series of tumble-down sheds in the rear.

The Polly Kendall house stood just north of Mr. A. C. Raymond's present residence on the corner of Central avenue,—it was similar to the house last described, and had luxuriant lilac bushes about it, and abundant "Bouncing Betsies" in the street.

Between these last two houses (on land now Raymond park) was the Wing house, once occupied by David Deming. Mr. Deming's wagon-shop stood just south of it. This place with other land on the south has been purchased by Mr. A. C. Raymond, who intends to lay out a park upon it, on the corner of Central avenue.

On Burnside avenue (then Bigelow Lane) lived William Bigelow, in the large house now standing on the south corner on Main street; he was a man of business, and acquired considerable property. Daniel Bigelow before him was one of those deeding Burnside avenue to the town. Samuel Hurlburt once kept a tavern on this site.

On this avenue settled the numerous Bidwells, some of whose descendants occupy the sites of their ancestral homes. In the first fork of the roads, going east, stood the house of Enodias Bidwell,—a sharp-roofed house with small diamond-paned windows.

Henry Cotton bought the tavern house and store just north of the road here, of the heirs of Enodias Bidwell in 1832. This is an old fashioned brick mansion now.

In the old house, west of the brook, on Burnside avenue, once lived Moses Bidwell. He died in 1840.

A similar old house, some rods east of the brook, now owned by Mr. E. F. Stager, was once Russell Bidwell's. He died in 1828.

The house next east of this, owned by Oliver W. Elmer, was the homestead of Jonathan Bidwell. He died in 1815.

Next west of Cotton's tavern stands the home of Makens Bemont, one of the few men in town who owned a chaise in 1800, an indication of his conspicuous wealth. This house has a gambrel roof, with dormer windows, and is a typical old-fashioned house.

West of this, and next east of the house of Mr. Ralph G. Spencer, was the old Russell Abbey place, so called, a small story-and-a-half brown house, hidden in lilac bushes. The lane next west of this was made a "right-of-way" by the persistence of people in passing across to the station.

On the south side of this avenue was the old George Burnham house, since made over into Mr. Horace B. Olmsted's. Next west of this stood an ancient red house, with a gable roof and low "lean-to," which has given place to the new house of Mr. E. C. Hills.

On this avenue, west of Mr. C. M. Bidwell's and nearly opposite "cow lane," was once a little hill, known as Benton Hill. On the north side of the road on this hill, under its elm tree, was the home of Mr. Elisha Benton, who was a soldier of the Revolution, as well as a poet, as we have seen.

In Burnside early settled the Eastons and the Forbes, and the Spencers at Spencer Hill, and on Spencer street beyond. At the foot of Benjamin's Lane (now Orchard street), on the southeast corner, lived Thomas Case, about the year 1800, or earlier.

South of here, on the corner of Mill street, stood the old house of the Bucklands, dating back nearly to the earliest settlements. It had a secret cellar under its east front room, entered by a trap-door from above. Its common cellar was on the west side.

On the west side of Main street, a little way north from the old meeting-house, stood the house of Jonathan Pratt, to which the "meetin' folk" resorted on cold Sunday noons, and to which the society meetings sometimes adjourned. Mr. Pratt was a tanner. He died in 1755. His son, Eliab Pratt, built a house on Silver Lane in 1740, on the site of the house now occupied by Mr. George W. Pratt. This house was taken down about 1858. Eighty rods south of this house stood an Indian wigwam, inhabited (about 1775–80) by a remnant of one of the tribes once living about here.

Russell Smith built a house on Silver Lane, nearly opposite to Eliab Pratt's and about the same time. West of this, on the corner of the mill road, lived Nehemiah Smith, in a house now no longer standing. This house had a double gallery across the front, which faced the west.

Jonathan Risley lived south of Silver Lane, near the southwest corner of Mr. G. W. Pratt's land. His son Timothy lived here after him. Timothy Risley was father of Eri Risley. Other Risleys lived on Main street near Willow Brook.

On Silver Lane, also, stood the old Benjamin Hills house (1731), now owned by Mr. Benjamin Sisson; here stood, too, the houses of John Hazeltine, and John Abbey, and, near the mill road, the old Roberts house, where Mr. Frank Roberts' house now stands.

The house next east of Mr. Benjamin Sisson's, lately owned by the Bidwells, was once owned by Lieut. David Little, who was committee on Sunday boating in 1784. Dr. Bidwell kept a tavern in it.

West side of Main street, south of the Hockanum River, lived the Warrens. Dr. Warren ran a cider-brandy still on the premises now owned by Mr. Horace Williams.

Capt. Samuel Wells lived in Hockanum (1700), in the place now owned by Mr. Reuben Brewer. He owned a tract of land, we are told, one-half mile wide, lying just north of Brewer Lane, and extending east to the three miles' end. His son, Capt. Samuel Wells, Jr., was a lieutenant in the army in 1757, during the French war. Col. Jonathan Wells lived on the James Hills place; Jonathan Wells, Jr., in what was lately the Levi Moody place.

The old house owned by Mr. Joseph Treat is a quaint old mansion, with a basement work-shop, and a gambrel roof with dormer windows. It has a large hall chamber, in which once stood an antique loom.

Hockanum was also the early home of a branch of the Roberts family, whose descendants still live here.

Jonathan Hills, Esq., lived near the meadow gate in Hockanum. He owned slaves, and was a prominent man in his day. He lived in the house now occupied by Mr. Pebbles.

On the East Glastonbury road lived the Porters. They opened this road about 1775, from near Brewer Lane southerly to Glastonbury. They are said to have owned eighty-four rods in width of the three mile lots.

Ashbel Roberts built the house now standing next south of the brook on this road.

David Porter once lived on the farm now owned by Mr. Philip Handel.

The Winslows settled on the corner of this road north of the brook, about one hundred years ago.

Daniel Pitkin lived in the Meadow, and kept a tavern and store, just north of the ferry road and landing, and south of the present bridge. When his house burned down his family moved to a house on the road running north by the present lumber yard, and afterwards lived on the Bridge Road, where they kept a tavern and a store. The tavern was burned down, and re-built only to be burned again; the store is now owned by Mr. G. W. Darlin.

In the North Meadow, Joseph Easton, one of the first settlers, lived about the year 1700.

Pomp Equality, once a slave of Daniel Pitkin's, owned a schooner, and was himself its master. He died in the house now owned by Mr. Obed Chapman, and owned some real estate.

Morse's Hotel was built or conducted for years as a tavern by Joseph Pantry Jones.

Earlier, John Pantry Jones kept a tavern on what was then the corner of the South Meadow Road, a few rods south of Mr. Chauncey Lester's.

Building lots in the Meadow once sold for high prices, the people believing it would grow to be "a second Brooklyn."

THE PITKIN FAMILY.

CHAPTER XXI.

SELDOM is it the fortune of any family to have numbered so many individuals raised to places of distinction in the affairs of a State, by their own abilities, as in the case of the Pitkin family of East Hartford. No other family in our commonwealth stood so constantly and for so long a time in the front of current events, unless it were the Wolcott family of Windsor (now South Windsor), which was also remarkable for the number of its prominent men. From 1659 to 1840 and later, the Pitkins were conspicuously represented in our church, town, and State governments, as well as in our military affairs and inter-colonial relations. From memoranda made by Gen. S. L. Pitkin we gather the following facts.

The pioneer of this family in this country was William Pitkin, already mentioned among the earlier settlers of our town. He was born in 1635 in Marylebone, without the walls of London, England. He came to Hartford in 1659. He was by profession a lawyer, and was appointed King's attorney for the colony in 1664. He was a representative in the assembly from 1675 to 1690, excepting during Sir Edmund Andros' brief authority; in 1676 was treasurer of the colony, and from 1690 until his death was a member of the council, and was otherwise prominent in the affairs of the colonies. He was sent with Samuel Willys to New York with a letter to Gov. Andros, asking him "to engage the Mowhawkes against our Indian enemies," etc. He died in 1694. His wife was Hannah Goodwin, daughter of Ozias Goodwin, the ancestor of the Goodwin family. His sister Martha married Simon, youngest son of Henry Wolcott, and was mother of the first Governor Wolcott, and ancestor of Oliver Wolcott, of Oliver Wolcott, Jr., and of Roger Griswold, who were also governors of Connecticut.*

The Hon. William Pitkin, son of the above, was educated by his father in his profession of the law, and married Elizabeth Stanley, daughter of Hon. Caleb Stanley. He was one of the Council of the Colony for twenty-six years; was judge of the county court, and of the probate court; and in 1703 was judge of the court of assistants; and after the establishment of the superior court in 1711, was a judge of that court until 1713, when he was made chief justice. He lived near the house of the late Capt. John Pitkin on Main street, south of the railroad, and about twenty-five rods from the street. He died in 1723. Prior to 1706 he owned the mill seats on the Hockanum, and built two fulling mills and erected a clothier's shop, carrying on the business largely for the benefit of his sons, William and Joseph, to whom he gave the mills.†

Of the second generation, also, was Hon. Ozias Pitkin, who was repeatedly elected to the legislature, and in 1725 received the appointment of associate judge of Hartford County until 1735, when he was chosen chief judge. He was a member of the Council of the Colony in 1727, and remained a member from that time until his death in 1746.

---

* William Pitkin left a brother, Roger, in England, an officer in the royal army. His sister, Martha, in 1660 or 1661 (she then being about 21 years of age), crossed the Atlantic in the hope of inducing her brother William to return from his wilderness life. She found him feeding his swine. She said, "I left one brother in England serving his king, and find another in America serving his swine." She met with a flattering reception in the colony, and was thought "too valuable to be parted with." It was a question what young man was good enough for her. Simon Wolcott, to their surprise, and perhaps her own, for her mind was still to return to England, succeeded in obtaining her hand. One account has it that so many young men wished to marry her that the matter was decided by lot, which fell on young Wolcott. She is said to be the ancestor of seven governors of this and other States.

† William Pitkin, 2d, is said to have been no less ready in repartee than he was able in argument. He was once opposed in a case by Mr. Eells, a brother lawyer. Eells, in his summing up, said that the court would perceive that "the Pipkin was cracked." "Not so much so, your honor," he replied, "but you will find it will do to stew Eells in yet."

Capt. Roger Pitkin, also of the second generation, was selectman of the town of Hartford, and captain of the first organized company on this side of the river. He died in 1748.

Hon. Col. Joseph Pitkin, son of William Pitkin, 2d, was selectman, and for many years a representative of Hartford. He was captain of our train-band in 1738, and afterwards colonel of the First Regiment. He was also a justice of the peace, and judge of the county court. His first wife was Mary Lord, daughter of Richard Lord of Hartford; his second wife was Eunice Chester, daughter of Hon. Col. John Chester of Wethersfield; his third wife was Madam Law, widow of Jonathan Law of Milford, once governor of Connecticut. He died in 1763.

Governor William Pitkin was son of William Pitkin, 2d. He had no college education, but was brought up in the clothier's business by his father, from whom he acquired a sound knowledge of business and of political affairs. He was chosen town collector in 1715, and in 1730 was captain of the train-band on this side the river. From this office he was promoted until he became colonel of the First Regiment in 1739. His talents, "aided by a natural courtesy and ease of manner," led him to take a prominent place in political affairs. He represented Hartford in the colonial legislature six years, and was speaker of the House from 1728 to 1734, when he was chosen assistant. He was a justice of the peace and of the quorum in 1730; presided as judge of the county court from 1735 to 1752; was elected judge of the superior court in 1741, chief justice and deputy-governor in 1754, and governor in 1766,* holding that office until his death. The inscription on his monument, written by good Dr. Williams, is as follows:

"Here lieth Interred the body of the Honorable WILLIAM

---

* Deputy-governor Pitkin was a strong advocate of colonial rights, and opposed the Stamp Act and other unpopular measures. The course of Gov. Fitch had made him unpopular, and in May, 1766, William Pitkin was chosen governor over him by a majority so great, says the *Connecticut Gazette*, that the votes were not counted. Hon. Jonathan Trumbull was deputy-governor.

Pitkin, Esqr, late Governor of the Colony of Connecticut. To the God of Nature indebted for all his Talents, he aimed to Employ them in Religion without Affectation, Chearfull, Humble, and Temperate, Zealous and bold for the Truth, Faithfull in Distributing Justice, Scattering away Evil with his Eye, an Example of Christian Virtue, a Patron of his Country, a Benefactor to the poor, a Tender Parent and Faithful Friend. Twelve years he presided in the Superior Court, and three years and an half, Governor in Chief. After serving his Generation by the Will of God with Calmness and serenity fell on sleep, the 1st day of October, A. D., 1769, in the 76th year of his age.

> "Walk thoughtful on that solemn shore
> Of that vast ocean thou art soon to pass."

Among Gen. Pitkin's memoranda is the following: "Gov. Pitkin was of commanding appearance, and highly affable and pleasant in his manner. His urbanity and courtesy were long remembered by those who enjoyed his acquaintance." A satire published many years ago makes use of his affability to represent him "bowing and scraping, and constant hand-shaking," graces we can certainly tolerate in one who scattered away evil with his eye. Gov. Pitkin's house stood on the site of Mr. L. D. Richardson's.

Col. John Pitkin, son of William Pitkin, 2d, was selectman of Hartford in 1735. He was lieutenant-colonel of the First Regiment of the forces raised for the expedition against Crown Point and Canada in 1755, "and served throughout the campaign with great credit to himself." The muster roll of his company is given elsewhere (see Early History, 1670–1774). He became colonel of his regiment in 1756. He was in the legislature many years, and died in 1790.

Of the fourth generation was the Hon. Col. William Pitkin, son of Governor Pitkin. In 1758 he was "major of the First Regiment of colonial forces raised for the expedition against Canada, under Gen. Abercrombie, and acquired the reputation of a faithful and gallant officer. He was colonel in the militia later; was often in the legislature, acting sometimes as its clerk; was sheriff of Hartford County for several years, and was elected to the Council from 1766 to 1785. He served as a member of the Council of Safety during the greater part of the Revolutionary War. In 1784 he was elected to the Congress of the United States. He died in 1789, after serving as judge of the Superior Court for nineteen years, "having lived during a very interesting period of our history, and taken a part in many of the important events by which it is characterized."

Col. George Pitkin, son of Gov. William Pitkin, served in the militia, and was commissioned lieutenant-colonel commandant of the Fourth Regiment of minute-men, and marched with his regiment to Roxbury, during the siege of Boston. He represented Hartford in the legislature of 1783, and East Hartford for two years afterward. He lived in what is now known as the Root house.

Elisha Pitkin, Esq., son of Col. Joseph Pitkin, was a trader, and lived on the corner of the South Meadow Road, near the site of the old meeting-house. His house had a reputation for hospitality, and was called the "ministers' hotel." Here Count de Rochambeau was entertained during the stay of the French troops in our town in Revolutionary times. Mr. Pitkin was a graduate of Yale, and for many years a magistrate and prominent citizen.*

Of the fifth generation was Maj. Samuel Pitkin, son of Elisha, who lived where Mr. John B. Smith's house now stands. He was a graduate of Yale; was major in the artillery, and town clerk and treasurer for thirty-five years. He was often in the legislature; was a deacon of the First Church, and superintendent of its first Sunday-school in 1819. He died in 1839, and is pleasantly remembered by many of our citizens. A gentleman of the old school, he wore to the last his knee breeches and silk stockings, and large silver buckles, a habit which had passed out of vogue. His long white hair was gathered in a queue and tied with a

---

* He was a typical old-times' justice of the peace, firm and exact in administering judgment. He had a sense of humor, too. One Evans, whose family had a bad name, was brought before him. "What is his name?" asked 'Squire Pitkin. "Evans," was the answer. "Evans! Guilty, then!" said the Justice.

black bow. It was said of him that he would have made a good duke. In manner he was courteous and genial, and beloved by the children. His wife was Sarah Parsons, a woman of many accomplishments, whose researches have preserved for us much that is valuable in the history of her husband's family. Her obituary notice was written by Mrs. Sigourney.

Samuel L. Pitkin, son of the above, was town clerk and representative, and prominent in business and military circles. He became major-general of the State militia in 1837, and in 1839 was appointed adjutant-general. He was a graduate of West Point, and died in 1845.

Capt. James Pitkin is said to have been captain of the first steamboat that came up the Connecticut River, one "election" holiday, prior to 1825.

Many others of this family have been distinguished by frequent election to office, and the commitment to them of important trusts.

CUSTOMS AND LAWS.

CHAPTER XXII.

THE government established by our fathers in the young Colony of Connecticut was in many respects a stern and exacting one. They of course felt it to be important to intrench themselves against the dogmas of the old world from which they had found asylum, and also to adopt a rigid policy against the many fanatical souls who sought these shores, half-crazed with a sense of unlimited freedom, as well as against the swarm of disreputable refugees and adventurers who sought refuge here from their own unsavory reputations across the sea. In this critical formative time of a new nation, it behooved its guardians to have a jealous care of the elements that sought to fuse themselves into it, and there is more occasion to thank them for their wise exclusiveness of whatever might prove a fatal element in the composition of the State than to reproach them for bigotry and intolerance, though that charge may with abundant justice be made against them. Probably to nothing does our government owe so much for its permanence and present stability as to the fact that it was founded upon the Puritan idea of absolute righteousness.

Still the early days of our commonwealth were a most uncomfortable time for lawless souls. Although the long-reviled "Blue Laws of Connecticut" have been proved a fabrication, there is enough in the actual code of 1650 to make a sinful nature shrink from contact with it. There were fourteen capital laws, based upon the Mosaic code, and all but one having a reference to scriptural authority attached to it. Other punishments were by the stocks, the pillory, and the whipping-post, or by the terrible disgrace of branding on the forehead or the hands, or by imprisonment in the house of correction. The old whipping-post in our town stood near the present sign-post in the Center District until within a few years, and some of our people remember the application of the lash to the bare backs of culprits who were tied to it.

Church membership was not absolutely essential to participants in the government of the State, although it had great weight in the determination of the reputation and standing of the citizen.

Among the early orders passed by the courts are many of curious interest. In 1636 it was enacted that no " yonge man y^t is neither married nor hath any servaunte & be noe publicke officer shall keep howse by himself, wthout consent of the town where he lives first had, under paine of 20s. p^r weeke;" nor could any master of a family harbor any such young man without incurring the displeasure of the court. To indicate still further how hard was the lot of bachelors at that time appears the record of a young man fined for inveigling the affections of a maid without her master's consent. Householders were forbidden to entertain strangers,—meaning Quakers, ranters, Adamites, and like "heretiques."

The price of labor was regulated by law ; excess in apparel was forbidden as "unbecoming a wilderness condition and the profession of the gospell, whereby the rising generation is in danger to be corrupted, which practices are testifyed against in God's holy Word." And any one wearing "gold or silver lace, or gold or silver buttons, silk ribbons, or other superfluous trimings, or any bone lace above three shillings per yard, or silk scarfes," the list-makers were to assess such persons or their husbands, parents, or masters, at one hundred and fifty pounds estate, and they were to pay accordingly, "as such men used to pay to whom such apparell is alowed as suitable to their rank." Magistrates and their families were exempt from the application of this law. The dress of the common people was sober in color, and of homespun texture. The magistrates until recently wore cocked hats, as a sort of badge of office.

Besides the Sunday services of our ancestors there was a public lecture upon a week day, upon which attendance was expected, and this was the usual day for the parade of culprits in the stocks, or upon the pillory, before the meetinghouse in Hartford.

Travel upon Sunday was forbidden, except upon the most urgent business, and even good Dr. Williams, of stern and venerable aspect, had to have his Sunday pass, signed by a justice of the peace, when he "exchanged pulpits" with neighboring ministers. One of his passes to New Lebanon, N. Y., is preserved; it is dated 1791, and is signed by William Williams, justice of the peace. It requests the "informing officers" not to interrupt or delay Dr. Williams upon his journey. Jonathan Hills, Esq., of Hockanum stopped Sunday travelers and kept them at his house until holy time was passed.

In the times of the Indian alarms, guards were ordered at all "meetings for religious use," and all soldiers were to "bring a muskett, pystoll, or some peece, wth powder and shott to ech meeting." Seats were provided for them near the door, and a sentinel was kept outside. As forts were ordered built on this side the river after our first meeting-house was finished, very probably our fathers went armed to meeting, and scanned the river swamp with watchful eyes. On week days, places of rendezvous were appointed in case of an alarm, and delinquents were fined or censured by the court. All men were subject to guard duty, and turns had to be taken as night watchmen.

The arms of the earlier days consisted of pikes, swords, guns, or muskets, and pistols. The guns were of rude construction, being known as match-locks—which were fired with a lighted piece of wood, and required to be aimed from a "rest," which the gunner carried,—or as snap-hances, the early flint-lock muskets. The soldiers often wore armor, or arrow-proof quilted coats.

In Hartford, in 1643, a bell was ordered rung by the watch every morning one hour before daybreak,—to begin at the bridge, on Main street, and go forth and back from Master

Moody's (Buckingham street) to John Pratt's (Pratt street), "and there shall be in every house one up and some lights within one-quarter of an hour after the end of the bell ringing"; in default of which "to forfeit 1s. 6d., to be to him that finds him faulty, and 6d. to the town." These were incentives to early rising which we do not have.

Before the days of newspapers and handbills the town crier, rising in public meetings to make his announcements, or perambulating the streets with his monotonous voice and his bell, was an institution in the larger towns. He announced the arrival and departure of vessels and other events of a public nature, and cried articles or children lost or found, the public sales of property, etc.

In 1707 every ratable person in the town was to kill a dozen blackbirds in March, April, or May, or pay one shilling to the town's use. A penny a head was paid for all extra birds killed. A bounty of 10s. a head was also paid for all wolves killed within three miles of the town.

The early towns were close corporations. For many years a person wishing to become an inhabitant of Hartford had to be formally admitted by a vote of the inhabitants, and was given a certain share in the common lands and other property of the town. To be made a freeman was a subsequent matter, and required the sanction of the courts and the taking of the freeman's oath. The attendance of freemen at town meetings was obligatory, and none could be excused except by consent of the entire meeting. The meetings were at one time held monthly, and all freemen were obliged to stay until the meeting adjourned. The selectmen of the towns were known as townsmen at first. It was among their duties to buy or hire bulls and boars for the use of the town. Forty shillings arising from the sale of a town-bull was given to the east side company for the purchase of colors in 1701.

Slaves were owned by the principal families, even to within fifty years of our own time. Elisha Pitkin owned slaves, and Dr. Williams, the Goodwins, Olmsteds, and Jonathan Hills of Hockanum, and others, though probably the total number was not large. In 1761 there were but 23 colored persons enumerated on this side the river. The following curious certificates are from our town records :

"These may certify that according to my best knowledge and belief, Tamer, a molatto girl in my family was born of my Negro woman, Flora, sometime in July, 1785, according to my minutes then made.

ELISHA PITKIN. *

"A true Record entered the 6th day of June, 1789.

Test, JONA[TH] STANLEY, Register."

"On the second day of March, A.D., 1790, in the Dwelling House of Euodias Bidwell in East Hartford, was born a Negro Male child in Lawful Wedlock, of a Negro woman belonging to me named Rose. The Father is Jack a Negro man, late the servant of the Hon[ble] William Pitkin, Esqr., deceased. Which is according to my best knowledge and belief.

"GEORGE PITKIN.

"A true Record, entered July the 28th, 1790.

Test, JONATHAN STANLEY, Register."

Some now living remember "Old Flo'," as she was called, who is named in one of these certificates. 'Squire Elisha Pitkin at his death left 200 acres of woodland in the Five Miles for her support, but she lived to so great an age that his son, Dr. Edward Pitkin, became tired of supporting her, and turned her on to the town. Thereupon 'Squire Pitkin's executors were summoned to answer to Lemuel White, Esq., and the rest of the inhabitants of East Hartford for her support according to the law,—and were probably obliged to provide for her. She lived in the old Warren house, south of the Hockanum Bridge.

"Old Sylvia," still remembered by some, was once the property of General Pitkin. She lived to be so old that she could not climb to the negroes' seats in the meeting-house on Sundays, and so sat upon the stairs that led up to them.

---

* Elisha Pitkin's slaves, as entered in the town book beneath his family record, are : Flora, born 1752 ; her children—Lill, born 1772, Sylva, born 1776, Nando, born 1779, Leah, born 1783 (married a white man in Albany), Tamer, born 1785.

Jin's children—Dinah, born 1783.

Matilda Scott ("Aunt Matty") was another thrifty relic of the kindly days of New England slavery. She once owned a house on Mill street, and is pleasantly remembered as a very helpful neighbor.

Memories are still alive of the stories told by these faithful old servants of our older families while sitting long evenings by the winter fire-place—weird tales of witches and hobgoblins, that made the children afraid to go to bed, as well as sunny reminiscences of their younger days.

It hardly seems possible to our younger generation, but slavery was not abolished in our State until the year 1848,* although it had for some time prior to that date practically ceased to exist.

The earlier conveniences for travel were clumsy ox-carts, or the backs of beasts,—the ladies riding oftenest upon the horses behind the men, on pillions. The first chaise brought to town was owned by Elisha Pitkin, Esq., we are told. Dr. Timothy Hall, when he began to practice here, had no horse; he carried his saddle-bags on his shoulders, as he trudged about among his patients. He afterwards came to own a chaise.

Chaises at first were counted a luxury, and their owners were taxed for them. In 1792 there were twelve returned by the lister in East Hartford; these were owned by Dr. Samuel Flagg, John Goodwin, Selah Norton, Aaron Olmsted, John Pitkin, Elisha Pitkin, George Pitkin, Widow Abigail Pitkin, and Widow Anna Woodbridge; and by Dr. Timothy Hall, and Elisha Risley, of Hockanum. Open-topped carriages and sulkies were owned by twenty-four persons at this time. Later the keeping of chaises was licensed by the United States government, subject to a duty of $4 each per year. The writer has one of these licenses issued to Major Samuel Pitkin in 1816.

At first the colony sought to encourage the growing of tobacco in the plantations; but in 1747 it ordered that "Forasmuch as it is obsearved that many abuses are committed by

---

* The importation of slaves into Connecticut was forbidden in 1771. In 1784 was passed an act declaring that all children of slaves thereafter born should become free on attaining the age of twenty-five years.

frequent takeing tobacco," no person under the age of twenty years, nor any other not accustomed to the use, should take any tobacco unless he obtained a certificate from a physician that it was useful to him, and also a license from the court. And such as had the habit were not to take it publicly in the street, nor in the fields or woods unless when on their journey at least ten miles, except at dinner time; nor above once a day any way, and then not in company with any person. This act was probably never very strenuously enforced, and hardly comports with the later history of a State which has won so high a reputation for tobacco culture as has our own.

Of the household arts of the days that are gone we have many traditions. There is hardly an old family in town but has still its reels and spinning-wheels, and perhaps its loom, standing idle in the cobwebs of the garret. The time was when the power mills in our town were subservient to the looms and wheels of the family fireside, carding the wool for them, or fulling the homespun fabrics they produced. There are those living who tell us of the "stints" at the wheels which met the girls at an almost tender age, and busied them through all their industrious lives. In a time when rugs and carpets and all textile fabrics were hand-made, the bride could indeed boast of her outfit, fashioned mostly by her own hands. There are many traditions of surprising achievements by the assiduous housewives of the past which we hope will long be perpetuated by their descendants. In our old families are still kept premiums and diplomas from the agricultural societies won by the good dames of a half century or more ago.

The prevalent conception of the boy of the past pictures him as standing by the wayside with his hat politely doffed, while the venerable citizen passes by. It is a conception which has done a deal of good in the world. But it is not altogether correct in its premises. A venerable member of the family of the writer, now many years dead, was once asked in what respect the later days were superior to those of the past. He replied, "In the better conduct of the young." In his younger days it was no uncommon thing for the young men of the leading families to be brought before the magistrates for the wild deeds in which they engaged. Sometimes a farmer's load of wood was run off in the night, and dumped in the swamp; or, perchance, some morning he found his cart lifted bodily astride of the ridge of his barn—a good forenoon's work for a half dozen men and boys to get it down again. And then there were the contests on Sunday noons under the hill east of the old meeting-house, where one of our first citizens confesses that he vanquished the champion of Hockanum in the halcyon days of his youth. But, for our part, we have no boast to make for the present in this regard. They had no Sunday-schools in those days.

A CASE OF WITCHCRAFT.

We had hoped to claim as residents of our side of the Great River the principal persons in a case of supposed witchcraft, for which Nathaniel Greensmith and his wife Rebecca were executed in Hartford in 1662. But the inexorable logic of the records has convinced us that, although Greensmith owned land in Podunk, he did not live there, but had a house on what is now New Britain avenue, in Hartford. The case well represents the dreadful belief in a real devil which prevailed, together with a certain conviction that he had his emissaries on earth, whose aim was to draw all men into horrible covenant with him. It was thought that these agents of his were especially active against the young and the pure. In the account of the case we have mentioned, it appears from Mather's Magnalia that one Anna Cole, "a person of serious piety, was taken with strange fits wherein her tongue was improved by a demon to express things unknown to herself. . . . . . Such and such persons . . . . . were consulting how they might carry on mischievous designs against her and others, by afflicting their bodies and destroying their good names." All answer the invisible speakers were heard to make was, "Ah! she runs to the rock!" Then the demons confounded her language, that she might tell no more tales, and she talked in a Dutch tone. One of the persons accused in this matter was Rebecca Greensmith, who was then in prison on suspicion of witchcraft. She was brought before the magistrates, and the ministers read Anna Cole's strange speech to her. She astonished them by declaring it true, and by further asserting that she, and others named in the papers, had familiarity with the devil. She had made no formal covenant with him, but only promised to go with him when he called her, "which she had sundry times done accordingly." At Christmas he had told her they would have a *merry meeting*, and then the agreement between them should be subscribed. She also acknowledged that when the ministers began to read she was in a great rage, and could have torn them to pieces, and resolved on denial; but after they had read 'twas as if the flesh were pulled off her bones, and she could no longer deny what they charged. She declared that the devil first appeared in the shape of a deer skipping about her, and that he came frequently to her.

She was indicted for "familiarity with Satan the grand enemy of God and mankind." Her husband, Nathaniel Greensmith, was also indicted with her. Upon her confession and "other concurrent evidence," they were both executed, the woman alone confessing. The other accused persons escaped to other parts of the country,—"whereupon Anna Cole was happily delivered from her troubles."

In explanation of the queer confession of Rebecca Greensmith, it may be said that confession was often the easiest way to escape the tortures of the water-trial and other fanatical tests which were tried upon the accused. One "method was to tie the thumb of the right hand to the toe of the left foot, and draw the victims through a horse-pond. If they floated, they were witches; if they sank, they were in all likelihood drowned." (*North American Review*, April, 1869.) Another reason for the confessions which were made by suspected persons was that they often seemed to believe in their guilt as firmly as did those who accused them.

There were other suspected cases of witchcraft in Hartford and its vicinity, and a number of executions took place, but at no time did the delusion expand to such frightful dimensions as it afterwards attained in Salem, Massachusetts.

What part the people living on our soil had in these superstitions we do not know, but probably they shared in the apprehensions of that dark, portentous time, and thanked

God that Satan was caused to withhold his hand from among them.

Eerie stories, and a half belief in witches, lurked in our chimney corners for many a year, and men trembled at the weird sounds of the night, and read many dark omens in the varying phenomena of the sky. Stories are still told of the witches who rode back and forth on the road west of Thomas Burnham's, braiding the manes and tails of the horses as they rode. So late as the Revolution the Hockanum Causeway, near the old meeting-house, was believed to be haunted by a gigantic spectre—an apparition higher than the tree-tops, cleaving the midnight air with a vast shadowy sword. And headless horsemen were seen in the swamp, near by, wandering aimlessly about, as such men naturally would, we suppose. Other "old crone stories" were told, and belated lovers used often to hasten their steps at a passing gleam upon the roadside pool, or at the clammy touch of a low-waving bough that brushed them as they passed. A venerable citizen tells us that once he courageously followed a fleeting figure in white into the burying-ground, where he found it to be a vagrant crazy woman.

INDEX.

⁂ An alphabetical list of early settlers will be found on pages 59 to 67. A list of town officers on pages 98 to 101. A list of soldiers in the war of 1861-65 on pages 208 to 211. All other names will be found in the following index:

Atlas, Hartford Co., x.
Arramamet, 17, 28, 29, 40, heirs, 34.
Attawanhood (Joshua), 30.
Adams, Jeremy, 46.
Apples, "Belle bonne," 89.
Apparel, Dr. Williams', 135.
—Major Pitkin's, 229.—Excess in, etc., 232.
Ayres, Jared A., 163.
Academy, 173.
Arms and armor, 233.
Apparitions, 240.
Allen, Mr., 26, 28.—Col., 29.—John, 45, 155.
Abbey, John, 73, 183, 222.—John, Jr., 78.—Stephen, 105.—Nehemiah, Jr., 203.—Russell, 221.
Anderson, Ira, 96, 199.—Norman L., 167, 214, 218.—John, 186.
Andrews, Wm., 46, 164.—Francis, 47.—Edward, 47, 52, 178, 214.—Sarah, 52.—Mary, 52.—Solomon, 52, 125.—Widow, 178.
Avery, Jonathan, 77.
Anecdotes of Ira Anderson, 96.—Of Cotton's tavern, 111-12.—Of Dr. Williams, 135-6.—Of Dr. Yates, 140.—Of Thos. Spencer, 146.—Of Bidwell's mill, 155.—Of Thaddeus Olmsted, 165.—Of Bear Swamp, 182.—Of Epaphras Pitkin, 217.—Of Wm. Pitkin, 2d, 226.—Of Elisha Pitkin, 229.
Alexander, W., 214.
Ackley, Elijah, 218.
Abercrombie, Gen., 228.
Alden, Maj. J. Dean, 241.
Alcott, Mr., 45.
Abbott, John, 103.
Arnold, John, 46.—117.—Jos., 95.—Mrs., 189.
Andrus, Wm., 19.
Andross, Gov., letter to, 54, 225.
Ash, George, 57.
Allyn, John, 155.
Arts, household, 237.
Almshouse, 102-3.
Articles of Confederation, 86.
Artillery Company, 199, 201, 202.—Sword exercise, 170.
Atkins, Thomas, 57.

Barnard, Barth., 27, 45, 54.—John, 45.
Barnes, Thomas, 45.
Bartlett, Robt., 41, 47, 52.
Blachley, Thos., 45, 57.
Barding, Nathaniel, 45, 55.
Base, John, 46.
Bacon, Andrew, 47.
Blasphemy, Case of, 53.
Blanchard, Richard, 57.
Bragg, Benjamin, 78.
Barbecues, 89, 182.
Brainard, Timothy, 95.—David, 203.
Baker, Sergt. Heman, 118.—William, 203.
Black cloth for funerals, 119.
Blackbirds, 234.
Baptists, 136,146.—Meetings, 145.
Bancroft, Stedman &, 163.—James, 167, 218.
Bathing, by-law, 191.
Barber, George, 199.
Bachelorhood, discountenanced, 232.
Betts, Widow Abigail, 45, 53.
Bemont, Levi, 170.—Makens, 221.
Beven, Benj., 57.
Brewer, Reuben, 74, 223.—Thos. Jr., 77.—Benj. Jr., 77.—Daniel, 77, 214.— —, 118.—George, 187.—Janeway, 187.—E. C., 189.—Samuel, Jr., 199.—Ashbel, 199.—S. A., 199.—John, 203.—Brewer lane, 186.
Benjamin's tavern, 109, 219.—Lane, 169, 222.—John, 77.—Jonathan, 105, 132.—Jas., 105.
Belding, Ebenezer, 78.
Belden, Thomas, 894.
Benton, Elisha, 85, 132, 221.
Benton hill, 221.
Bell, school house, 170.—To be rung, 96.—New, 143.—Before daybreak, 189.
Best chamber, Wells' tavern, 109.
"Bees," road-making, 112.
Bearers at funerals, 119.
Bear swamp, 145, 182.
Bidwell, Nath., 33, 69.
Bidwell, Daniel, 35, 71, 72, 73, 126, 151, 156.—Euodias, 36, 111, 235, 221.—Ozias, 37, 103.—John, 45, 49, 58,

73, 155, 168, 182.—Thomas, 156.—Dr. Epaphras, 83, 109, 222.—Capt. Zebulon, 85.—, 117, 221.—John, Jr., 151.—Joseph, 151.—Timothy, 160.—Samuel, 169.—Daniel, Jr., 182, 183.—Wm. 182.—Chas. M., 191, 221.—Moses, 221.—Russell, 221.—Jonathan, 221.—Bidwell's lane, 50, 73. (See Burnside ave.)
Blise, Thos. Sr., 43, 46.—Thos. Jr., 43, 46.
Birchwood, Thos., 45.
Billings, Thos., 47.
Bridgman, Jas., 47.
Bissell, Ozias, 77.
Bishop, Samuel, 158.
Bird, Thomas, 179.
Bigelow, Hall, 188.
Bigelow, Daniel, 182, 221.—William, 220.
Bridges, 71.—In Hockanum, 108, 176.—Burnside, 181.—Hockanum, 71, 181.—South Meadow, 187.—Carried off, 190.
Bridge Co., Hartford, 195-7.
Biers, 119, 119, 119.
Brick-making, 162.
Bog wall, 42.
Boundary extended, 68, 177.—Northern, 69, 70.—With Five Miles, 75, 80.—With Bolton, 75.—Lines run out, 75-6.—With Glastonbury, 79.
Bolton, bounds with, 75.
Brown, Wm., 77.—Benj., 95.
Brooker, Abraham, 78.
Brooks, Peter, 162.
Boston embargo, 82.—Company to relieve, 82, 229.
Boston or Middle turnpike, 188.
Boats impressed, 90.—For Ferry, 194, 195.—Horse, etc., 196.
Boswell, Keeney & Co., 156.
Boars, town, 234.
Brownell, Dr. Pardon, 160, 173.
Boyle, Wm. H., 171, 217.
Bonds, town, 206.
Bounties, to soldiers, 86, 206, 207.—For blackbirds, 234.—Wolves, 234.
Boy of the past, 237-8.

Burnham, Thomas, 27, 28, 30, 33, 45, 53, 59, 69.—Heirs, 70, 150-2; 175, 188, 214.—John, 28, 185.—Julius, 33, 53, 188, 214.—John A., 53, 175.—Richard, 56, 151, 181. —Samuel, 70, 185.—Asa, 77. —Gurdon, 82.—Augustus, 83.—Aaron, 84.—Z. Arthur, 113, 188, 214.—Phineas, 116, 214.—Thomas and Mary, 116.—George, 120, 221.— Thomas, 159, 189, 240.— John, Jr., 185.—Jabez, 185. —Charles, 185.—Caleb, 185. —Cornelius, 214.—Joshua, 214.—Samuel P., 214.— Timothy, 185.—Joseph, 186.—Patrick, 218.
Burnham's station, xii.
Burnham's road, 175, 188.
Burnside, xiv, 154, P. O., 172. —Indians in, 37.—Bridge, 181.—Public house, 109.— School, 166; house, 168, 172.—District extended, 169; bounds changed, 171; divided and united, 172; Baptist meetings, 146.
Burnside Avenue, x, 50, 73, 176, 182, 220.
Buckingham, Thos., 31, 68.
Blumfield, Wm., 43, 46.
Burr, Benj., 45.
Burying-Grounds, 114-122.— Center, 34, 74, 114-117, 207. —Wanted in Burnside, 118.
Buckland's corners tavern, 112.
Buckland, Wm., 56, 73, 179. —Chas., 77.—Capt. Stephen, 85.—Elisha, 95.—Timothy, 189, 203.—House, 222.
Burton, Rev. Dr., 141, 142.
Buffum, Rev. F. H., 142.
Bull sold, 201.—Town, 234.
Bull, Joseph, 35, 49, 155.— Thomas, 47, 58.—John C., 216, 217.
Bunce, Thos., 45.——, 117, —— Susanna, 184.
Butler, Richard, 46.—Moses, 82.—& Hudson, 160.
Buckler's tavern, 109, 219.
Bryant, Timothy, 95.—Ebenezer, 95.—Henry, 170, 216.
Blue-laws, 231.

Charter of 1662, 40, 171.—For ferry, 194.
Case, Thos., 43, 105, 121, 134, 192, 222.—Richard, 45, 55. Austin, 89.—John, 126.— ——, 182.
Clark, Joseph, 220.—Seth, 201.—Nich., 45.—John, 45. Andrew, 78.—George, 82.— Abraham, 84.—Doctor, 168.
Callsey, Wm., 45.
Cadwell, Thomas, 58, 194.— Widow, 194.—John, 58, 95, 184.—117.
Caldwell, Capt. John, 205.
Chandler, Samuel, 77.—Moses, 147.—William, 84.
Crain, Ezra, 78.
Carter, Joseph, 78.
Chatfield, Jesse, 78.
Call, Daniel, 84.
Chapman, Reuben A., 97, 215, 217, 219.—Obed, 224.

Chappel, Geo., 108.
Carrington, John, 120.
Catechism in the public schools, 139.
Clancey, Rev. Wm. P., 148.
Carding-machines, 160, 161.
Carver, Joseph, 199.
Cannons, 201.
Cady, Jemison, 203.
Carney, L., 217.
Captain Jack, 219.
Canada, Expedition, 228, 228.
Chaises, 236.
Cheeney, Benj., 151, 182.— Brothers, 159.
Chestnut Hill, 155.
Chester, Eunice, 227.—Hon. Col. John, 227.
Center District and schoolhouses, 169-170; line changed, 170.
Central Avenue, 190.
Childs, Dr. S. L., 161.
Chimney-viewers, 212.
Chittenden, Reuben, 77.
Cogrenossett, 17.
Crow, John, 33, 41, 45, 49, 52, 58, 69, 70, 75, 154, 176, 179, 214.—John, Jr., 49.— Nath'l, 49, 57.
Crow Hill, 49, 214.
Cohas, 33; a child of death, 34.
Cowles, Goodman, house burned, 33.—Dea. Timothy, 57, 73, 169, 184, 217.—house, 170, 218.—Dea. Wm., 186, 217.—Wm. C., 202.—Anson, 203, 218.—Ashbel, 218.— Reuben, 218.
Cole, Jonathan, 151.—Anna, 238.—Mr., 47.
Connecticut river, forded, 180.
Connecticut, charter of, 40.
Congress, encroachments of, 87.
Crook, Sarah, 45. 57.
Cornwell, Wm., 45.
Constable, 71.
Commons, wood on, 74, 151.
Crown Point, expedition, 77-78, 228.
Cone, Daniel, 77.—Stephen, 95.
Cotton-mills, 160.
Cotton, Henry, tavern, 111, 221.—John, store, 113.
Corning, Mr., 112, 182.
Coffins, 119, 120.
Colleague for Mr. Woodbridge, 127.
Coloring the meeting-house, 130.
Choristers, 132.
Crosby, David, 135.
Cooley, Dr. Wm., 204.
Cockburn, Admiral, squadron, 141.
Conference room, 143.
Clock, tower, 143.
Copper-mines, 149, 151, 157.
Clothiers' works, 156, 160, 162, 216, 218, 226.
Comstock, Perez, 161.—Wm. G., 217.
Colt's ferry, 162.
Cook, Aaron, 179.
Corbett, Wm., 183.
Composer, Timothy Olmsted, 219.

Cow lane, 221.
Church, Richard, 45.—James, 150.
Cullet [Cullick?], Mr., 46.
Curtis, Geo., 161.
Customs and laws, 231, 240.
Church membership, 232.

Day, Robert, 45.
Davis, Stephen, 55.
Daton, Joseph, 78.
Dances, French, 89; social, 170.
Darlin, George W., 113, 223.
Draft, 1813, 203, 205.—1863-65, 206-7.
Drafted men, list of. 211.
Deming, Timothy, ix, 192, 203, 204.—David, 220.
Deerfield, assailed, 72.
Dewey, Nathl., 77.
Democrats, a sturdy few, 96.
Disbroe, Nich., 45, 55.
Dix, John. 56, 74, 178.
Dibble, Josiah, 57.
Dickerson, Daniel, 129, 151. —Joseph, 143.
Dignifying the meetinghouse, 129; verses on, 132.
Dinah, 235.
Dowd, Thomas, x, 200.
Dowd's grove, 47, 52, 214.
Dodge, Wm., Jr., 78.
Dutch Point, 19, 20, 38.
Drunkenness, fined for, 49, 55.

Easton, Agis, x, 147, 177.— Joseph, 41, 44, 45, 47, 56, 73, 224.—John, 56, 189.— James, 73.—Silas, 84, 167. Timothy, 151.—Sam'l, 151. —Daniel, 203.—222.
Easton's hollow, drained, 75.
East Hartford, description, xii (see Town); center, xiv; part of Hartford, 38; early bounds, 41, extended, 68; no Indian deed, 40; settled, 48; bounds with Five Miles, 75, 80, 151, 153; with Bolton, 75; ferry and contest with Bridge Co., 194-197; town history, 92-101; incorporated, 93; first meeting, 94; first officers, 95; division of property, etc., 95.
East Hartford Manuf'g Co., xiv, 155, 156.
East Glastonbury road, 190.
Evans, Benoni, 77, 83.—Moses, 77.—Samuel, Jr., 77.— Samuel, 77.—Marvin, 203. —Orrin, 203.—229.
Edwards, Thos., 30, 176, 177.
Ephraims, Ezra, 78.
Earthquake, sermon on, 138.
Equality, Pomp, 179, 224.
Ecclesiastical Society, first (3d of Hartford), 59, 124-145; functions, 59, 124; set off, 125; bounds, 125, 143; opposes Orford, 153.
Ecclesiastical History, 123-148.
Election sermons, 127, 138.
Eells, Mr., 226.
Eliot, John, preaches to Indians, 26.
Elmore, G., killed, 33.

INDEX.   245

Elmer, Edward, 43, 45.—
  Thos.,186.—Oliver W., 221.
  —117.
Ely, Nathaniel, 45.
Ensign, James, 47.—Ralph,
  53, 178.—Moses, Jr., 199,
  203.—118.
Elger, Abner, 77.
Epitaphs, 85, 116-17 ; by Dr.
  Williams, 139 ; on Gov.
  Pitkin, 227-8.
Episcopal Societies, 147.
Eldridge, Eri, 189.
Ellington road, 188.
Elms, street, 90, 192-93.
Elm brook, 191.
Eddy lot, 214.

Franklin, Daniel, 78.—Gov.
  Wm., 86, 90.—Thomas C.,
  199.
Flagg, Dr. Samuel, 98, 104,
  105, 115, 219, 236.
Fairchild, Rev. Joy H., 140,
  202.
Farnham, Andrew, 163.
Fares, on ferry, 194.
Fence, meadow, 43, 54 ; viewers, 44, 70 ; protected, 191 ;
  68, 177.
Ferry, Connecticut river, 58,
  93, 95, 194-7 ; two, 195 ;
  Sunday, 143, 222 ; over
  floods, 190.
Ferry road straightened, 187.
French and Indian war, 77 ;
  neutral French, 79.
French here in Revolution,
  88-91, 229 ; place of camp,
  241.
French, Ichabod, 78.
Freemen, admission of, 234.
Five miles, purchase, 31, 68,
  149 ; settled, 74 ; bounds,
  75 ; preaching in, 79, 143 ;
  made Parish of Orford, 80,
  143 (which see); taken
  possession of, 150; division
  of, 150-152 ; difference
  about, 150 ; encroachments, 151 ; survey, 152 ;
  school in, 167.
First Society, 143 (see Ecc'l
  affairs).
Fitch, James, Jr., 31, 68.—
  Joseph, 69.—Govern'r, 227.
Fireplaces, taxed, 212.
Fort Hill, 18, 21, 23.
Forts, etc., 32, 34, 72, 213.
Fort Henry, sermon, 138.
Forbes, Mr , 36.—James, 57,
  183.—David, 74, 165 —Hanmer &., xiv, 49, 154, 156,
  156, 157.— Daniel, 74.—
  Captain Moses, 95.—118,
  222.—Uncle Hick, 120.—
  Wm., 151.—Mahlon, 168,
  172.— Elijah, 189. — Timothy, 199.— Chas, 199.
Fox, Gideon, 78.—Jedediah,
  78. — 117, 162. — Leonard,
  203.
Foxen, 24, 28.
Flora, 103, 235, 235.
Frog Brook, 108, 177.
Forge, the, mills, 157, 158.
Foot stoves, 72.
Funeral customs, 118-120.
Funeral, a queer, 122.
Fulling mills, 156 (see mills).

Glastonbury, South, 32 ; line,
  79.
Garrison houses, 32, 49, 53.
  69.
Gaines, Simon, 77.—Sergt.
  Samuel, 45, 55, 168.
Grant, Seth, 45.
Garrad, Daniel, 45.
Grave, George, 46.
Grave-stones, study of, 116,
  117.
Graves, isolated, 118.
Gardner, Samuel, 47.
Grain, etc., as currency, 87,
  126, 134.
Grand list, 1769 and 1774, 92.
Galleries in meeting-house,
  129, 131.
Grace Church, 147.
Glass factories, 158, 160.
Great Hills. xiii.
Gennings, John, 45.
Geer, Gen. Elihu, 200.
Gleason, Stephen, 203.
Greensmith, Nathl. and Rebecca, 238-9.
Gilbert, Corp. Jonathan, 26,
  28, 155.
Gilbert's Island, 109, 179, 180.
Gilman, Solomon, 28, 150,
  152.—Richard, 73, 151, 167,
  187.—Epaphras, 83.—Benj.,
  84.—George,95, 217.—Capt.
  John, 118, 167.—Sergt. Elias, 218.—Ralzaman, 218.—
  218.
Gilman's landing, 188.
Griswold, Dr. Geo., 37, 103,
  105, 153.—Gen. Shubael,
  97-8, 110, 156, 158, 200, 219.
  —Capt. Josiah, 204.—Gov.
  Roger, 226.
Gibbins, Wm., 46, 55.
Gridley, Thos., 46.
Griffin, Wm., 84.
Goodwin, Henry L., xi.—Mrs.
  Edward S., xi.—Edw'd O.,
  xi, 219.—William, 39, 45,
  49, 54, 154, 184.—Elizabeth,
  49.—Nathl., 58.—John, 58,
  73-74, 104, 114, 184, 236.—
  Ozias, 58, 225.—Levi, 84,
  95, 109, 199, 217.—Joseph,
  89, 96, 115, 115, 192, 216.—
  Dea. Geo.,96,147. George,
  156. Caleb, 106, 184, 216.—
  Richard, 111.—Samuel O ,
  store, 113, 192, 216.—Capt.
  Joseph, 120, 192, 199, 215.
  —Hezekiah, 120.—Edward
  S., 130.—Rev. Patrick, 148.
  —Goodwin & Co., 154.—
  Goodwin & Hudson, 156.
  —John, Jr., 184.—Daniel,
  185, 186.—Andrew K., 202.
  —Buckland, 217.—Hannah,
  225.—Slaves of, 234.
Goodman, Richard, 45, 57.
Government, early, 231.
Goose pond, story of, 165.
Guns, sold, 96 ; cast, 157 ; old
  time, 233.
Guernsey, Lewis, 121.
Guards, at meeting, 233.—
  Guard duty, 233.
Gulf, the, formed, 190 ; error
  corrected, 242.

Hayden, Henry R., xi, 110.
  —William, 45, 58.—Dea.

Edward, 163.—Edward W.,
  190.
Haynes, Mr. John, 41, 46.
Hanmer, Francis, xi.—&
  Forbes Co , xiv, 49, 154.—
  & Forbes, 154, 156, 156,
  157.—William, 147, 190.
Hazard Powder Co., xiv, 157.
Hartford, settled, 38-89 ;
  bounds, 38; extended, 68 ;
  called Newtown, 39 ; deed
  of land, 39 ; line with
  Windsor, 70 ; with Glastonbury, 79 ; opposes setoff, 92 ; York sent to. 103.
Hartford Bridge Co., 195-197.
Hat factories, 160, 161, 216.
Hall, Samuel, 45, 57.—Thos.,
  45.—John, 46.—Dr. Timothy, 104, 105, 200, 236, 236.—
Hallaway, John, 45.   [118.
Hart, Stephen, 45.
Haywards, 55, 70.
Hamlin, John, 75.
Harding, Israel, 78.—Thos.
  H., 147.
Hamilton, Gen., 86.—Alexander, 88.
Half-covenant, 124.
Hale, Benoni, 134.—Joseph,
  160.
Haseltine, John, 151, 183, 222.
Harris, Thos , 155.
Hallet, tannery, 161.
Harrison, Mrs. Lucinda, 174.
Harrington, Edward P., 202.
Handel, Philip, 223.
Hearses, 118, 118, 120 ; house,
  118.
Hermits, 219, 219
Hill, Wm., 32, 33, 46, 48, 52,
  57, 70, 198, 214.
Hills, Lieut. Jona., 35, 36, 72,
  74, 126, 143, 223, 233, 234.—
  John, 57, 70, 166.—Ebenezer, 74.—David, 95.—Benj.,
  109, 183, 222 —Dudley, 109.
  —Capt., 112.—117, 118.—
  George, 147.—Capt Jona.,
  land, 152.—Abraham, 167
  —Samuel,183.—Ashbel,188.
  —Martin O., 202.—Leonard, 203.—Edwin C., 221.
Hills' mill, 160.
Hilliard's mills, 160.
Hillyer. Maj. Drayton, 241.
Hide, Wm , 45, 55.
Higginson, John, 45.
Hoadley, Chas. J., x.
Horse R. R. Co., xii.
Horses and mules shipped,
  204.
Hockanum, river. xiii, 49, 56,
  154, 158, 160, 161.—pound,
  42, 45, 46.—District, xv ;
  school, 166 : houses, 167,
  168 ; name changed, 172.—
  Bridges, 42, 71, 108, 181.—
  Meadow, 38, 42 ; fence, 44.
  —M. E. Soc'y, 147.—Eccl.
  Soc'y,148.—Causeway,181.
Holmes, Lieut., 17, 20, 38.—
  Rev. T. J., 131, 142.—Henry
  U., 188.
Hollister, John, 32.—Lieut.
  Thos., 33.
Holton, Wm., 47.
Hooker, Mr., 46 —Thos , 39,
  and 39, line 23, instead of
  John.—Nath'l, 114.

Hopkins, Mr., 46.—John, 46.
Hosmer, Thos., 46, 47, 152.—
  Capt. Stephen, 152.
Hop Brook, 58, 109, 155, 168.
Homan, Peter, 78.
Horse Neck, defense of, 87.
Home life of Dr. Williams,
  136-7.
Houses, Dr. Williams', 137;
  early, 175; old, chapter on,
  212-224.
Household arts, 237.—goods,
  50-51.
Houghten, Wm., 178.
Hubbard, George, 46.—Hou.
  R. D., 98, 174, 241.
Hull, Lemuel, 77.—Ezekiel,
  78.
Hudson & Goodwin, 156, 156;
  mill, 156.
Hudson, Butler &, 160.
Hughes, Robert, 158.
Hurd & Perkins, 163.
Hurlburt, John, 82, 95, 106,
  118, 167, 218.—Samuel, 83,
  105, 106, 109, 221.—Joseph,
  106.—Jared, 181.
Hutchins, Edward, 78.

Inhabitants, admitted by
  vote, 41, 234; chapter on,
  48-67; alphabetical list of,
  59-67.
Indians, chapter on, 17-37;
  Mohawks, 54, 225; woman,
  103; cider, sold to, 107;
  wigwam, 222; alarms, 233.
Inventory, estate of Richard
  Risley, 50.
Inoculation with small-pox,
  104-6.
Industries in Five Miles, 152,
  154-163.
Island road, 175, 188.
Inns (see Public Houses).
Iron slitting, etc., 157.

Jamus, 35.
Jamstone Plain, 150, 168.
Jack, 235.
Jin, 235.
Johnnot, 33.
Johnson, Col. Richard M.,
  111, 202, 241.—Gen. Wm.,
  78.
· Jones, 84, 117.—John P., 111,
  224.—Joseph P., 111, 199,
  202, 224, 242.—William, 202.
  —James, 77.—Amos, 78.
Joshua, 30, 53.—lands, 31, 68.
Judd, Thos., 46.
Jupiter, 103.

Keeler, Ralph, 47.
Keeney, Alexander, 55, 77,
  168.—Richard, 57.—Joseph,
  74, 77.—John, 77.—Benj.,
  77.—Thos., 78.—117, 117.
  —T., 188.—Hosea, 188.—
  David, Jr., 203.
Kellogg, Nathaniel, 45.
Kelsey, Reuben, 78.—Aaron,
  78.
Kendall, Polly, 120, 220.
Kennedy, Sam'l, 84.—John,
  202.—117.
Kentfield, 118.
Kilbourne, Alfred, xi.—Alfred E., 19.—James, 82.—
  Thos., 74, 184.—Russell, 95.
  —John, 183.

Kimball, Dr., will, 119.—
  Ebenezer P., 201, 202.
King, Gideon, 77.

Labor, price of, 232.
Ladders, roof, 212.
Lake George, battle, 78.
Land, bought of Indians, 39,
  40; division of, 40; shares
  in, 41; owners must settle,
  41; divided, 42; for poor
  men, 42; grants to mills,
  43, 154-155; Indian, fenced,
  43; waste divided, 44; 3
  miles divided, 44-47; Podunk, 53, 69; equivalent,
  59, 70, 150; Five Miles divided, 149-152; survey of
  part of Five Miles, 152.
Landing place, 179, 180.
  " Gilman's, 188.
Latymore, John, 43, 47.
Law, Madam, 227.—Jonathan, 227.
Laws, customs, etc., 231-240.
  —Capital, 231.
Lawrence, John, 82.
Lafayette, Gen., tour of, 88,
  91, 110.
Lay (Leary?), Edward, 46.
Lyman, Elihu, 78.—Richard,
  47.
Leah, 235.
Lecture, week-day, 233.
Ledyard, John, 82.—Watson
  &, 158.
Lester, Chauncey, ix, 111,
  187, 189, 224.—Isaac, 96,
  146, 162.—118.
Liebig Mfg. Co., 162.
Lining the Psalms, 132.
Lill, 235.
Lister, east side, 76.
Little, Lieut. David, 222.—
  118.
Little River, bridge in Hartford, 194.
Long Hill, xiii.—District,
  171; bounds changed, 171;
  made union district, 171.—
  Road, 190.
Looms, 237.
Loomis, Benoni, 77.—Maj.
  Henry A., 241.
Lord, John Haynes, 152.—
  Mary, 227.—Richard, 227.
Lotteries granted, 158, 158.

Mann, Benj, 45.
Manchester, 38, 149-153 (see
  Orford).—Green, 112.—
  companies, 199, 200.
Main street, 68, 71, 177, 178.
McAloon, Patrick, 113.
McMahon, Rev. John T., 148.
Map of town, referred to, x.
Marble, Ebenezer G., 203.
Marsh, 117.—John, 45, 71,
  181.—Daniel, 82.
Marvin, Nath'l, 45, 54.
Mason, Maj., 29,
Mashinott, 33.
Masseeckcup, 40.
Matross company, 201.
Mawley, Timothy, 84.
May, George, 189.
Maynard, John, 45.
Meadow District, xv, 170.
Meadows, filled up, 179; road

north in, 175, 180, 188.—
  training field, 198.
Mead, Rev. Asa, 140.
Meakins, Lieut. John, 45,
  55, 73, 75, 151, 156, 182.—
  Joseph, 115.—Ensign, Samuel, 151, 182.—house, 220.
Memorial day, 208.
Menageries, 110.
Mentor, Simeon, 78.
Menowniett's examination,
  33.
Meeting-house, 71, 126; first,
  129; second, 129-134, 144;
  new, 96, 143; three, 143;
  Spencer st., 146; Hockanum M. E., 147; Burnside M. E., 147; Episcopal,
  147; Catholic, 148; Hockanum Eccl. Soc'y, 148; in
  Orford, 153.
Merriman, Joseph, 72, 219.
Merideth, Rev. Richard, 142.
Merrow, houses, 219; barn,
  201.
Metcalf house, 220.
Methodists, 145, 146.
McKey, 117.
Middle turnpike, 188.
Mills, saw, 154, 160, 160, 160,
  161, 163; in Five Miles, 74,
  151; land for, 49, 71, 237;
  near meeting-house, 144;
  Burnside, etc.,154-163,226;
  fulling, 156, 162, 182, 183,
  226; oil, 156, 160; snuff,
  157; paper, 154-8, 160, 160;
  cotton, 160, 160; grist, 154,
  156, 156, 160, 160, 161, 161,
  163; nail, 160, 161; powder, 155, 157, 157, 160;
  woolen, 160; plaster, 161;
  shoddy, 162; sorghum, 163.
Mill road, north, 187, 189;
  south, 189.
Mill street, x, 163.
Mill district (see Burnside).
Miller, Amariah, 156.
McIntosh, Dr. L. W., 162.
Military affairs, 198-211;
  French and Indian war,
  77-8; sword exercise, 170;
  review of 1813, 241; colors
  bought, 201, 234.
Ministers, 71, 73, 125, 126,
  134, 141-143; house, 126;
  pew, 127, 130; "hotel,"
  145, 229; to have land, 149.
McCook, Rev. John J., 147.
Mohawks, 25, 225.
Monroe, President, 110, 192.
Moody, John, 47, 234 —
  Chas. C., 182.
More, Philip, 57.
Moore, Arthur P., 129, 215.
Morse, Luke, 111; hotel, 224.
Mudge, Jeruise, 43.
Mulcahy, Rev. J. A., 148.
Munger, Rev. T. T., 143.
Murder, in Manchester, 112.
Music, Sundays, 131.
Muster roll, 1755, 77; days,
  110, 111, 205.
McClure, Rev. David, 139.
Mygatt, Jacob, 27, 53, 54.—
  Joseph, 46.

Nail cutting, 160, 161.
Nando, 235.
Narragansett war, 31, 69.

INDEX. 247

Naubuc, garrison, 33, 69 ; 108, 161.
Nayage, 32.
Nelson, Mr., Baptist preacher, 146.
Nessaheagen, 29.
Newell, Rev. Samuel, 127, 134.
New London turnpike, 187.
New London, defended, 203.
Newtown, called Hartford, 39.
Nipmucks, 31.
Niantics, western, 30.
Nichols, Capt. Cyprian, 71, 114, 181.—John, 78.
Non-importation measures, 82.
Noonings, Sundays, 144-5, 238.
Norton, Selah, 82, 105, 132, 236.—Job, 82.
North District and schoolhouses, 170. — bounds changed, 171, 171.
North Meadow Road, x, 176, 179-180.

Organ, in meeting-house,143.
Olmsted, Aaron G., x, xi, 152, 217, 217.—Dr. H. K., x, xi.—Col. Chas. H., x, 52, 202.—Dea. Joseph, 35, 72, 73, 125, 127, 165, 181, 215.—Geo. J., 36, 192.—John. 45.—James, 45, 132.—Richard, 45, 73, 151.—Timothy, 82, 218.—Wm., 82. 215.—Ashbel, 162, 181, 215.—Nath'l, 82.—Epaphras, 82, 96, 215.—Gideon, 83-4, 215.—Capt. Aaron. 84, 215, 236.—Stephen, 85, 167. —Geo., 95, 95, 161.—Jonathan,95, 215.—John L.. 98, 109, 219.—Ralph A., 109, 178, 217.—Wm. H., 161, 216, 218.—Asahel. 82, 161.—Col. Giles, 161, 202, 202, 203, 220.—Thaddeus, 165.—Col. Solomon, 171, 173, 202, 202, 217.—Eli, 199.—Elihu, 215. —Persius,215.—Col. Aaron F., 202.—Horace B 221.— house 220.—land, 152.—slaves, 234.
Oldham, Capt., killed, 20.
Omnibus, xiii.
Oil Mills, 156 (see mills).
Orford, Parish of (see Five Miles); town meetings there, 96, 153; set off, 80, 143.—account of, 149-153.—collector in, 153.—made Manchester (which see), 153.—mills in, 157 (see mills).
Ordinaries (see public houses).
Orchard street, x, 190.
Overton, Delos, 52, 214.
Owen, Gen. Geo. C., 241.
Ocolo, old, 106.
Olcott, Mr.,45.—Lieut.Thos., 58, 73, 75, 109, 166.—John, 73.—Sidney, 109.—Josiah, 152.—Samuel, 179, 180, 180 —land, 152.—117, 168.
Old red store, 112, 188.

Pratt, Geo. W., xi, 37, 222.—

Wm., 45.—John, 45, 234.
Jona., 73, 144, 167, 222.—Aaron,77.—Gen. James T., 202, 241.—Luther, 113.—Geo. E., 191.—Eliab, 222.
Park, Raymond, xv, 220.
Parker, Wm., 45,54.—Elisha, 77.—Rev. Dr. E. P., 136.
Parties, old time, 110.
Pantry, Wm., 41.—John, 45, 58, 74, 114, 180.
Pantry's pond, 187.
Paper mills (see mills).
Parsons, Sarah, 230.
Pardee, Dwight W., 241.
Pasco, Amos, 199.
Plant,on meeting-house site. 145.
Psalmody. 132.
Pebbles, Watson, 223.
Peck, Paul, 47.
Pekoath, 20.
Perpetual motion, 162.
Perce, John, 47.
Pest-house, 104-106.
Perkins, Hurd &, 163.—Edgar, 173.—place, 214.
Pewter Pot Brook, 41, 160.
Preaching in Five Miles,152 ; other, 145.
Prescott, Gen., 86.
Phelps, Samuel G., 77, 201, 219.—Henry, 110, 120, 121, 220.—Geo. S., 120, 121, 122, 144.—Edward. 121.—Sal'n, 174.—Store. 220.
Pigeon Hill, 36, 53, 214.
Pirate Hill, xiii. 170.
Pillions, 145, 236.
Pitch-pipe. 131.
Phillips. Wm., 45.
Pitkin Family, 81, 225-30.—Wm., 27, 30, 44, 45, 49, 54, 70, 124, 156, 164, 176, 179, 182, 213, 225, 226.—Elisha, Esq., 49, 89, 95, 103, 105, 115, 115. 144, 144, 145, 157, 158, 161, 186, 199, 201, 216, 229, 234, 235, 236, 236.—Hannah, 57, 119.—Capt. Roger, 58, 70, 73, 184, 227.—Col. John, 73, 77, 82, 183, 186, 199, 217, 228.—Capt. Ozias, 75, 119, 184, 199, 226.—Col. Joseph, 78, 82, 127, 143, 156, 157, 182, 183, 183, 199, 216, 226, 227, 229.—Gen. Samuel L., 82, 97, 144, 199, 199, 200, 217, 225, 228, 230, 235.—Col. George, 82, 94, 157, 162, 199, 204, 217, 229, 235, 236.—John, Jr., 84, 199, 199, 236. —Wm. (4th), 86, 95, 157, 158, 217, 228, 235.—Daniel, 94, 95, 95, 102, 109, 111, 113, 223, 224.—Capt. Richard, 94, 95, 95.—Ashbel, 95, 216. Richard, Jr., 95.—David, 95, 216.—Maj. Samuel. 97, 102, 202, 217, 229, 236.—Mrs. Samuel, 230.—Jonat'n, 102. —Gov. Wm , 137, 138, 156, 184, 199, 216, 226, 227.—Capt. John, 122, 199, 213, 217, 226.—Wm. (2d), 34, 35, 71, 72, 73, 75, 125, 156, 165, 181, 199. 213, 226, 226, 227, 228.—Capt. James. 230.—Col. 152.—Elisha, Jr., 157, 158.—J. R., 158.—Samuel,

& Co., 160.—A. P., 161.—J. H. & W. L., 163.—Capt., 132, 165.—Nathl., 184.—Addison, 186.—Martin, 199.—Geo.Jr.,202.—Nathan, 202, 216,218.—Walter, 216.—David, 216.—Dr. Edward, 216, 235.—Geo., 216.—Charles, 216, 218.—Epaphras. 216.—Roger (2d), 217.—Joshua, 217.—Ezekiel. 217.—Dennison, 217.—Osmyn, 217.—Leonard T., 220 —Martha, 225, 226. — Roger, 226.—Widow Abigail, 236.—In Manchester, 217.
Pitkin's Falls, and Mills, 154, 156, 157, 187.
Privateers, 83-84, 204.
Prison ships, 85, 204.
Prisoners of war, 86, 90, 193.
Pock-house Hill, 104-5.
Podunk. 38.—River. 17, 18, 42.—Meadow, 44.—Indians, 17-37.
Pomp Equality, 179, 224.
Population, 1774, 81, 92.
Popo, 28.
Poor, town's, 93, 102-3, 104. —House, 102.
Porter, Wm. S., 44, 52.—Thos., 47.—Hezekiah, 74.—Joseph H., 108, 177.—Wm., 202.—David, 223.—Ira W., 177.—John, 147.—117, 118. 223.—Land, 152.
Post, Stephen, 45.
Pounds, 42, 45, 46, 70.
Pondrette fact'y, 162.—Lane, 217.
Powder Mills, 155, 157, 157.
Prospect st., x, 176.—North, 181.—No. 2, 190.
Provisions, embargoed, 86.
Public Houses, 58, 74, 75, 107-113, 202, 217, 219, 221, 222, 223, 224, 242.
Purcas, John, 45, 55.—Elizabeth, 55.
Puritans, a word for. 123.
Punishments, 76, 231-232, 233.
Putnam, Stillman, 181, 218.
Plymouth House, 17, 20, 38.

Quanampewet, 30.
Quebec, sermon, 138.

Raymond, Albert C., xi, xv, 120, 217, 220.—Park, xv, 220.
Raiment, Amos, 77.
Ranney, J. H., 190.
Rag-toes, 198.
Rathbun. Sala J., 203.—Erastus, 203.
Ryant, John, 78.
Rebellion, war of, 205-211.
Redfield, Peleg, 77.—James, 78.
Refreshments at funerals, 119.
Representatives, how chosen, 97 ; list of, 98.
Revolution, 81-91, 229.
Review of 1843, 202, 241.
Reynolds, John,82.—George, 122.—Capt. Amherst, 202, 203, 220.
Richards, Thos., 46.
Richardson, L. D., 216, 228.

Riley, Walter A., x.
Risley, Richard, 41, 47, 50.—
  Sarah, 51.—Samuel, 51.
  Richard Jr., 51, 52.—John,
  74.—Thos., 74.—Levi, 85.—
  Timothy, 189, 222.—Elisha,
  199, 236.—Harvey, 203.—
  Horace, 204.—Jonat'n, 222.
  Erie, 222.—118, 222.
Ritter, Mr., 169.
Roads, 71, 175-191; primitive, 175; repairs of. 190;
  let out, 190; by-laws, 191;
  —Near Willow brook, 178-9.—South to Bolton. 183.—
  North to Bolton, 184-5.—
  Along Windsor bounds,
  185-186.—"New," in Podunk, 186.—To Pratt's ferry. 187.- Old ferry straightened, 187.—Ellington, 188.
  —From Jacob Williams,
  188.—From mills to Silver
  Lane, 189.—North from
  Bridge Road, 189.—Hillstown, south, 189.—In Meadow, 189.—In South Meadow, 189, 189.—On Neck,
  189.—Mill, north, 189.—A
  right-of way, 221.—other
  roads, 190.
Roberts, Martha, x.—Ira T.,
  xi.—Ozias, 33, 49, 98. 144,
  204, 214, 215.—Wm., 56, 57,
  73, 83, 215.—Dorothy, 57.—
  Benj., 57, 99, 104, 135, 145,
  183, 161, 215.—John, 83.—
  Elijah, 84.—Ashbel, 89, 223.
  —Jason, 89.—Jerusha, 99.
  —Hezekiah, 104, 145, 215.—
  Wm., 114.—Jona., 132, 199.
  George, 144, 215.—Joseph,
  151, 184.—Samuel, 169, 187.
  Osmyn, 178.—Frank, 214,
  222.—118, 223.
Rochambeau, Count de, 88,
  229, 241.
Rogers, Stephen, 82.
Rood, Rev. John, 71, 126.
Root, Thos., 45, 50.—Jas.,
  house, 162, 217, 229.
Rooley, Thos., 78.
Rowley, Israel, 78.
Roman Catholic Soc'y, 148.
Rose, 235.
Ross, Wm., 77.
Roxbury, Company to, 82, 229.
Ruscoe, Wm., 45.

Sables, John, 46.
Sadler, John, 108, 177.
Sage, John, 202.
Sailors, many once, 204.
Salaries, ministers, 143.
Salt, quota of, 86.
Sandford, Goodwife, 56.
Saw-mills (see mills).
Saw-Mill River (see Hockanum).
Sargent, Wm., 216.
Slater, John O., 203.
Slaves, 103; seats, 130; 131, 223, 234-236.
Slavery, abolished, 236.
Small-pox, hospital, 104-106 graves, 118.
Spar Mill Swamp, 155.
Squatters, in Five Miles, 74
Standift, Josiah, 77.

Stage coaches, 110.
Stager, Edward F., 221.
Stanley, Wm. M., x, xi, 170,
  218, 218.—Hon. Caleb, 45,
  226.—Thomas, 45.—Wm.,
  73, 218.—Nath'l, 75.—Theodore, 82, 95, 96, 218.—Jonathan, 94, 95, 95, 105, 134,
  158, 235.—Elisha, 98, 218.—
  Martin, 161, 199, 216.—Col.
  Ashbel, 199, 218.—James,
  218.—Elizabeth, 226.—
  Clothiers' shop, 162.
Stanton, Thomas, 45.—Wm., 77.
St. Mary's church, 148.
State appropriation for schools, 172.
Strangers, 232.
Seacnt, 29.
Seating the meeting-house,
  129, 129-30, 131; verses,
  132; seats for guards, 233.
Second North District and school-houses, 170; bounds changed, 171.
Second South District school houses, 167, 168; bounds changed, 168.
Secret cellar, 222.
Selectmen, east side, 81; first,
  94, 95; by ballot, 97; list
  of, 100; license liquors, 112;
  called townsmen, 234.
Sentry, Sunday, 72, 233; in forts, 72.
Selden, Thos., 47.
Sequassen, 23, 39.
Servants, run-away, 35; 59.
Sermons, Dr. Williams', 138.
Settlements, 38, 39.
Settlers, chapter on, 48; list of, 59-67; in Five miles, 152.
Sewers, orchard st., 191; in Burnside, 191.
Seymour, Lt., Col. T. H., 241.
Sextons, 120-122.
Sheat, 17.
Shepard, Jona., 78.
Shields, Daniel, 78.
Skeleton, exhumed, 18, 191.
Spectre, 240.
Spencer, Ralph G., xi, 221.—
  Thos., 45, 52, 84, 109, 156,
  183, 220.—Widow, 45, 50, 55.
  —John, 73, 84.—Judah, 78.
  —John, Jr., 199.—Joseph,
  130.—Thos., 146.—Thos.
  Jr., 151.—Disbrowe, 151.—
  Timothy, 146.—Silas, 169.
  James, 199.—Col. N. W.,
  202.—Solomon, 203.—117, 222.
Spencer Hill, xiii; street,
  222.—street burying-ground, 117. — meeting-house, 146.
Steele, John, 39.
Stebbins, Edward, 78.
Stevens, Jeremiah, 77.—
  Thos., 78.—Abraham, 78.
  —Aaron, 78.
Stedman, Timothy, 95.—
  Nathan, 95.—& Bancroft, 163.—Reuben, 203.
Steeple to meeting-house, 130.
Stewart, John, 220.
Shipyard, 162.

Shipman, Horace, 202.
Sidewalks, protected, 191; built, 191.
Sign-posts, 76, 232.
Sigourney, Mrs., 230.
Silk culture, 158, 160; mills, 159.
Silver Lane, x, 89, 90, 109, 183-4.
Simons, The, 168.
Singers' seats, 130, 131.
Sisson, Benj., 109, 222.
Skinner, John, 45.
Smith, Russell, 222.—John
  B., 217, 229.—Arthur, 46.—
  Giles, 47.—Philip, 73, 74,
  108. - Capt. Samuel, 95, 95.
  —Nehemiah, 146, 189, 222.
  —Widow Simeon, 147.—
  Samuel, 151, 183.—Lewis,
  203.—Hon. John C., 205.
Smith's lane, 49, 214, 215.
Spinning wheels and reels, 237.
Spirituous liquors, 107-113.
Spring, Rev. Dr. Samuel,
  140-142, 205; ancestry, &c., 141.
Stiles, President, induction of, 139.
Swine, restricted, 43; damage by, 56.
Solomon's river, xiii.
South East District, xv, 169, 172.
South Middle District, 169, 172.
South Middle Burying Ground, 117.
South Burying Ground, 117.
South Meadow Road, x, 187.
South Windsor, prisoners in, 86, 90.
Sounding-board, 130.
Societies, four, 146.
Sorghum mill, 163.
Soldiers, provision for, 86-7;
  quota, how filled, 87; monument, 117, 207; Record,
  207; lists of, 77, 82, 199,
  202, 203, 208-211.
Sowgonosk, 30.
Scott, Thomas, 45.—Matilda, 236.
Scott's swamp, 45.
Scotland, xiv, see Burnside.
Scout, Maj. Treat's, 31.
Scoville, Abner, 78.
Schools, 54, 164-174.—houses,
  144, 165, 165, 167; four, 167,
  168; divided, 168-218; in
  Five Miles, 152.—Support
  of, 166, 168, 172, 173.—Dame
  and master, 166.—Wood
  for, 164, 166, 194.—Society,
  170-171; fund, 167.—Other
  fund, 171, 172-3.—Districts
  formed, 168-172; made corporations, 171; names, 172.
  —The Academy, 173.—
  Other schools, 174.
Spoon shop, 163, 217.
St. John's Parish, 147.
Stone, Samuel, 39, 45.—Capt. killed, 20.
Stoughton, Ancient, 41.—
  Augustus, 203.
Stocking, George, 46.
Stores, sold liquors, 112.—
  Elisha Pitkin's, 144.—Old

INDEX. 249

red, 112, 188.—Goodwin's, 113, 216.—Griswold's, 219.
—Old yellow, 219.
Stove, in meeting-house, 130, 144.—foot, 72, 144.
Substitutes for drafted men, 87, 206, 207, 211.
Suckheiom, 78.
Suckiaug tribe, 39
Sunday-schools, 142, 229.—services, 238.—travel, 233.
Surveyors, 70, 95.
Snuff mills, 157.
Squinimo, wife of, 29, 31.
Sylvia, 235.
Symouds, John, 95, 151.—land, 152.—117.

Tantinomo, 13, 23, 53.
Tanneries, 49, 71, 160, 161, 161.
Tamer, 235, 235.
Taquis, 28.
Talcott, Maj., 68.—John, 154.—Joseph, 185, 186.
Taylor, John, 82.
Tarbox, Rev. I. N., 174.
Taverns (see public houses).
Tract, against seceders, 136, 146.
Train band, 48, 52, 198.—Training fields, 198.
Treat, Maj. Robt., 81.—Henry, 52.—Matthias, 74, 125, 214.—Stephen, 95,—Sylvester, 203.—Joseph, 223.—52, 118, 214.
Treasurers, town, list of, 101.
Trees, old oaks, 156, 193; elms, 90, 192-193; on causeway, 181.
Trespassers in Five Miles, 151.
Terry, Loren C., 216.
Timber, for mills, 49, 154: on commons, 74.
Tin ware, manufactory of, 162.
Third Soc'y of Hartford (see Eccl. affairs).
Trill, Thos., soldier, 34, 55, 114, 151.
Tobias, Indian, 37.
Tobacco, Dr. Williams smokes, 136; 236-7.
Tobacco avenue, x, 189.
Tolland turnpike, 185, 188.
Thomas, Elijah, 78.
Thornton, Thos., 151.
Town (see E. H'fd), farm, 44, 102-3.—officers, 81; list of, 98-101.—history, 92-101. poor, 93, 102, 103, 104.—first meeting, 94-96; in Orford, 96, 153; compulsory attendance, 234; now held, 96; method of voting, 96-7. — center, 144. — Deposit fund, 172-3.—Bonds, 206.—crier, 234.
Townsmen (selectmen), 234.
Total abstinence, 140.
Tryon, Frank, 216.

Trumbull, Hon. Jona., 227.
—Maj. Henry C., 241.
Tudor, Samuel, 70.
Turner, Isaac, 77.—Reuben, 78.
Tubbus, Lebbens, 78.—Benajah, 73.
Turnpikes opposed, 188; abandoned, 188.
Tyler, Col. H. A., 200.
Tythingmen, 95, 131.
Uncas, 23, 26, 29.
Uncle Rues, 219.
Uniform, artillery, 201.
Upper-quag plains, 198.
Van Dorn's hotel, 111.
Vehicles, early, 175, 236.
Volunteers, equipment of, 206; list of, 77, 82, 208-11.
Vier, Ed., 119, 120.
Village Improvement Soc'y, xv.
Wacile, James, 43, 47.—Henry, 43, 46.
Wadsworth, Allen, x, 161.—Wm., 45.—Capt. Joseph, 114.—T., 189.—117, 117.
Wade, Robert, 45.
Walker, Rev. Mr., 142.—F.R., mill, xiv, 157.
Wagunicut, 17, 20.
Wakeman, Sam'l, 41, 46.
Warner, Andrew, 46.—John, 45.
Ward, Nath'l, 46.
Watts, Richard, 46, 52.—William, 43, 47.
War, debt paid, 87.—of 1812, 203-205.—of Rebellion, 205-711.—post, 206.
Warren, 52; house, 89.—William, 52, 55, 70, 125, 151.—Andrew, 73.—Thos., 125.—Ashbel, 162.—Austin, 162.—Edward, 203.—Jas., 203.—Nath'l, 89, 219.—Doctor, 223.—118, 135, 192, 223.
Warfield, Ephraim, 203.
Washington in Hartford, 88.
Waterhouse, A. A., 216, 220.
Watson & Ledyard, 158.
Watchmen, 233.
Whalen, John, 218.
Weaseapono, 23.
Weautwose, 23.
Weaver's shop, 109, 219.
Wethersfield, settled, 38.
Webster, Mr., 45.—Selah, 162.—Norman, 162, 170, 218, 219.—Ezekiel, 168.
Webb, Richard, 45.—James, 78.
Wells, Mr., 45.—Samuel, 52, 74, 78, 165, 166, 186, 223.—Thos., 52, 54.—Col. Jona., 85, 117, 200, 223. — Capt. John, 95, 95.—Capt. Samuel, 152, 223.—Wm., 152.—Jona. T., 174.—118.—Tavern, 109, 173, 219.
West Hartford, deed of, 40.
Westwood, Wm., 45.

Westover, Jane, 32.
West India trade, 204, 215.
Wesley, Wm., 46.
Willow Brook, 161, 214.—District, xiv (see 2d South).
Willys, Mr., 33, 46, 69, 152.—Samuel, 40, 128, 225.—Col. Samuel, 86.—Thos., 83.
Williams, Sergt. Wm., 35, 72, 73.—William, 44, 57, 59, 70, 150, 152, 233.—Timothy, 52, 151, 186.—Jane, 57.—John, 73.—Gabriel, 73, 151.—Gabriel, Jr., 151.—Joshua, 83, 218.—Jacob, 83, 151, 188, 218.—Dan'l, 83, 151.—Matthew, 108.—Rev. Stephen, 121.—Rev. Eliphalet, 134-139; ancestry, 139; 192, 213, 215, 227, 233, 234.—William, Jr., 151.—George A., 168.—Jonah, 185, 218.—Samuel, 199.—Horace, 224.—35, 52, 214.—Israel, 258.
William Street, 189.
Wilcox, John, 43, 47.—Giles, 78.
Wiley, Sylvester, 199.
Willerton, Gregory, 47.
Wing, house, 220.
Winslow, 223.—Gov'nor, 20.
Windsor, 17, 20, 38; line, 70.
Windrop, John, 40.
Witch stories, 236, 240.
Witchcraft, case of, 238-9.
Whiting, Mr., 46.—Col. John, 152.
White, Jno., 46.—Capt. Lemuel, 85, 220, 235.
Whitmarsh, Samuel, 159.
Whipping-post, 76, 232. — Public, 108, 108, 232.
Wright, Miles, 78.—Moses, 78.—Theodore L., 173.
Wolcott, Wm., 186.—Simon, 225,226.—Henry,225 —Gov'rnor, 225.—Oliver, 225.—Oliver, Jr., 225.
Wolves, bounty, 234.
Wood, Obadiah, 34, 56, 114, 151.—John, 186.
Wood, for minister, 127, 134, 135.—For schools, 164, 166, 194.
Woodbridge, Deodat, 37, 108.—Rev. Samuel, 26, 73, 126 -128, 165; ancestry, 128.—Samuel, 82.—Russell, Jr., 84.—Russell, 167, 199.—Alfred, 199.—Widow Anna, 236.—Tavern, 109, 219; in Manchester, 112.—Avenue, 190.
Woodford, Thos., 45.
Woodruff, Benj., 34.—Erastus, 173.
Woolen mill, 160.
Work-house, 102-103.
Wyles, John, 95.

Yates, Rev. Andrew, 139-40.
Young, Mathew, 59.
York, Negro, 103.

www.ingramcontent.com/pod-product-compliance
Lightning Source LLC
Chambersburg PA
CBHW071429150426
43191CB00008B/1086